Eat Not This Flesh

"Of their flesh shall ye not eat, and their carcase shall ye not touch; they are unclean to you."

Leviticus 11:8

Eat
Not This Flesh

FREDERICK J. SIMOONS

Food Avoidances
in the Old World

GREENWOOD PRESS, PUBLISHERS
WESTPORT, CONNECTICUT

Library of Congress Cataloging in Publication Data

Simoons, Frederick J
    Eat not this flesh.

    Reprint of the ed. published by University of
Wisconsin Press, Madison.
    Bibliography: p.
    Includes index.
    1. Food habits. 2. Meat. I. Title.
[GT2850.S57 1980]   394.1'6   80-22232
ISBN 0-313-22772-1 (lib. bdg.)

This is a reprint of the second printing (paper), 1967.

Reprinted with the permission of University of Wisconsin
Press.

Reprinted in 1981 by Greenwood Press
A division of Congressional Information Service, Inc.
88 Post Road West, Westport, Connecticut 06881

Printed in the United States of America

10 9 8 7 6 5 4 3 2 1

To Eduard Hahn,
Edwin Loeb, Carl Sauer,
and Elizabeth

PREFACE

This book was stimulated by the lectures of Edwin M. Loeb and Carl O. Sauer at the University of California in Berkeley, and by my experiences in northwest Ethiopia during a period of doctoral field research in 1953–54. In Ethiopia my curiosity was aroused by the discovery that Christians and pagans as well as Jews and Moslems consider pigs unclean and reject pork as food. Ethiopian Christians reject camel flesh as well, regarding its use as a Moslem trait and so serious a violation of their customs that an offender may be excommunicated from the church. All Ethiopians avoid horseflesh, and some of them refuse to eat domestic fowl. In traveling across Africa from Ethiopia to Nigeria, I noted that there were large areas where a particular flesh food was used and others where it was avoided; and that those who rejected a food had strong feelings on the matter.

At the first opportunity I began to investigate the question of flesh avoidance, working first in the Public Library at Newark, New Jersey, and continuing research in the Human Relations Area Files at Princeton and in the libraries at the Ohio State University, the University of California (Berkeley), and the University of Wisconsin. My intent was to write a short article on the use and avoidance of flesh foods in Africa. Gradually I was drawn to consider other parts of the Old World, other flesh food avoidance that seemed important and widespread, and the question of the origin and subsequent diffusion of avoidances over the large areas where they are now found. Thompson Webb, Jr., encouraged me to develop the material into a book.

I make grateful acknowledgment to the Ohio State University and the Graduate School of the University of Wisconsin which supported parts of the research; to Walker Fesmire, Robert di Bartolomeo, Paul English, and Janet Ritchie, who assisted me in various phases of the work; to Randall Sale and other members of the University of Wisconsin Cartographic Laboratory for preparing the maps; to Mary Jane Johnson and her staff for typing; and to the Whitbeck Fund for Research for aid for the index. Suggestions for improving the manuscript were made by Karl Butzer, Donald Crim, Dorothy R. Jutton, Edwin M. Loeb, David Lowenthal, James J. Parsons, Carl O. Sauer, Jonathan Sauer, Gwen M. Schultz, Philip Wagner, and Paul Wheatley. Andrew Clark suggested the final form of the title. Roberta W. Yerkes, the editor, made many substantial contributions. And my wife Elizabeth helped with the research and gave editorial assistance. To all of these go my warm thanks.

F.J.S.

Madison, Wisconsin
December, 1960

CONTENTS

ix

ILLUSTRATIONS

Following page

Eat Not This Flesh

1

INTRODUCTION

The problem of feeding the world's people is becoming increasingly serious. To the need for alleviating the widespread dietary deficiencies that already exist are added new demands for food to supply the rapidly growing world population. In view of the urgency of the problem, it is odd that few social scientists have been seriously concerned with the nature and distribution of man's foodways—the modes of feeling, thinking, and behaving about food that are common to a cultural group. The foodways determine which of the available food resources a group eats and which it rejects; through cultural preference and prejudice they may present major barriers to using available food resources and raising the standards of nutrition. It is not rare for the foodways to lead men to overlook foods that are abundant locally and are of high nutritive value, and to utilize other, scarcer foods of less value. Beef, chicken flesh and eggs, dogmeat, and horse and camel flesh comprise such important potential sources of animal protein that their more general use might contribute substantially to reducing the widespread and serious protein deficiency that prevails in large parts of the Old World. Yet today the threat to proper nutrition sometimes grows when Western food prejudices are adopted by non-Western peoples, as part of the process of Westernization which has pervaded much of the world. In such cases the use of the food is viewed as symbolic of membership in an "uncivilized" group, and rejection is seen as symbolic of a man's

3

progressiveness. Though the symbolic role of food is quite varied in society, in ceremonial life and as a status symbol within the group,[1] its position in symbolizing ethnic and religious groups has been most important in the diffusion of food use and avoidance and is emphasized throughout this book.

In considering the influence of man's foodways on his use of food resources, anthropologists have principally followed the functional approach, typified by Audrey Richards' admirable *Hunger and Work in a Savage Tribe*. This involves analysis of the interrelations between the foodways and other aspects of a particular society and culture. The present study, by contrast, introduces the approach of the cultural geographer to the understanding of foodways. It has two purposes. The first is to consider the use and avoidance of certain foods of animal origin in the Old World, and to explain their occurrence in historical terms. The second is to demonstrate that the foodways behave like other culture traits. They have origins. They may be diffused. They may develop independently in different places. And they may be modified through time by various means.

In the Western literature, on which this study is based, there are abundant references to the use and avoidance of foods of animal origin. This results from the strong feeling surrounding such foods and the disgust many observers feel when confronted with departures from their own foodways. Some writers include such information in an effort to shock the reader. Thus Shakespeare concocted a witches' broth for Macbeth largely of strange and revolting animal products:

FIRST WITCH Round about the cauldron go;
In the poison'd entrails throw.
Toad, that under cold stone
Days and nights hast thirty-one
Swelter'd venom sleeping got,
Boil thou first i' the charmed pot.
SECOND WITCH Fillet of a fenny snake,
In the cauldron boil and bake;
Eye of newt, and toe of frog,
Wool of bat, and tongue of dog,
Adder's fork, and blind-worm's sting,
Lizard's leg, and howlet's wing,
For a charm of powerful trouble,
Like a hell-broth boil and bubble.

THIRD WITCH   Scale of dragon, tooth of wolf,
                      Witches' mummy, maw and gulf
                      Of the ravin'd salt-sea shark,
                      Root of hemlock digg'd i' the dark,
                      Liver of blaspheming Jew,
                      Gall of goat, and slips of yew
                      Sliver'd in the moon's eclipse,
                      Nose of Turk, and Tartar's lips,
                      Finger of birth-strangled babe
                      Ditch-deliver'd by a drab,
                      Make the gruel thick and slab:
                      Add thereto a tiger's chaudron,
                      For the ingredients of our cauldron.
SECOND WITCH   Cool it with a baboon's blood,
                      Then the charm is firm and good.[2]

A drawback of this literature is the ethnocentrism of the writers. They take more note of foodways that differ from Western ways (i.e. the eating of dogs, the rejection of beef, chicken and eggs, and pork) than of those that are similar (the rejection of dogflesh, the eating of beef, chicken and eggs, and pork). Accordingly the principal emphasis in this book is sometimes on the use of a food (dogflesh) and sometimes on its rejection (beef, chicken and eggs, etc.). Another drawback is unequal treatment, and the deficient coverage of some Old World peoples. Contrast the thoroughness of the accounts of the few hundred surviving Toda of India with the paucity of those dealing with the millions of people living in the Indo-Gangetic Plain. This has seriously handicapped the maps showing foodway distributions, for units of varying size and coverage have had to be used. The maps should be regarded only as approximations, to be delimited in greater detail by further searching of the literature and by intensive field work.

Numerous references in the literature are but brief mentions of use or avoidance, without account of reasons or other circumstances. Hence many questions cannot be fully answered, and the functional relations of the foodway to other elements of society and culture cannot usually be determined. In one case an avoidance may be associated with mere indifference; in another it may involve strong prejudice and the imposition of severe sanctions, even death, for violations. Yet the account may not reveal this. This book nevertheless attempts to show the manifestations of the foodway, whether it is universally observed in a society or held only by certain groups or individuals, whether or not it is observed at all times, and what intensity of feeling surrounds it. Although functional material is included in some places, the work remains primarily a study in cultural geography. It is hoped that the approach will demonstrate the feasibility of dealing in distributional terms with the nonquantifiable aspects of nonmaterial culture that limit man's use of available resources, a subject which has largely been ignored in the past in favor of the tangible and measurable.

The primary divisions of this work, following the background material presented in Chapter 2, are by individual foods, each of which is considered in a separate chapter. Within each chapter the consideration is by region, delimited according to similarity of observance; this is followed by discussion and evaluation of the theories of origin that have been advanced, and the means of diffusion. The conclusion of the book presents generalizations on the nature, manifestations, origin, and diffusion of group avoidances of flesh food.

2

THE USE AND POTENTIALITIES
OF FLESH FOOD

Vegetarians claim that food of animal origin, such as meat, fish, eggs, and milk, is not essential for adequate nourishment. Their claims are valid in that vegetarian diets can be satisfactory if they are carefully selected to provide all necessary nutritional elements. However, foods of plant origin are commonly poorer in protein than animal foods. And vegetable proteins, because they have fewer of the essential amino acids, cannot be converted into body protein as readily as animal proteins; they must therefore be consumed in larger quantities for adequate nutrition. The danger in a purely vegetarian diet is that through either ignorance or poverty the necessary amino acids will not be supplied in sufficient amounts to meet dietary needs. It is as a compact source of easily digested protein that animal foods are important in the diet.

Striking differences in physique and state of health among neighboring peoples are often found to correlate with the amount of animal protein consumed. The people of northwest India, who eat more foods of animal origin than people in other regions of India and have a higher protein intake, are generally healthy, vigorous, and well developed; many peoples of the south and east are poorly developed, disease-

ridden, and lacking in energy. The pastoral Masai of Kenya, whose
diet includes substantial amounts of milk, blood, and flesh, are tall,
vigorous, and healthy, whereas their agricultural Kikuyu neighbors,
who live almost exclusively on millet, maize, sweet potatoes, and yams,
are smaller, weaker, and less resistant to certain tropical diseases, as
well as to tuberculosis and pneumonia.* In fact the average Masai
woman is as strong as the average Kikuyu man. The form of economy
is the major factor in the Masai's greater intake of animal protein and
superior nutritional state. That these are more than isolated instances
is suggested by Vilhjalmur Stefansson, whose life with the Eskimos
convinced him that profound nutritional differences exist between
hunters and pastoralists on the one hand and farmers on the other. In
the United States only people who can afford abundant "hunting man's
food, like beef steaks and chicken, or a lot of monkey food, like fresh
fruit and raw vegetables ...," escape deficiency troubles. Stefansson
also contends that "No people of the past or present are known who
had complete freedom from tooth decay unless they were hunting, fishing, pastoral in their way of life, and got little or none of their food
direct from the vegetable kingdom."[1] Because of his Arctic experiences,
Stefansson believes that men can successfully live solely on flesh food
for long periods of time. To convince others, he and a companion
named Andersen undertook a controlled experiment of living for a year
entirely on meat and fish. They planned to exclude from their diet not
only all vegetable food but also eggs, milk, and milk products. Though
Stefansson found it necessary, in traveling around the country, to eat
products in the egg and milk category, Andersen used neither eggs,
milk, nor milk products during the entire year. Both completed the experiment without injury to health.[2]

In historical times most of mankind has become increasingly dependent on plant food, and has had available but small quantities of animal
foods—meat, of them all, being in shortest supply. Some groups obtain
flesh only on rare occasions, as when an animal is sacrificed ceremonially. Curious manifestations of desire for flesh are displayed. The
Bemba of Northern Rhodesia have a special word, *ubukashya*, for the
craving for meat. Their reaction to its presence "is quite out of keeping

* The Masai, Kikuyu, and most other Old World peoples and places mentioned in the text
are located on Maps 7–13. To determine on which map a group or place appears see
Map 6 or the index at the back of the book.

with its purely physiological value"; when meat is abundant they dance through the night and work again the following day, in an outburst of energy which they attribute to the strength gained from eating meat.[3] If the Lele of the Kasai region of the Congo have no meat or fish to eat, they may choose to drink palm wine and go to sleep without eating. Lele discussion of social occasions centers on the quantity and type of meat served, and understandably they consider it an insult to offer a meal of vegetable food to a guest.[4]

Despite the nutritional value of foods of animal origin, attitudes and customs restricting their use are widespread. In large areas of East and South Asia and of tropical Africa, for example, people refuse to drink milk, a practice as defiling in their eyes as drinking urine would be in ours.[5] The most important restrictions derive from those religions, such as Buddhism and Hinduism, which preach vegetarianism, and which base their teachings on belief in the sanctity of life. Because many ancient scholars were involved in religious pursuits, they became staunch supporters of these beliefs, which have descended to their emancipated successors, as in western Europe.

India exhibits the most extreme manifestations of vegetarianism. Among the Hindus, who in early times sacrificed and ate animals openly, there was a slow growth of vegetarianism, which was tied to the principle of nonviolence and was stimulated by those offshoot competitors of Hinduism: Buddhism and Jainism. In keeping with their beliefs, Brahmans, the priestly castes of Hindus, today commonly refuse meat and fish. They have a moral obligation to be tender to animals and to avoid injuring them. Some other castes share the attitudes of the Brahmans. Gandhi, a member of the Bania caste, abhorred flesh food. His one attempt at eating it, encouraged by hatred of the British rulers of India, was a fiasco:

"It began to grow on me that meat-eating was good, that it would make me strong and daring, and that, if the whole country took to meat-eating, the English could be overcome...It was not a question of pleasing the palate. I did not know that it had a particularly good relish ...We went in search of a lonely spot by the river, and there I saw, for the first time in my life—meat. There was baker's bread also. I relished neither. The goat's meat was as tough as leather. I simply could not eat it. I was sick and had to leave off eating. I had a very bad night afterwards. A horrible nightmare haunted me. Every time I dropped off to sleep it would seem as though a live goat were bleating inside me, and I would jump up full of remorse. . . . If my mother and father came to know of my having become a meat-eater, they would be deeply shocked. This knowledge was gnawing at my heart."[6]

The Jains, a sect of dissenters from Hinduism who follow strict rules in their efforts to attain spirituality, take five vows, of which the first is not to kill. The orthodox Jain sweeps the ground before him as he walks lest he destroy living creatures; he wears a veil to avoid inhaling insects; he believes that it is best not to eat in the evening or at night, for these are times when he might inadvertently eat some living thing; "he rejects not only meat," says Westermarck, "but even honey, together with various fruits that are supposed to contain worms, not because of his distaste for worms but because of his regard for life."[7]

Even more effective in propagating humane feelings toward animals and vegetarian observances than Hinduism and Jainism has been Buddhism, which diffused these traits far into Southeast Asia, inner Asia, and the Far East. An extreme statement of the Buddhist position, as put by Westermarck, is that a Buddhist "may not knowingly deprive any creature of life, not even a worm or an ant. He may not drink water in which animal life of any kind whatever is contained, and must not even pour it out on grass or clay."[8] Though Buddhists generally are opposed to taking life, not all of them are reluctant to eat flesh. In many Buddhist areas, including Tibet, Ceylon, Burma, and Thailand, even Buddhist priests eat meat. In China, where both Buddhist and Taoist influences have encouraged kindness to animals and vegetarianism, people believe that the gods do not like the killing of animals, that eating flesh is incompatible with the highest degree of purity, and that vegetarian practice will aid one to a better afterlife. In spite of this, pure vegetarianism has generally been practiced in China only by clergy, devout laymen, and by widows, though others would eat vegetarian meals once or twice a month. An exceptional case is the island of Pootu (Puto Shan) off the coast of Chekiang, where in 1935 more than half the population was Buddhist monks, who were strict vegetarians. Neither eggs nor meat could be purchased on Pootu, and there was a prohibition against importing meat products of any kind.[9] In China, and in Japan as well, traditional attitudes have given way rapidly in modern times; today economic considerations rather than cultural prejudices are mainly responsible for the small per capita consumption of flesh.

In the Middle East and the Mediterranean area too, vegetarian practices have generally been observed scrupulously only by clergy and the very devout. Vegetarianism was common in ancient Persia only in the priestly and learned class of the Magi.[10] The Chaldean Christians of modern Turkey, Iraq, and Iran still require that a candidate for the patriarchate of their church shall never have eaten meat, and that his mother shall not have done so during her pregnancy and nursing.[11] An occasional religious group, such as the followers of Mani,[12] forbade flesh food to all believers, but this was exceptional. Even where vegetarianism was not widely followed, there sometimes occurred, as in ancient Greece,[13] the belief in a former golden age when men killed no animals and abstained from flesh food; and animal food was thought not to promote either individual temperance and frugality or piety and the contemplative life.

There have been vegetarians in northwest Europe as well, though their numbers, which include both the religious-minded and others, have been less impressive than has their vociferousness. The eighteenth-century English scholar Joseph Ritson contended that even the "sight of animal food is unnatural and disgusting," that meat reminds the thoughtful person of a dead body along the road being eaten by vultures or ravens, or perhaps even of a cannibal feast.[14] He argued that animal food is not necessary for attaining strength or size, and in fact injures health and mental well-being, as well as that killing animals for food develops cruelty and ferocity and leads to human sacrifice and cannibalism.[15]

It is interesting that there is no sharp line dividing vegetarians from meat eaters in their attitude toward slaughter of animals. In fact, many meat eaters share with vegetarians the belief that slaughter is immoral and degrading, and that it contaminates the slaughterer. An example is the Mandaeans of Iraq and Iran, who are apologetic about animal slaughter and regard it as a sin.[16] Another example is the widespread phenomenon of professional butchers. The only one, in some groups, to slaughter animals, the butcher is placed in a position of danger and impurity but other people are thereby protected from contamination. The Bemba of Northern Rhodesia consider the hereditary official who kills most of the animals used for ritualistic purposes at the principal chief's court a daring fellow for performing such dangerous work. For his own protection he undergoes purification ceremonies after the slaughter.[17] The Guanche of the Canary Islands did not allow their professional butchers to enter the homes of other people, to handle their property, or to associate with anyone but those of their calling.[18] In Japan members of the butchers' caste, the Eta (Yeta), are regarded as unclean and kept from contact with other people.[19] The professional butchers in Tibet have been the most despised of all classes, regarded as professional sinners because they violate the Buddhist precept against taking life.[20]

Differences in wealth and status very generally lead to inequities in the distribution of available flesh food. Some groups, it is true, have customs which tend to offset these differences and bring about a wider distribution of the food; but as a rule pronounced inequities persist. In many of the Pacific islands and in the Northern Territories of Ghana chiefs and other officials are singled out for preferential treatment in the distribution of flesh. Elsewhere it is members of prestigeful groups who have preferential status. All-male cult groups among the Lele of the Congo have prior rights to hunt certain animals or to eat specific parts of them; only a few small animals such as birds, squirrels, and monkeys are left for ordinary people to hunt and consume at will.[21] In other groups older men are given special treatment when the flesh food is divided. The Nuba of the Sudan treat the old men as privileged guests at feasts; when the flesh of game is available a large share of it is presented to them as a matter of politeness or because they need it for various rituals. Nuba women receive but small portions of meat or none at all.[22] On Alor in Indonesia flesh food is viewed as the property of the men. At feasts, the principal times when meat is available, it is distributed to households according to the men in them; these share it with their dependents, the women and children. The system of distribution thus reinforces the prestige of the men in society.[23] Such situations are so common in the Old World as to deny to many women an adequate supply of protein, although as bearers of the young they are in particular need of it.

3

PIGS AND PORK

The Middle Eastern Center of Pork Avoidance

As one might expect, the principal center of pork avoidance in the Old World today is the Middle East (see Map 1), where Moslems, who vigorously reject swine, account for a large part of the population. The distribution, however, cannot be explained simply in terms of Islam, for pork is also strongly rejected there by such other groups as the Orthodox Jews, the Yezidi, the Mandaeans of Iraq and Iran, and the Christian and pagan peoples of Ethiopia. Where strong feeling against the use of pork occurs elsewhere in the Old World, it can frequently be traced to Middle Eastern influence, whether through diffusion of Middle Eastern religions; through a return to the ways of the old religions, as among the Seventh-Day Adventists; or through the spread of Middle Eastern cultural attitudes unrelated to religion.

Early History.—The widespread occurrence of pork rejection in the Middle East today and the strength of feeling about it contrast curiously with the ancient situation there. In late Paleolithic times many peoples of the region apparently hunted wild pigs and ate pork. This hunting probably continued in the area through Neolithic times into later periods. But at some point in prehistoric times—exactly when is not known—the domestic pig appeared in parts of the region, and its flesh presumably supplemented or replaced that of its wild brethren. That

13

Map 1—Pork Eating

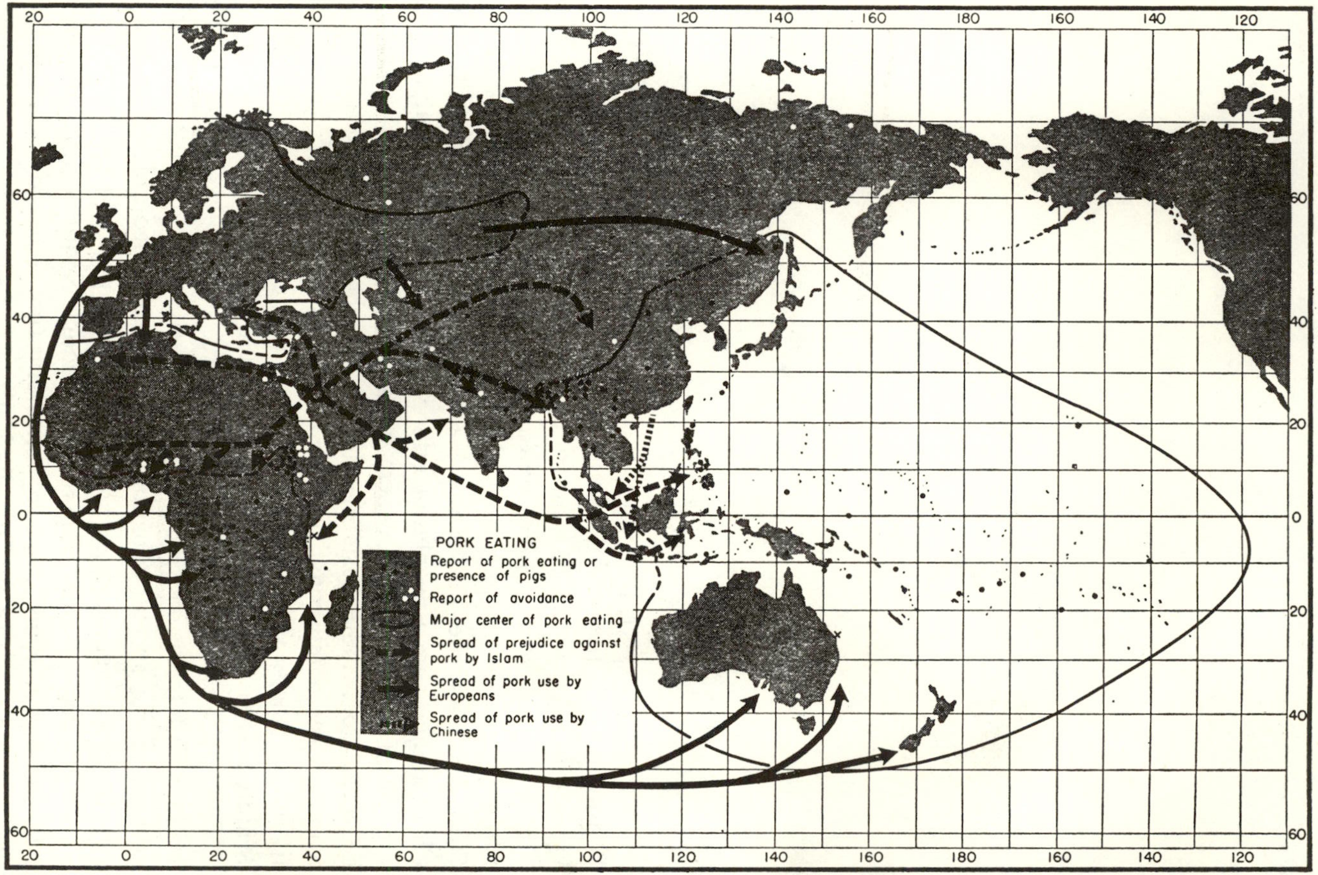

PORK EATING

Report of pork eating or
presence of pigs

Report of avoidance

Major center of pork eating

Spread of prejudice against
pork by Islam

Spread of pork use by
Europeans

Spread of pork use by
Chinese

14

pork came to be widely used in the Middle East is suggested by the occurrence of pig bones in an impressive number of prehistoric and early historic sites from North Africa to the Indus Valley. In some cases they were from wild animals, but in others, it is asserted, they belonged to domesticated individuals.[1]*

The historical record confirms the widespread early occurrence of pig keeping and pork eating in the Middle East. At the western end of the area, the Guanche aborigines of Tenerife in the Canary Islands ate pork at the time of first European contact.[2] Although the pig is seldom found portrayed in Egyptian ruins, clay pigs dating from predynastic times have been uncovered along the Nile Valley. The first mention of domestic pigs in Egyptian history dates from the Third Dynasty (c. 2686–2613 B.C.). Later King Sesostris I (c. 1972–1928 B.C.) appointed an official to care for the royal farms and named him "Overseer of Swine."[3]* Pictures from tombs of the Eighteenth Dynasty (c. 1567–1320 B.C.) at Thebes show pigs being driven over fields of newly sown wheat, to tread it in (Fig. 1).[4] And King Amenophis III (c. 1417–1379 B.C.) presented a thousand hogs and a thousand young pigs to the Temple of Ptah at Memphis. Facts such as these indicate the importance of pigs in Egyptian life.

There is no hint of negative reaction to pigs or pork throughout the early period of pig keeping in Egypt. That the king himself possessed pigs, that he presented them to the temple, and that they were bred in the temple grounds at Abydos,[5] most sacred place in all Egypt, suggest, on the contrary, a respectable position. By the time of Herodotus (c. 484–425 B.C.), however, the status of the pig in Egypt apparently had altered. It was regarded as so unclean that a man who brushed against one rushed to the river and plunged in without undressing, to cleanse himself. Swineherds belonged to a separate class and were considered too defiled to enter the temples.[6] People, of course, did not generally eat pork. But the Egyptians sacrificed pigs and ate pork once a year, at a celebration to the moon and to "Bacchus" (Osiris). Poor people who could not afford to buy pigs for this celebration made and baked pigs of dough and sacrificed them.

After the time of Herodotus the position of the pig in Egypt continued to be ambivalent. According to Plutarch, Egyptian priests re-

---

* An asterisk in combination with a note number here and throughout the rest of the text indicates that the note contains discursive material expanding the text material.

garded the pig as unclean and refused its flesh, though pigs were still sacrificed at every full moon.[7] Aelian (c. A.D. 200) stated that pigs were abhorrent to the sun and moon, and that the Egyptians sacrificed them at no time but the annual lunar festival.[8] Though this may seem to confirm the lowly position of the pig, the Greeks Aristides (c. A.D. 125), Clemens (c. A.D. 150–215), and Cyril (c. A.D. 376–444) all believed that the pig was sacred to the Egyptians!

Several ideas have been advanced to explain the strange duality in the position of the pig in Egypt. One plausible suggestion is that the animal fell from a position of respect because of the ascendancy of the god Horus over his rival Set, with whom it may have been associated.[9] Support for this may be claimed in the legend that Set, disguised as a pig, attempted to destroy the "eye of Horus," probably the moon, and that Horus avenged himself by establishing pig sacrifice to the moon.[10] The fact that by the time of the Greek observers the Egyptians considered both the pig and Set symbols of evil[11] lends credence to this hypothesis.

Frazer, discussing the duality of feeling toward some animals, points out that the Egyptians may have regarded the pig not simply as a foul and disgusting creature but as one possessing significant supernatural powers, and may have held toward it "that primitive sentiment of religious awe and fear in which the feelings of reverence and abhorrence are equally blended."[12] The change in the position of the pig in Egypt may reflect a conquest of one facet of this duality of feeling by the other, the awe or reverence, which at one time may have been the stronger, being gradually dominated by the abhorrence. Whether this came about through the struggle between Set and Horus or in some other way remains a mystery.

The ancient Jewish attitude toward the pig, though less ambiguous than that of the Egyptians, was not altogether consistent either. Leviticus and Deuteronomy picture the pig as unclean and forbid its flesh;[13] other Bible passages such as the proverb likening a "beautiful woman without taste" to "a golden ring in the snout of a sow,"[14] indicate the lowly position of swine. There are, however, some curious statements in Isaiah,[15] in sections probably added to the book from 400 to 200 B.C., which suggest that the Jews had secret religious meetings at which they ate pork. Greek observers were puzzled by the Jewish attitude toward swine. They noted that although Jews were not permitted to eat pigs—which suggests uncleanness—neither were they permitted to kill them—which suggests sanctity.[16] But it was the feeling that the pig is unclean that prevailed among the Jews, and that caused the avoidance of pork to become symbolic of the religion. During the reign (175–163 B.C.) of the conqueror Antiochus Epiphanes, who put strong pressure on the Jews to abandon their religion in favor of the Greek gods, they were tested to determine their willingness to accept the new ways by being required to sacrifice swine and eat pork.[17] In one instance the old scribe Eleazar was forced to put pork in his mouth, but he spat it out, choosing rather to die than to break the law of his faith.[18] Some Jews evidently did acquiesce in pork eating, for a little later when John Hyrcanus I was high priest (c. 135–105 B.C.), he found it necessary to issue a decree prohibiting the practice.[19] There are various references to pigs and pig keeping in New Testament times, among them the story of how Christ cured the madman (or madmen) from across the Sea of Galilee by driving the demons who possessed him into a herd of swine.[20] These pigs probably belonged to Gentiles, for the Jews continued to regard pig keeping as the lowliest of occupations.

Some peoples in ancient Southwest Asia had none of this feeling. In Mesopotamia wild and domestic pigs were mentioned in inscriptions and pictured on seals and on wall reliefs.[21] At Tell Asmar pig bones were so plentiful that Max Hilzheimer concluded the pig was the most important Sumerian domestic animal raised for food.[22] In Babylonia Hammurabi's code of laws (c. 1900 B.C.) set a penalty for theft of pigs belonging either to temples or householders.[23] To judge from one Hittite text,[24] the Hittites also kept pigs, although their position is not stated. In Mesopotamia after the death of the Persian pretender Cyrus in 401 B.C., the Greek mercenaries and their Persian allies pledged allegiance to each other by slaughtering a bull, a ram, and a boar, dipping their weapons in the blood, and swearing an oath.[25] On their march up country to safety the Greeks obtained hogs' lard and pork in Armenia and encountered pigs among the Drilai in Pontus.[26] Thus we know that, from the time of the Sumerians down to the March of the Ten Thousand, pigs were present and their flesh was eaten by numerous peoples in Southwest Asia.

In spite of these facts, there also existed an ambiguity of feeling toward pigs in this part of the Middle East, similar to that found in Egypt. Often the ambiguity resulted in the rejection of swine, but whether because they were sacred or unclean is not certain. It has been conjectured that in Nippur, a city south of Babylon, the pig was sacred to the god Bel; and Peters says that the pig seems to have been taboo or unclean there, in the sense that its "flesh was forbidden for unhallowed use."[27] The student of Mesopotamian religion, Morris Jastrow, sees evidence that in parts of Babylonia the boar was a sacred animal—though there were two aspects to its sanctity: on the one hand it was too sacred to be sacrificed to the gods and on the other it was considered unclean.[28] In Haran in northern Mesopotamia the inhabitants were forbidden to eat pigs, but on a certain day every year they sacrificed swine, offered them to their gods, and ate as much pork as they could lay their hands on.[29] According to Lucian (c. A.D. 120–180), at Hierapolis, a city in northern Syria sacred to the nature goddess Atargatis, where people neither sacrificed pigs nor ate pork, some said it was because pigs were abominable, others because they were holy animals.[30]

Several of the religious cults of Asia Minor clearly were foci of pork avoidance. At Comana in Pontus, in northern Asia Minor, a city which was a center of the worship of the ancient Anatolian goddess of fertility Ma, the people, in order to maintain the purity of the temple, neither ate pork nor permitted it in the city.[31] Similarly, at Castabus in the Carian Chersonese in southwest Asia Minor, people who had eaten pork or come into contact with pigs were forbidden entry to the sanctuary of Hemithea.[32] Contact with swine constituted one of the first categories of impurity for the followers of Men Tyrannus, an Asiatic deity worshiped widely in Asia Minor. Foucart presents evidence that there were followers of Men in Phrygia, Lydia, Pisidia, Caria, Pontus, and Pamphylia.[33]

Perhaps best known of the cults in Asia Minor is the Phrygian cult of Cybele, the mother goddess. Worship of Cybele originated in prehistoric times, and became important in Galatia, Lydia, and Phrygia early in historic times. Julianus (A.D. 331–363) said that the followers of Cybele abstained from pork during their sacred rites because the pig was regarded as an animal belonging to the earth and because its flesh was impure and coarse.[34] Pausanias (c. A.D. 175) reported that the people of Pessinus in Galatia, the most sacred city of the cult of Cybele, "abstain from swine"; and he recounted the explanation given him, which centers on one of the myths of Attis, Cybele's son and lover, who figured prominently in her worship.[35] This was the account of a poet of

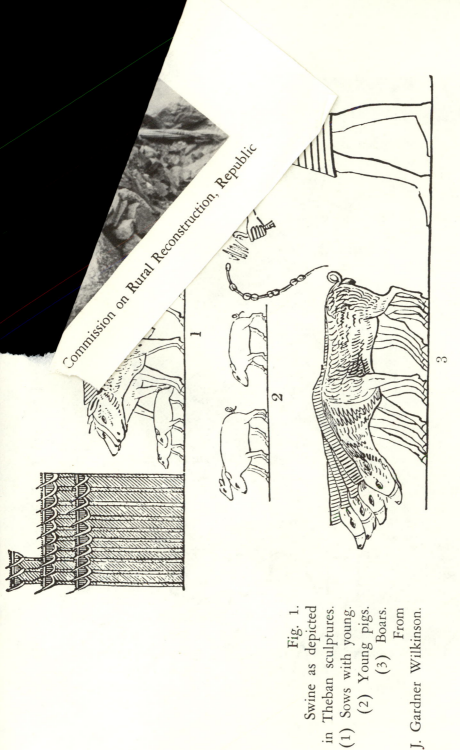

Fig. 1.
Swine as depicted
in Theban sculptures.
(1) Sows with young.
(2) Young pigs.
(3) Boars.
From
J. Gardner Wilkinson.

Fig. 2. Pig keeping on Quemoy. Courtesy Joint [Commission on Rural Reconstruction] of China.

the fourth century B.C., Hermesianax, who said that Attis was a Phrygian who migrated to Lydia and was so honored by the Lydians that Zeus sent a boar to destroy their fields. The boar killed Attis and some of the Lydians; hence the Galatians of Pessinus abstain from swine. Frazer comments that although this myth might indeed have found expression in the refusal of the people of Pessinus to eat swine, it might also have been invented later to explain the practice.[36]

The paragraphs above indicate no sharp regionalization of attitude toward pigs and pork in ancient Southwest Asia. W. M. Ramsay has argued that there were striking differences between eastern Asia Minor, beginning with Pessinus, and western Asia Minor and Greece.[37] He considers the Halys River to be roughly the boundary between the two regions: to the east were the pig haters, to whom "the very presence of a pig in the holy city" was "a profanation and an impurity"; to the west the pig eaters, who used swine in their holiest ceremonies and who made images of the pig to bury with their dead. If a line of demarcation is possible at all, it must be more carefully drawn than along the Halys River: pigs were considered a profanation in parts of western Asia Minor, and as we shall see, pork was prohibited in Crete. Nevertheless, Ramsay's theory that in Asia Minor the religion that originally prevailed did not regard the pig with horror, but that Semitic influence, probably from the Assyrians, subsequently introduced abhorrence and spread it westward warrants further investigation.

In the Aegean region people seem to have kept sizable numbers of pigs from Neolithic times on.[38] The works of both Greek and Roman writers indicate that pork was a favorite meat and was considered more nutritious than other foods. Hippocrates (c. 460 B.C.), for example, spoke of pork as providing more strength than other types of flesh.[39] Galen stated that if professional athletes went for one day without pork and were given instead an equal amount of any other food, they immediately became weaker; and if this persisted for several days, they lost weight. Aëtius, Oribasius, and the authorities succeeding Galen agreed in his judgment.[40] Pliny commented that in Rome the flesh of both domestic pig and wild boar was much esteemed, and that hogs' fat was highly regarded for medicinal purposes.[41] Martial wrote of his fondness for young milk-fed pigs;[42] and Juvenal and other writers of the period mentioned wild boar as a favorite delicacy of Roman epicures.[43]

While Greeks and Romans regarded pigs primarily as a source of flesh, the Greeks made them sacrificial animals,[44] the customary victims in purificatory rites;[45] and the Romans sacrificed them on special occasions.[46*] Cato suggested that before thinning a grove of trees the farmer should sacrifice a pig to the deity of the place to win his favor.[47] The pig was associated particularly with Demeter, Greek goddess of the grain, and was regularly sacrificed to her. At one of the rites of Demeter, the Thesmophoria, people sacrificed pigs, ate some of the flesh, and kept some until the next festival, when it was sown with the seed to assure a good crop. Apparently the eating of pork in this ceremony was a solemn sacrament in which the worshipers symbolically ate the body of the deity.[48] In Crete, like Greece a center of the worship of Demeter, the pig was also considered sacred, but one report indicates that nothing could induce people to eat its flesh.[49] This suggests the possible intrusion into the Greek and Roman world of Asian influences, for Crete was one of the avenues by which Oriental elements entered the Mediterranean world.

If pork rejection was present in Greece and Rome, it may have been introduced with Asian deities who had some connection with the matter —precisely what is not clear. Likely candidates are the Syrian Adonis, and the Phrygian Cybele with her lover Attis. Of these, Cybele is the more likely, for she was introduced to Rome in such a direct and auspicious way that Oriental elements might readily have been accepted with her.[50*]

Since the Rise of Christianity.—Christianity, despite its derivation from Judaism, did not adopt the Jewish view that the pig is an unclean animal whose flesh should not be eaten. In fact it spread the use of pork, both through conversions from Judaism and through the gradual elimination in the Greek and Roman world of earlier cults associated with the rejection of pork. Even in Egypt, with its ancient and curious attitudes toward the pig, the animal apparently became acceptable again; pork eating, too, became more general following the rise of Christianity and the decline of the ancient gods.

Yet old attitudes and avoidances persisted in Judaism and perhaps, too, in some of the unchronicled cults that survived in the Middle East and Mediterranean. And with the establishment of Islam there arose a new champion of the ancient negative attitudes toward the pig and pork. The Islamic attitudes may have derived originally from pastoral or Jewish prejudice, but the immediate source was the Prophet Mohammed himself, who may have adopted them in order to distinguish Islam from its major adversary, Christianity. Mohammed repeated more than once in the Koran his specific prohibitions against pork;[51] and from the seventh century on they were rapidly diffused by the faithful from an essentially pigless Arabia into regions of pig keeping in Asia, Africa, and southern Europe. Islamic rejection of the pig and pork was commonly accompanied by strong feelings of revulsion, and some Moslems, such as those of Egypt,[52] so abhorred swine as to consider everything touched by them contaminated and worthless.

The difference between Moslem and Christian practice has made the pattern of pig keeping and pork eating fairly simple in the Mediterranean and Middle East. Christians on the north shores of the Mediterranean generally keep pigs and eat pork, though the Moslems of Albania do not. To the east of the Mediterranean, pork is rejected by Moslems and Orthodox Jews; by the Nosairis of Syria,[53] whose religion appears to be a syncretism of the ancient Haranian religion and Islam; as well as by the Yezidi "devil worshipers" of Kurdistan[54] and the Mandaeans of southern Iraq and Iran.[55] The Christians of Syria and Lebanon eat pork.[56] It has been substantiated, too, that the Druses do not hesitate to eat it, and that if they seem to abstain, it is during their stay in the cities and by imitation or from fear of the Moslems.[57] In Israel both Christian Arabs and emancipated Jews eat pork. Pig keeping has even been adopted by certain Jewish farmers, and pork is sold in some butcher shops. This has understandably disgusted the Orthodox Jews; in 1960 legislation was pending which would enable local governmental units to prohibit Jews from keeping pigs. In North Africa pork is eaten by Christians, including both the European settlers who are found in various places and the Coptic Christians of Egypt.[58*]

In view of the strong official rejection of pigs and pork by Moslems, it is surprising that the use of wild and domestic pigs as food survived at all in the Islamic world—yet it did. Certain Moslem groups have eaten the flesh of wild pigs for food;[59*] others have eaten domestic pigs surreptitiously. Most Moslem authors, it is true, condemn pork, but two tenth-century Persian doctors apparently upheld its use. Thus Avicenna included pork in his classification of foodstuffs among those that "enrich the serous humour";[60] and Haly Abbas spoke favorably of it as food.[61] Among the Indonesians and certain Berbers of North Africa people persisted in pig keeping and pork eating long after becoming Moslems. For example, Xavier de Planhol states that "the Ghomara,

Riffian heretics of the Middle Ages, permitted the flesh of female pigs and boars to be eaten";[62] and formerly people raised swine in most of the mountain core of the Rif. It was only a few generations ago, in fact, that the Berbers of Iherrushen and Ikhuanen in northern Gzennaya, Morocco, stopped raising pigs, after one of their leading men returned from a pilgrimage to Mecca. Elsewhere among the Berbers of Morocco pig keeping apparently persisted even later, although people were very secretive about it; Carleton Coon could not say with certainty whether people kept swine in the Rif or Senhaja when he was there in the late 1920's, but he suspected that they did. The pigs were bred from animals trapped in the mountains and brought home. They fed on acorns and roots on the mountainside during the daytime and were kept in the house at night; people were careful to remove them before guests arrived, and never took them to market or admitted keeping them.[63] In Coon's time pork, apparently from wild boars, was also made into sausages or dried in the sun to form kadids. Because some people ridiculed the eating of pork kadids, connoisseurs in some places ate them secretly and in others called them by different names when strangers were present.[64] It is worth noting that this survival occurs in the oak woods of the Atlas Mountains, an environment eminently suited since antiquity to pig keeping.

Today the prejudice against pork is somewhat on the decline in the Middle East, following the weakening of traditional religious beliefs. As a result the meat is available, in limited amounts, in most parts of the area, among Moslems and Jews as well as Christians. Pork, it is asserted, can be found in Israel, Iraq, Iran, and Turkey, as well as Egypt, and is probably entirely absent only in the Arabian Peninsula (except for Bahrein, Dhahran, and probably Kuwait).

In addition to the survivals and revivals of the use of pork for food, there is a perhaps more general medicinal use of the flesh of the wild boar. In Morocco, for instance, people eat the liver of the wild boar to gain the animal's strength.[65] They also believe the flesh of the boar to be bracing for children, to be a remedy for syphilis, and to make a man insensitive to pain.[66]

Non-Mediterranean Europe

Among the earliest European farmers cattle and swine were the most numerous livestock. Cattle usually predominated in the western sections, including southern England and the lower levels of the Swiss lake dwellings; and swine in the northern sections, especially among coastal groups.[67] Though sheep increased in importance in the Late Bronze and Early Iron ages, pigs continued to occupy a significant position in the agricultural life of non-Mediterranean Europe, and people have continued to eat their flesh until the present time. Except for temporary penetrations by Islam into the Iberian Peninsula and the Balkans, and the settlement of non-pork-eating Jewish migrants in the region, the area at first remained largely isolated from the great struggle between those who used pork as food and those who rejected it.[68*] With the period of colonial expansion, however, non-Mediterranean Europeans took a more active part, in favor of pig keeping and pork eating.

Africa South of the Sahara

Africa south of the Sahara, on the contrary, has long been deeply embroiled in the controversy over the status of pigs and the acceptability of pork as food. There is no evidence that the pig was ever domesticated south of the Sahara (though wild forms of the common pig, Sus, are found in the Sudan) or that it was present in the earliest Sudanese agricultural sites.[69*] Nevertheless, domesticated pigs were introduced to the Sudan from Egypt long before Europeans arrived. This was accomplished by way of the string of Nubian agricultural villages that cling to the banks of the Nile. Once pig raising reached the more humid country south of Khartoum, it spread freely into regions away from the river.[70*]

There is no certainty that in pre-European times the domestic pig was diffused farther into Africa than the Sudan. Why it should have failed to spread farther cannot now be determined precisely. One probable factor is the presence to the south of tsetse-borne sleeping sickness, to which the pig is susceptible. Another is the resistance of the Ethiopians, who since antiquity have looked on pigs as unclean and refused to keep them or to eat pork. There is no record of any Ethiopian people, except a few pagan Negroid groups along the Sudan border, ever having kept pigs. The antipathy occurs not only among Moslems and Jews (Falasha) but also among Christians and unassimilated pagan Cushites such as the K'amant.

Pig keeping in the Sudanese area was attacked from the north starting in the seventh century, when the Moslems overran Egypt. Although the Nubian Christian kingdoms along the Nile held out for several centuries, as Islam gradually spread southward they were overthrown one by one, and pig keeping was abandoned. After the capitulation of the Nubian Christians at Ibrim in 1173, the Moslem conquerors performed two acts symbolic of their victory over Christianity: they jailed and tortured the priests and killed the pigs.[71] Nevertheless, pig keeping probably persisted farther south in Nubia until the fall of Dongola in the fourteenth century and of Alwa in the early sixteenth century. The further expansion of Islam has brought about a continuing recession of pig keeping in the Sudan. It has survived only among those marginal groups that have remained pagan, such as certain peoples of the Nuba Mountains. Even these are now coming under increasing pressure from Islam. Many already have abandoned pig keeping and speak with contempt of their unconverted brethren who continue to eat pork.[72] A similar abandonment of pig keeping occurred along the border between the Sudan and Ethiopia, where the pagans have been under pressure not only from Islam in the Sudan but from Christianity in Ethiopia.[73*]

At the same time that Islam was bringing about the decline of pig keeping in the Sudan, Europeans were introducing domestic pigs to Africa, following the Portuguese voyages of exploration in the fifteenth century.[74*] From the west coast pigs spread into the interior, except where sleeping sickness or Islamic and other prejudice blocked their way.[75*] In East Africa the introduction of pig keeping was hindered by the Arabs of the coastal trading settlements, and there and in South Africa by the reluctance of certain other peoples to accept them. Though in some cases this may simply have been due to the strangeness of the animal, in others it seems to have been a more positive contempt developed by cattle people for a beast unsuited to their way of life. As in the Middle East, some groups who rejected the flesh of domestic pigs nevertheless ate the flesh of wild pigs, whether bush pigs, wart hogs, or common pigs.[76*]

Whatever their initial objection, many non-Moslem groups of Africa have since given way to European example and influence.[77*] Pig keeping and pork eating have thus been widely adopted by native groups, especially along the Guinea Coast and in the Congo and Angola.[78*] Not only is the keeping of domestic pigs widespread, but a few peoples of West and Central Africa have tamed and kept the bush pig or the red river hog (*Potamochoerus*) for eating. This may be an interesting step

toward the domestication of an animal that would fit into the same ecological niche in African life as the domestic pig.

Iran and Inner Asia

Iran and inner Asia represent another major arena of struggle between pig peoples and anti-pig peoples. Not only does the region contain both pastoral and settled groups, who traditionally have been major
protagonists in the struggle, but it occupies a zone between the European and Chinese centers of pig keeping on one hand and the Middle
Eastern center of pig and pork rejection on the other. At an early date
farming peoples in at least parts of the region kept pigs; the bones have
been uncovered in a number of archeological sites. Other early groups,
however, developed an antipathy to the pig. According to Herodotus
the Scythians, who migrated from here into the Ukraine, used no pigs
for sacrifice, and did not allow them in their country;[79] for the early
Turks also swine were "taboo."[80] But it was Islam that brought about
the great decline in pig keeping and pork eating in the region from
the seventh century on.

In Iran today neither Moslems nor the few surviving Zoroastrians[81]
eat pork. When a European in Iran eats ham or bacon, the Iranians call
it "nightingale's flesh" to save face for the cook who prepares it.[82]
Iranians also regard the wild boar as unclean. A pious Moslem killed by
a wild boar, it is said, has to remain in the fires of hell for five hundred
years to become purified.[83*] In view of their antipathy toward pigs, it is
odd to find Iranian grooms whenever possible keeping a wild pig in the
stable, in the belief that pigs protect horses from the evil eye and that
their breath is good for horses.[84*]

In inner Asia pork is rejected by all Moslem groups, and by certain
non-Moslem peoples there and in neighboring areas: in the last century
among the Christian Cheremis who lived along the Volga River in
European Russia,[85] among the Votyak (a Christian Finnic group of the
Vologda region of European Russia), among the Lapps, and among the
Yakut of Siberia.[86] With the Cheremis and the Votyak, the rejection of
pork was apparently in imitation of Moslem groups, but the diffusion
of Moslem ideas seems less certain for the Lapps and the Yakut.

Inner Asia nevertheless is transitional in its attitudes toward pigs and
pork. Although the Selkup Samoyed, for example, apparently keep no

pigs themselves, pickled pork is eaten in wealthier homes during wedding celebrations.[87] The Kara-Kirghiz (Burut) farmers, who live northeast of Afghanistan from the Pamir region into Chinese Turkestan, keep pigs.[88] Mongols have a strong bias against pigs, which, it has been suggested, may be the normal reaction of a "nomadic" people to an animal that they cannot herd; nevertheless, they have no prejudice against pork and usually will eat it whenever they visit a city like Peiping. And when they do settle down to farming they start at once to keep pigs, which then become their sole source of meat.[89]

Tibet presents an even more confused picture of transition. Tibetan Lamaists believe that pigs were guilty of great wickedness in their previous life, and are unclean in their present state, partly because they destroy other forms of life in feeding.[90] Because of this, Lamaist law forbids eating pork,[91] and some Tibetan monks abstain from it.[92] The nomads constitute another strong sector of pork rejection.[93*] Nevertheless the people of central and eastern Tibet[94] do eat pork to some extent, especially in places like Lhasa and Dartsendo (Kangting), where foreign habits are imitated.[95] Even monks sometimes eat pork, and there is one report of its being served in the monasteries.[96]

Often in the past the peoples of inner Asia who kept pigs have been under strong pressure to abandon the practice. Today the struggle is going in favor of the pig, for China and Russia are dominant in the area and Islam and the pastoral way of life are on the decline. Where pigs are found in the region, they have apparently been introduced: to western Turkestan by the Slavs, and to eastern Turkestan, or Sinkiang, from China.[97]

The Far Eastern Center of Pig Keeping

China contains an estimated fourth of the world's pigs: 114,000,000 animals in 1957. Like Europe, it has been a major center of pig keeping[98*] and a place from which the practice has been diffused into neighboring areas.

Swine were an important feature of every northeast Chinese culture from the Neolithic down to and including the Shang people (c. 1520– c. 1030 B.C.). Pig bones, in fact, are found in such enormous numbers in Neolithic sites that pork is believed to have been the principal staple of Neolithic men. The Shang people, who kept both domestic pigs and an occasional wild boar in sties, also ate them in large numbers.[99] In later times the number of pigs has varied according to group and period; but the pig has remained one of the most common domestic animals in China, and pork has been a prized and important flesh food, among aborigines as well as Chinese.[1]* Not only was the flesh consumed, but in some parts of China it was customary to cook pig ribs in a sweet and sour sauce of sugar and vinegar, which made the calcium in the bones digestible; this provided an invaluable source of calcium for pregnant women.[2] The New Year's pig is as dear to the Chinese as the Thanksgiving turkey is to Americans.[3] Perhaps the best illustration of the importance of the pig in China is the fact that the ideograph meaning "home" consists of the signs for "roof" and for "pig."

The pig in the traditional Chinese economy was a household scavenger which survived on table scraps and chaff (Fig. 2). In many places pigs were actually quartered in the family garbage pit and regularly fed human excreta and garbage. Thus they not only converted into flesh certain plant nutrients that the human digestive system could not absorb directly, but may actually have performed an important health function, too: human parasites such as hookworm may have been destroyed in the pig's intestine.[4] It was rare for one farmer to raise a pig from infancy until it was ready for market; instead, some specialists bred pigs, others purchased young pigs and raised them, and still others fattened them for slaughter.[5]

Pressure in China against keeping and eating pigs has come principally from the sizable Moslem minority (estimated at 5 per cent of the population), most of whom are of Turkic, Mongol, or Arab extraction, and who are especially numerous in western China. For these pious Moslems the very presence of the pig is an irritant; it defiles the ground and pollutes the air.[6] The strictest Mongol Moslems refuse even to enter an ordinary Chinese house.[7] The people of the Moslem quarter of one town destroyed all their utensils to avoid defilement after they had been used by Russian soldiers billeted there, who presumably were unclean.[8] Some Moslems avoid the very word "pig," and refer to the animal as "the black one." Chinese Moslems also use the oath "pig-defiled"; it seems to puzzle non-Moslem Chinese, who do not regard the pig as an abominable animal.[9] In some regions Chinese Moslems drink river water to avoid using the same well as their pig-eating Chinese neighbors.

Though they publicly avoid pork, in private Chinese Moslems are sometimes quite lax. Many will eat pork freely if it is called "mutton" or some other name. A popular Chinese jibe is that "One Moslem travelling will grow fat, whereas two on a journey will grow thin."[10] Thus the Chinese may have weakened Moslem resistance to the Chinese way, as they have traditionally done with other alien groups. They have also resisted Moslem pressure in China proper, they have carried pigs wherever they have migrated, and have encouraged other people to raise them. In Tibet pigs are kept mainly by the Chinese;[11] in Inner Mongolia most Chinese families have a pig or two, and pork is their commonest meat.[12] In Formosa both Chinese settlers and some aboriginal groups keep pigs, and pork is the most important source of animal protein.[13]

Elsewhere in East Asia pig keeping is important in many areas. Among the Manchu, as among the Chinese, pigs are valuable, prestigeful animals. Not only are they used to pay the bride price and for ransom but pork is the principal flesh food, and is offered to the spirits on ceremonial occasions.[14] The Koreans keep pigs in much the same way as the Chinese, though pork is too expensive for most people except on important occasions.[15]

In Japan proper the situation is different. Bones of domestic swine have not been found in Neolithic sites of the Jomon culture (3000 B.C.– 0 B.C.?), though they appear in some sites (of that period?) in the Ryukyu Islands.[16] Thus pigs must have been introduced rather late; and vegetarian feeling encouraged by Buddhism apparently kept consumption of pork low. Today, though traditional attitudes have broken down, relatively small numbers of Japanese have come to like pork because it is fatty and out of keeping with the greaseless cooking typical of the country.[17] It is true that many farmers in Japan now raise pigs, feeding them largely on waste and garbage; but for the most part they sell them for consumption by town and city people. In the Ryukyus pig keeping is of greater importance than in Japan: not only is the pig the most important sacrificial animal, but a remnant of an ancient cult survives in which pig skulls are associated with ancestor worship.[18]

The Indian Subcontinent

The Indian subcontinent stands in sharp contrast to China as an area of small, sparse pig population: about 4,400,000 animals in 1951. This is due not to environmental limitations but to cultural attitudes. The pig could fill just as important an ecological niche in India as in China. But Hindus as well as Moslems object to pig keeping and pork eating.

Hindu feelings involve the notion that the pig is an unclean animal, perhaps more than the idea of the sanctity of life. The feelings are shared by many lower as well as upper castes. It is true that the members of some low castes keep pigs and eat pork,[19*] but other Hindus regard these people as unclean in consequence. In Rampura village, Mysore District, members of the pig keepers' caste live on the outskirts of the settlement; other people refuse to eat food prepared by these swineherds, to drink water from a vessel they have touched, or even to come into contact with them.[20] A number of low castes have understandably given up pigs and pork. In Kerakat Tahsil, Uttar Pradesh, a Hindu caste of untouchables, the Bhars, has recently renounced pig keeping in an effort to raise their status.[21] In Kotah State two subcastes within the Chamar caste have rejected pork as food, though one inferior subcaste, which apparently derives its name from the word "pig," still eats pork.[22]

Many of the aborigines of the subcontinent keep pigs and eat pork without prejudice, and clearly regard pork as a delicacy.[23*] The Angami and Sema Naga castrate male pigs to encourage their fattening.[24] Some aborigines feed pigs table scraps and chaff to supplement what they obtain scavenging in village and woods. The possession of numerous pigs gives high social status among aborigines, whereas among Hindus the very possession of pigs is a sign of low caste.

The pig-keeping tribes of Assam, most of those of Bihar and Orissa, and many of those of central India offer pigs to their gods.[25] The Reddi of Hyderabad, for example, breed pigs for sacrifice to the Earth Goddess at the first sowing of the crops, believing that the blood fertilizes the seed—an interesting parallel to the practice of the devotees of Demeter, who stored the flesh of the sacrificed pig and sowed it with the seed to assure a good crop. The Reddi also sacrifice pigs on other ceremonial occasions, use them for paying fines, and regard the flesh as their favorite meat.[26]

Despite the general pattern of pig keeping and pork eating among Indian aboriginals, some groups have restrictions on these practices.[27*] Some of the restrictions are probably associated with ancient magical or totemic observances, which involve belief in a special relationship between the group and a totemic animal that is held in high respect. Other restrictions can be related to Hindu influence. Thus, while pigs and pork are important in Reddi culture generally, one entire group of Reddi neither keeps pigs nor eats pork. This is believed to be the influence of Hindu religious teachers who have convinced these people that the pig is unclean.[28] Among the Ho, too, social reformers loudly denounce pork and have succeeded in getting the upper classes to abstain from it.[29] It is clear that the anti-pig attitudes, fostered by Moslems and Hindus alike, are continuing to make progress in the subcontinent. One small reversal of the trend has developed in Portuguese Goa, where pigs are numerous in Christian villages and pork is a favorite Christian food and major source of animal protein.[30]

Southeast Asia

Scholars place the first domestication of the pig in Southeast Asia. From there pig keeping spread in prehistoric times westward across India and the Middle East to Europe and Africa, and north and east to China, Japan, and the Pacific islands.[31] Despite the antiquity of the pig in Southeast Asia, and the fairly general occurrence of pig keeping and pork eating,[32*] there appear never to have been such dense populations of pigs or such intricate systems of pig care and breeding as developed in Europe and China. On the contrary, in Southeast Asia, as among the aborigines of India, the pig is a free-ranging household animal and village scavenger. In many places the housewives own the pigs and develop strong ties to them.[33*] Among the Karen of Burma, where such ties exist, a woman's pigs are killed when she dies so that their spirits may accompany her into the next world.[34] A Thai household has no pigs if it does not have a woman capable of caring for them.[35] This pattern has led some observers to assert that pigs were first kept by women as pets and only later were used for other purposes.

The people of Southeast Asia seem to raise pigs as much for sacrifice to the gods, particularly in connection with divination and agriculture, as for food. The Karen, for example, keep pigs chiefly to propitiate evil spirits;[36] a Karen guilty of adultery or fornication must atone for his trespasses by sacrificing a hog to make the land fertile again.[37*] Divination may involve using the pig's liver or gall bladder, or may simply require drinking the animal's blood. The Karen use the gall bladder; a full and round bladder is a sign that the spirits are pleased and that good fortune, health, and abundance will follow.[38] The Sea Dyak of Borneo ask the pig an important question to be relayed to the supreme being; the deity inscribes his answer on the pig's liver; after slaughtering the pig, the old men examine its liver, gall bladder, fat, and tendon to obtain the answer.[39] The Minahasa of Celebes follow a somewhat different procedure: the priest thrusts his head into the dead animal, drinks the blood, and begins to prophesy.[40] It is not known whether the need for animals to serve in sacrifice and divination was responsible for the domestication of the pig in Southeast Asia. It is clear, however, that peoples there make more extensive use of sacrifice and divination than groups elsewhere in Eurasia.

There seems to have been little pressure by Buddhism and Hinduism for the abandonment of pig keeping and pork eating in Southeast Asia.[41] On Bali, a surviving outlier of Hindu culture, pigs are still raised and pork relished by the general populace, though some Brahmans abstain from animal food altogether. In Burma and Thailand pork is eaten by Buddhists; and in Indochina, where Buddhist influence is also strong, pig keeping and pork eating are widespread. The only apparent change made by the Thai to conform with their Buddhist beliefs is their refusal to slaughter pigs themselves—a refusal encouraged by the government's imposition of a slaughtering fee. They obtain young pigs from local Chinese, fatten them, and sell them back to the Chinese. This has not led the Thai to regard pork as any less a delicacy.

In contrast with Hinduism and Buddhism, the intrusion of Islam into the Malaysian part of Southeast Asia has brought about a considerable reduction in pig keeping and pork eating. The Cham of Indochina, who are mainly Moslems, do not keep pigs, and they refuse pork.[42] The Malay Peninsula became a land without domestic pigs; even today pigs are not found and pork is not eaten in Malay villages.[43] Anti-pig attitudes were also carried by Islam through Indonesia and into the southern Philippines, where the Moro of Mindanao have given up pork.[44] The abandonment has not been complete, however, in Malaya and the islands of Southeast Asia, for non-Moslem natives and Chinese as well as lax Moslems[45]* have continued to eat pork.

This calls to mind the important role played by Chinese settlers in counteracting Islamic influence and in encouraging pig keeping and pork eating. The Chinese in Malaya not only raise pigs but in the past imported numbers of swine from abroad.[46] Pork is also very popular among the Chinese of Java;[47] many own pigs and maintain them on the outskirts of settlements with the help of Javanese herdsmen.[48] Chinese restaurants provide lax Moslems with the readiest source of the forbidden flesh. It is apparently because of Chinese influence, too, that parts of Indochina have the highest development of pig keeping in Southeast Asia. In the Tonkin Delta almost every Annamese house has its square piggery enclosed by a crude railing and covered with a thatched roof. Pork and pork fat are so important in the delta that a woman does not return from market without pork; and the whole pig is consumed, skin and all.[49]

Australia and Tasmania, Melanesia, Micronesia, and Polynesia

Domestic pigs were not introduced to Australia and Tasmania until European settlers arrived in the eighteenth and nineteenth centuries, for the aborigines lived entirely by hunting, gathering, and fishing. Long before, however, pigs had spread from Southeast Asia to the east, along a southern route through Melanesia to the Fiji Islands, and along a northern route at least into the western end of the Micronesian chain of islands. Credit for introducing them into the eastern Pacific belongs to the Polynesian peoples, who pushed eastward, either from Melanesia or Micronesia, at a date presumed by some to be about the fourth or fifth century. It is not certain whether they carried pigs with them in their initial movement into western Polynesia or obtained them later, perhaps from the Fijians. Eventually they did carry them across Polynesia as far as Samoa in the southwest, the Marquesas, Society, and Austral islands in the southeast, and Hawaii in the north. There were, however, certain places in Polynesia where pigs were not present in pre-European times: in New Zealand and Easter Island, on the fringes of settlement; on the coral atolls (including, among others, Pukapuka, Manihiki, and Raka-hanga north of the Cook Islands), where, some claim, there was too little food to maintain them; and on individual high islands such as Aitutaki and Mangaia in the Cook Islands, and on Mangareva in the Tuamotu Archipelago.[50] Traditional accounts on Mangareva suggest that pigs were present earlier but had become extinct,[51] which may have happened on other high islands, too.

In any case the absence of the domestic pig in certain Pacific islands had nothing to do with Islam, which never entered the area. People were free to develop their own patterns of pig keeping—and when the Europeans arrived the practice was greatly stimulated: peoples who kept pigs were encouraged by new economic opportunities, and pigs were introduced to most Polynesian groups that had lacked them. The Maori of New Zealand, for example, began to rear pigs extensively for food and for market,[52]* and were delighted with their acquisition.

Despite European encouragement a few peoples, such as those of Tikopia in Melanesia,[53] have not taken over domestic pigs, from indifference or other reasons. There are also scattered reports of group rejection of pork. In Australia, where European settlers introduced pigs, certain aborigines, such as those of Victoria and Queensland, developed a repugnance for pork and pork fat, and refused to eat it.[54] The people of Tamara, an island off New Guinea, refuse pork because they believe that souls of the dead sometimes pass into the bodies of pigs.[55] Other cases of pork rejection apply only to particular types of animals or to particular members of society and are based on magical, religious, or totemic beliefs. Among the Kai of New Guinea, for example, agricultural laborers refuse pork for fear the flesh of the dead pig in the laborer's stomach will attract live pigs, whether wild or domestic, to destroy the crops in his field.[56] No inhabitant of Osiwasiu village, a settlement of the northern Massim of New Guinea, will eat wild pigs, though men eat domestic pigs without hesitation; the flesh of wild pigs, people believe, would make one's stomach swell.[57] At Boitaru village one Massim clan, the Malasi, whose totemic animal is the pig, avoids the flesh both of the wild pig and of domestic pigs that are yellowish-brown in color. They sell or exchange their brown pigs with men of other clans.[58] Most of the avoidances mentioned above do not represent a rejection of pork by an entire people, and are therefore not at all similar to the pork avoidance of the Moslems. They are little different from similar observances of non-Moslem aboriginal groups in Southeast Asia.

Methods of pig care in Melanesia, Micronesia, and Polynesia also resemble those of Southeast Asia. The pig is a household animal which in some places is permitted to run loose and to scavenge for its food, and in other places is restricted in its movements. Some Melanesians permit their boars to run wild but blind their sows to keep them from wandering too far.[59] On Ifalik in Micronesia and in the Society Islands in Polynesia, on the other hand, hogs are commonly tethered to trees and fed.[60] In Manua, Samoa, people apparently permit pigs to run loose in the plantations but construct low stone walls to keep them from entering the village.[61] Elsewhere in Samoa large, stone-walled community pig-enclosures are used ordinarily; to fatten their pigs, however, some people confine them in small stalls near the dwellings and feed them leftovers.[62]

Another similarity of the Pacific area with Southeast Asia is the importance of pigs for sacrifice to the gods, and for slaughter on ceremonial occasions such as wedding and funeral feasts.[63*] But the pig is far more involved in the prestige structure of society. Certain persons with prestige commonly enjoy preferential rights in keeping pigs, in slaughtering them, or in eating their flesh. On Kiriwina in the Trobriand Islands, for example, the paramount chief is the only one permitted to own pigs, though lesser chiefs and important headmen sometimes enjoy similar privileges within the areas of their control.[64] On Tonga large pigs are reserved for people of high rank,[65] and the flesh of pigs sacrificed to the gods was formerly eaten by the priests.[66] On Pukapuka the chief obtains a special portion of the slaughtered pig, though otherwise the pork is distributed without reference to rank or status.[67] At a feast in the Cook Islands, reports P. H. Buck, the head of the slaughtered pig is set before the high chief as "the symbolic portion appropriate to his rank."[68*]

Reports of restrictions on women eating pork further confirm the association of pork eating with a position of prestige in society. The Biara of New Britain did not permit women to eat pork,[69] nor did the Society Islanders.[70] Among the Buin of Bougainville in the Solomon Islands, though one of a woman's most important duties is to raise pigs, she rarely eats pork, and then only as a special favor of her husband.[71] In the Marquesas Islands pork was forbidden to women at certain times,[72] whereas in Hawaii it was forbidden except in special cases.[73] I have found only one reference to pork being completely forbidden to children,[74*] but they generally get lesser portions.

Further manifestations of the importance of pigs in the prestige structure are found in the high value commonly placed on them, the desire to increase their number, their use as a medium of exchange, and their sacrifice to gain social advancement. For the Koita of New Guinea the pig is among a man's most valued possessions.[75] In Lesu village on New Ireland pigs are almost always bought in connection with a ritual feast, and are the usual objects of trade.[76] The southern Massim of New Guinea so often use pigs in paying for valuable objects that they may almost be considered currency.[77] On Sakau in the New Hebrides pigs

are the chief concern of the people and their standard currency; by lending their pigs to one another they establish complicated patterns of
indebtedness, and they trade pigs with other islands.[78] The people of
Malekula, another of the New Hebrides, use pigs to exchange for wives
and other goods, and a man's status depends on the number and value
of his pigs, which he tries to increase by careful lending and borrowing.
Here pigs are life, progress, and power; without them, the Malekulans
assert, they would simply exist.[79] In Malo, one of the New Hebrides,
when a man has sacrificed a thousand small pigs to the souls of his ancestors, he attains the highest nobility.[80]

Many of these Pacific island practices provide interesting parallels
with East Africa, where cattle occupy a similar position in the prestige
structure of cattle peoples. The New Hebrideans' concern with the size
and shape of their boars' tusks suggests the interest some East African
peoples take in the size and shape of cattle horns. It is not so much the
size of the animal as the size and curvature of its tusks that determine
a boar's value. Preferred tusks curl around to make two or three complete circles.[81] The people of Malekula take out the top canine teeth of
their best male piglets when they are almost a year old, to encourage
growth of the tusk teeth; should the pig reach the three-circle tusk
stage, it is said to be "surcharged with power, its tusk is the coiling
snake and the spirit of earth."[82] Though I do not know of people elsewhere in the Pacific islands showing this sort of interest in their boars'
tusks, the report that the Polynesians wear the long tusks of their boars
for ornament[83] suggests the possibility.

Another parallel between the Pacific islands and East Africa is the
attachment that develops between the people and their animals: The
Papuans of the Trans-Fly in New Guinea not only take genuine pride in
their mature pigs but show strong affection for them; the woman who
feeds the pig fondles and pets it, and when finally it is killed she cries
freely. The owner does not kill the pig, for as the Papuans say, sorrow
would make his arm too weak to use the bow.[84] Similarly, a man of the
northern Massim sometimes has a remarkable fellowship with his pig;
there is one delightful record of a pig's doglike attachment to its master
which led it to persist in following him on a trip despite all his efforts
to send it home.[85] The ultimate in affection seems to be displayed on
Sakau and on Ifalik, where small pigs have been suckled by the

women.[86] In former days childless Maori women of New Zealand some-times carried and nursed young pigs as substitutes for their own off-spring.[87]

That the pig is the most celebrated animal in Oceanian fable, as cattle are in East African song, is an appropriate expression of its position in the Pacific islands. According to one tale, giants sailed from Tahiti to fight a man-eating pig; another tale tells how Hiro, born of the sun, killed this pig.[88]

Origin and Diffusion of the Pork Avoidance

The earliest historical records of group avoidance of pork in the Old World are for India and the Middle East. In India, contrary to some statements, the avoidance was not derived from Islam, for pork was forbidden in pre-Moslem times.[89]* Despite the antiquity of the Indian prohibition, which may be as old as those that developed in the eastern Mediterranean area, pig keeping and pork eating have persisted as common practice among some low-caste Hindu peoples and most abo-riginal groups up to the present time. It seems likely, therefore, that the prohibition was imposed from above by high-caste Hindus and not from below. Unfortunately, it cannot now be determined how high-caste Hindus came to have a negative feeling about pigs and pork. Did they inherit it from their Aryan predecessors who may, when they in-vaded the subcontinent about 1500 B.C., have held the typical pastoral-ists' scorn of pigs; did they adopt it from the aborigines of the subcon-tinent, as they may also have done in incorporating the pig into the Hindu pantheon as one incarnation of Viṣṇu; or did they develop it independently of the aborigines but within India, perhaps influenced by their belief in the sanctity of life and vegetarianism? Though the last possibility cannot be dismissed entirely, the feeling against pork appears to be more than vegetarian bias, for not only is eating pork looked down upon but pigs themselves are regarded as unclean, unlike many other domestic animals whose flesh is avoided by Indian vegetar-ians. Though many aboriginal groups eat pork, others reject it for rea-sons apparently independent of Hindu influence. It remains possible that the Hindus adopted their restrictions from one of the latter groups of aborigines, but it seems more plausible that the feeling against pork was brought to India by some ancient conquering tribe of pastoralists from inner Asia, who scorned the pig as a strange and unclean animal.

In antiquity the ban on pork was widespread in the Middle East. Many people hold that the Jews originated it. Some say that they came to regard the pig as ritually unclean because it was associated with alien gods; others, that the rejection dates from the Babylonian captivity, when the Gentile masters of the Jews sacrificed and ate pigs; still others, that the rejection is for esthetic reasons, because the pig is a gross and sensual animal. Perhaps the most persistent and popular explanations are that the ancient Jews rejected pork on hygienic grounds, either (1) because pork decays rapidly in the high temperatures that supposedly characterize the Middle East; (2) because the scavenging pig, which eats all kinds of filth and is itself physically dirty, may be dangerous as food; or (3) because of danger of trichinosis. The first explanation is completely without support. Temperatures in Palestine are no higher than in many other areas where pork is commonly eaten and where rapid decay presents no problem. If it did, the Jews, like many other peoples of the world, could have consumed the flesh in one great feast. That the rejection springs from the eating habits or physical dirtiness of the pig is equally questionable. If the Jews were really concerned with the indiscriminate eating habits of the pig, why did they not ban chickens too as food? The chicken is as aggressive a scavenger as the pig and it will eat just as many things that are repugnant to humans. Both Old and New Testament accounts assert that pigs were kept in herds out of doors, conditions in which they are not much "dirtier" than other animals. The water buffaloes of modern Palestine like to wallow in mud as much as pigs do, yet are not looked upon with the same horror.[90]

That the fear of contracting trichinosis led the Jews to ban pork is so widely believed as to require more detailed evaluation. Several points must be borne in mind. Neither the Jews nor any other peoples of the Middle East knew of *Trichinella spiralis* or of the relationship of the parasite, the pig, and man; this was not discovered until the nineteenth century. It is possible that they or some other group by common-sense methods associated the first-stage symptoms (vomiting, diarrhea, fever, and general malaise) of acute trichinosis with eating pork. Such associations have been made. There were early cases in which ham was suspected, and in which the illness was actually called "ham poisoning."[91] On the other hand, the association is not easy to make, for often people do not sicken immediately, and during the several days between exposure and the first symptoms suspicion can easily fall on other causes. This is illustrated by the German school inspection commission which ate together at an inn in 1845. One of the members had only a glass of red wine. The other seven drank white wine and ate a meal, which included ham, sausage, and cheese. The first member was unaffected, but the seven became ill, and four of them died. A judicial investigation was then made in which both the innkeeper and the meal were suspected, and in which the white wine was tested. The inquiry led to no conclusion, but the innkeeper could not dispel public suspicion and eventually was obliged to emigrate.[92] Moreover, in many cases of trichinosis the symptoms are mild or absent. It has been estimated that in the United States there are 350,000 new infections each year, that only 4.5 per cent may show symptoms, and that but a few hundred are reported.[93] Doctors have found trichinosis difficult to diagnose, and correct initial diagnosis is the exception rather than the rule. In fact researchers have listed fifty diseases which have been mistakenly diagnosed in individuals suffering from trichinosis; the list ranges alphabetically from acute alcoholism to undulant fever.[94]

My search reveals no records indicating that Middle Eastern peoples had knowledge of the association. The amount of trichinosis in human populations is now known to be directly related to the incidence of trichinae in the pigs whose flesh is consumed;[95*] and pigs which are permitted to run loose and are not fed garbage have a very low incidence of trichinae.[96*] In the Middle East pigs generally derived considerable food from woodland and field, and apparently were not confined to sties and fed garbage. The probable low incidence of human trichinosis makes knowledge of the association still less likely.

A group that had detected the relationship between pork and trichinosis might also have made the further comparatively simple discovery that long, thorough cooking of pork completely eliminates the danger of contracting the disease; this would have provided a better solution to the problem than abandoning pork. In modern times, despite knowledge of the relationship between the disease and pork eating, there have been few serious suggestions that pork be banned. In the United States, in spite of high rates of infection,[97*] pork is not even examined microscopically for trichinae, though the Germans have required such inspection since the last century. The government and the meat packers take the stand that such inspection could not determine absolutely whether pork were free of trichinae, and would only serve to lull the public into a false sense of security.[98] Recurrent epidemics of trichinosis clearly show the imperfection of the German inspection system, yet people there continue to eat certain pork products in a raw or rare state. It is also interesting that since the discovery of the relationship between pork and trichinosis, not only has there been no general decline in pork eating but even Jews are increasingly accepting pork as food.[99]

The history of our knowledge of the disease casts further doubt on the trichinosis theory. Before the discovery of *Trichinella spiralis,* the Jewish ban on pork was attributed to fear of tapeworms,[1] an illustration of the tendency to seek explanations in terms of disease. Discovery of the parasite *Trichinella spiralis* came about not, as is often the case in medical history, by looking for the cause of a disease but by discovering an organism and step by step finding that it was harmful. In 1835, when the parasite was first found in human muscle, the conviction somehow spread that it was a harmless organism, and physicians in general soon ceased to have an interest in it.[2] It took twenty-five more years of fitful investigation to determine that trichinae could be transmitted to man through eating pork, and to recognize that these parasites could lead to fatal illness;[3*] yet medical men jumped to the conclusion that the ancient Jews had preceded them in this discovery. At first the suggestions were tentative, and the idea was considered merely plausible. As time passed, however, the statements by medical writers changed, and rather remarkably. Asa Crawford Chandler, for example, in earlier editions of his *Introduction to Parasitology* wrote: ("There can be little doubt that this worm, with the pork tapeworm as an accomplice, was responsible for the old Jewish law against the eating of pork") but by the 1955 edition, "there can be little doubt" had become "without a doubt."[4] In the mind of Chandler and of the public as well, an assumption which fitted with Western preconceptions had gradually evolved into accepted fact, despite the absence of documentation of any sort.

Casting further doubt on the trichinosis theory is the observation of Walter J. Harmer that all of the hygienic explanations fail in certain respects: (1) They overlook the fact that Jewish legislation banned the eating of more than thirty kinds of animals; to some of these the hygienic explanation seems inapplicable, whereas some of the approved animals seem questionable on these grounds. (2) They disregard the fact that the core concept of the Jewish ban is that the pig itself has a

defiling nature, of which the refusal to eat pork is only one manifestation; the problem, then, is to explain how the pig came to be considered
defiling and contact with it a sin.[5]

The anthropologist Carleton Coon, after rejecting the hygienic explanations of the Jewish dietary law against eating pork, suggests instead that it derives from population increase and environmental deteri-
oration. According to his view, the pig was a splendid animal in the
regional economy at an early period when the environment was unex-
ploited and the animals could feed in the oak and beech woods on
acorns, beechnuts, and truffles. With the increase of population and the
stripping of the oaks from the landscape to make room for olive trees,
the ecological niche of the pig was destroyed; it could survive in the
new situation only by consuming foodstuffs that could be better used in
feeding the people directly. Under the changed conditions, says Coon,
any man who kept pigs would be displaying his wealth and disturbing
the balance of the group in which he lived. In this way, he says, the pig
was displaced.[6]

Although it has been firmly established that man and his domestic
animals have indeed destroyed much woodland in the Mediterranean
and Middle East, the roles played by the various agents and the se-
quence in destroying the woodland have not been established with certainty. Instead of the destruction of woodland leading to the ban on
pork, it may be, as the geographer Xavier de Planhol has argued, that
the banning of pork had a part in opening the Mediterranean wooded
country to sheep and goats, which led to significant deforestation. De
Planhol calls attention to the fact that deforestation is particularly no-
ticeable in the Islamic sections of the Mediterranean; and that in Albania, in passing from Moslem to Christian sections, where pigs are
kept, the amount of woodland immediately becomes much greater.[7]
Whatever the succession may have been, it does not follow that the pig
has lost its usefulness as a result of deforestation. On the contrary, it
could still have filled a valuable niche as a scavenger, eating man's
refuse in much the same way that it does in East and South Asia. This
argument is buttressed by the experience of modern Israel. Various independent Jewish farmers there, as well as communal settlements, have
taken over pigs because they fit excellently into the local agricultural
system, converting into flesh waste products that otherwise would
simply be discarded. The pending threat to Jewish pig keeping in Israel

comes not from environmental factors but from cultural prejudice. Certainly the pig would be more beneficial as a scavenger than the dog, which performs this function in much of the area today, since the dog is valued there neither for its flesh nor its by-products. The second part of Coon's argument, that the abandonment of pig keeping occurred because men did not want to display their wealth, also is unlikely in psychological terms. Coon's interesting argument thus seems to be as questionable as the hygienic theories he rejects. Nor does there seem to be any better support for it in the historical and contemporary ethnographic record.

The hypothesis I prefer is that the prejudice against the pig and pork developed first among pastoral peoples in the arid or semi-arid sections of Asia, and was diffused to the settled peoples with whom they had contact. According to this hypothesis the transition of the pig from sacred to profane, and of pork from acceptable to unacceptable food, among various of the Middle Eastern peoples stretching from Egypt to Phrygia was initiated by pastoral influence. Why and how this may have come about is suggested by several observations. The pig is unsuited to the pastoral way of life in arid and semi-arid lands and is not generally kept by pastoral peoples in Asia or elsewhere. It was, on the other hand, widely diffused among agricultural peoples in Europe, Asia, and North Africa in ancient times, as we have seen. There is a long history of conflict between pastoralists and settled people, the former holding the latter in contempt for their manual labor, their carefully regulated lives, their lack of spirit and of individual courage in battle.

From these facts it is logical to suppose that pastoralists living in arid regions developed contempt for the pig as an animal alien to their way of life and symbolic of the despised sedentary folk, and came to avoid its flesh for food. It is fairly common for ethnic, religious, or other groups to be associated with a particular animal or plant food. One recalls that the Americans in World War I referred to the British, French, and Germans respectively as "Limeys," "Frogs," and "Krauts." The Tibetans of the Kansu-Tibetan border identify religions with particular food habits, and when they hear about other groups they ask, using the word "mouth" symbolically: "Is their mouth the same as ours, or is it like the mouth of the Moslems, or do they have some other mouth?"[8] From this sort of identification it is a short way to the rejection of foods simply because they are associated with a rival group.

Many Ethiopian Christians, for example, refuse to eat the flesh of camels because they regard this as a Moslem habit; a century ago Ethiopian Christians also resisted the use of coffee for a similar reason, as have other groups—unsuccessfully—in the past. The association, in many parts of the Old World, of the pig with settled people, and, where it was a sacred animal, with the worship of agricultural deities such as Demeter, makes it an ideal symbol for pastoralists to use for their settled rivals. That this may indeed have taken place is illustrated by the Mongols. Though they do not reject pork, they have a prejudice against the pig which Owen Lattimore contends may be "a spontaneous nomad reaction" to the fact that they cannot successfully herd pigs, as sedentary people can.[9] They also seem to regard the pig as symbolic of the Chinese, for they call pigs "black cattle" and the Chinese "herders of black cattle,"[10] just as in the fifteenth century the followers of Tamerlane called the Emperor of Cathay the "pig emperor."[11]

As perhaps in India, the prejudice against pork may have been introduced to settled groups by pastoral conquerors, becoming entrenched by the example of the pastoral nobility and through incorporation into the religions of the settled people. There must have been a long period of transition, however, as the practices associated with the ancient agricultural gods were broken down and gradually gave way. During this time survivals of ancient attitudes and practices respecting the pig created a situation which was both ambiguous and confusing. Generally, however, pork remained a main food only of lower castes and classes.

Such information as is available suggests that if the prejudice was indeed introduced in this way it may have occurred in the countries at the eastern edge of the Mediterranean sometime after 1400 B.C., at a time associated with a notable rise in strength of the pastoral groups living on the fringes of the great civilizations. There is little if any prejudice against pork, one observes, in places where pastoralists have had small influence, such as Western Europe, along the Guinea Coast, in the Congo Basin, in Southeast and East Asia, and on the Pacific islands. Moreover, among the Hindus of India pork is avoided particularly by upper-caste groups, who have perhaps been more influenced by the ancient pastoral Aryans than have other Hindus. In China, on the contrary, where the Mongol and other pastoral invaders were thrown off or more effectively absorbed, pork is relished by upper and lower classes alike, except among the Moslem minority.

With the expansion of Islam from the seventh century on, came the final and decisive spread of the prejudice against pork, at Mohammed's instigation. Even among Moslems, however, the elimination of pork eating was incomplete, for the flesh of domestic pigs is surreptitiously enjoyed in a few places and the flesh of wild pigs of various sorts is sometimes eaten without hesitation.

Map 2—Beef Avoidance

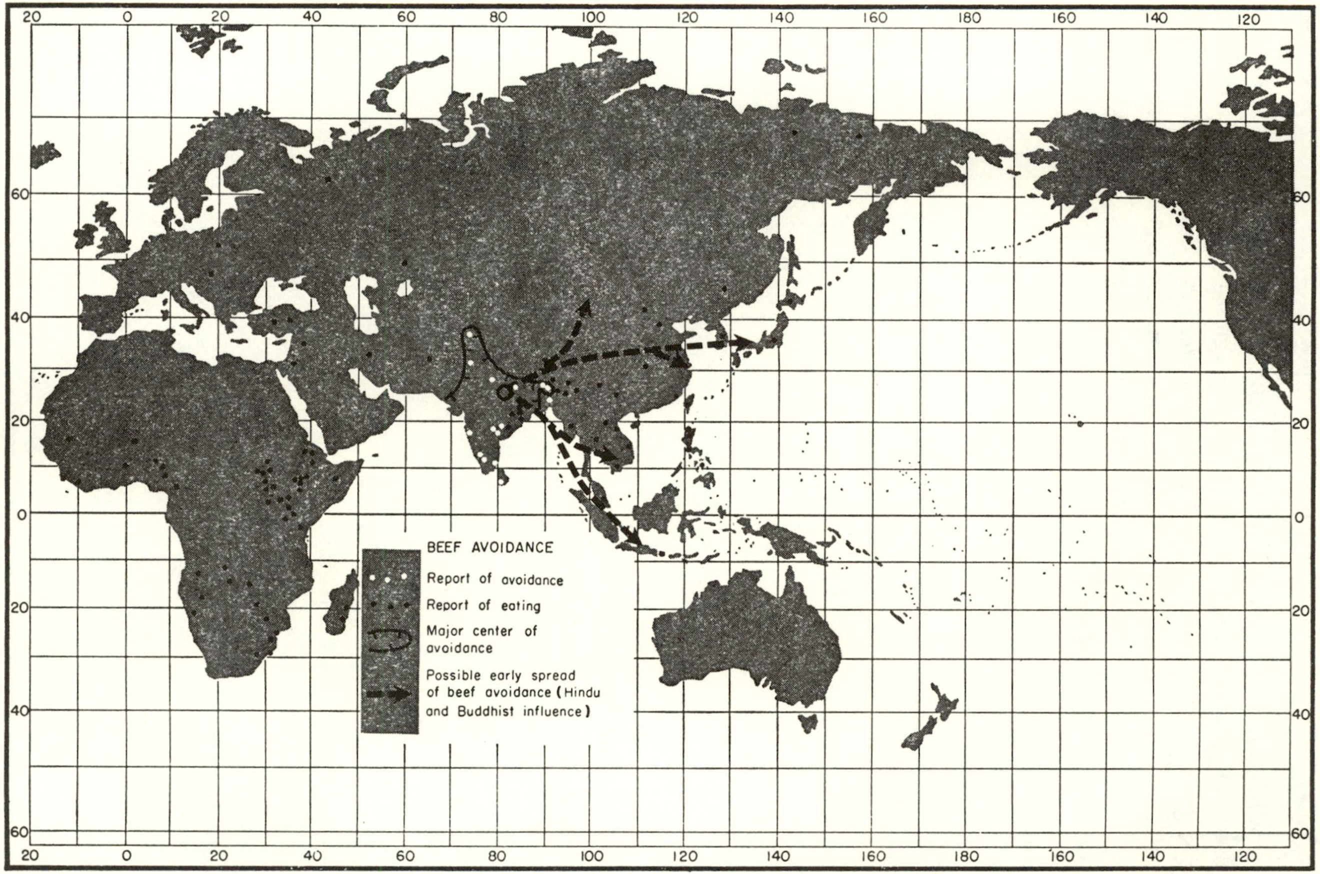

BEEF AVOIDANCE

Report of avoidance

Report of eating

Major center of avoidance

Possible early spread of beef avoidance (Hindu and Buddhist influence)

4

BEEF

*T*he *Indian Center of Beef Avoidance*

In 1956 India had a cattle population of 159,000,000—about a fifth of all the world's cattle. However, neither number of animals nor the unquestioned dietary importance of milk and dairy products gives an adequate impression of the position of cattle as a source of food in India, for the country is the center of beef avoidance in the Old World (Map 2). In accordance with religious precepts which declare the sacredness of cattle,[1*] the Hindus not only refuse to eat beef but vehemently oppose the slaughter of cattle and use every means, legal, moral, and ritualistic, to protect them from harm. In parts of India, for example, people perform rites to honor or protect the cattle. In some they pray to local Hindu gods for their welfare. In others the cowherds go around singing and begging contributions for their animals. In some places cattle are worshiped, then bathed and anointed with oil, colored with dyes, garlanded with flowers, and fed dainty food.[2] And in a few instances pigs are sacrificed to benefit the cattle.

Since they hold cattle sacred, it is reasonable for Hindus to be incensed at the idea of killing them and to do everything possible, through organized opposition and individual action, to stop it.[3*] When thirteen people were arrested in Bhopal in north central India in 1957 for violating the state prohibition against slaughtering cattle, Hindu opinion

45

was so aroused that public meetings were held, and several zealous Hindus started a hunger strike in protest.[4] In the past the feeling has been even more intense. In 1802 the ruler of one Indian state, on losing some territory to the British, offered to cede additional land if they would agree to prohibit slaughter of cattle in the area they had already taken from him. Elsewhere in India, when an epidemic broke out, people attributed it to cattle slaughter and formed a popular movement to suppress the practice.[5] The orthodox Hindu not only refuses to slaughter but objects to selling his cattle lest they fall into the hands of a butcher;[6] in 1772 a man caught selling a bullock to a European was impaled alive.[7] To kill an ox accidentally was an offense requiring compensation by such acts as feeding Brahmans and going on pilgrimage.[8]

Curiously at variance with general practice are the low Hindu castes which eat beef. These include the leatherworkers, some of the scavenger castes, and other untouchables;[9] they do not slaughter cattle, but obtain beef from animals that have died and which they are obliged to remove from the village. Other Hindus have the utmost contempt for them and even accuse them of poisoning cattle to obtain beef. Certain of these castes have given up eating beef, in an effort to make themselves more acceptable to the general Hindu community. The Chamar caste of Kotah State in northwest India, for example, abandoned beef eating in the present generation, and expelled members who persisted in the practice.[10]

Hindus not only look down on members of their own religion who violate their sensibilities about cattle slaughter and beef eating, but put pressure on others to abandon these practices. The Moslems, the largest religious minority, find themselves in an unaccustomed position here. Instead of being vigorous propagators of an avoidance, as they are with pork, they are on the defensive. In deference to the Hindus, certain Moslem rulers of India have urged their coreligionists to protect cows, and have passed legislation designed to preserve cattle.[11] But in spite of this and of the actions of Moslem cow-protection societies, most Indian Moslems reject the Hindu view of cattle. In predominantly Moslem sections they do not hesitate to eat beef or to sell old or infirm cattle for slaughter. In Hindu areas, however, they act with greater caution, in some places giving up the slaughtering of cattle and eating of beef in order not to offend their Hindu neighbors. In other places, as in the village of Shamirpet in Hyderabad,[12] they continue to eat beef, but slaughter their cattle outside the village, to respect the feelings of the Hindu majority and to avoid trouble. Their fears are based on a long series of incidents in which outraged Hindus have severely punished Moslems for their transgressions. In Srinagar in Kashmir, for example, a group of Moslems was imprisoned for years by the Hindu rulers for having slaughtered and eaten cattle during a famine.[13] Moslem cattle slaughter continues to create friction with Hindus today, and there is little likelihood that the differences will soon be reconciled— though now that the Indian subcontinent is divided between India and predominantly Moslem Pakistan there will be more clear-cut areas of beef eating and avoidance.

The behavior of other groups in the subcontinent with respect to cattle slaughter and beef eating is varied. The Sikhs, whose religion is an offshoot of Hinduism, have a reverence for cattle similar to that of the Hindus, and do not eat beef; in fact they have been among the strongest opponents of cattle sacrifice, and hence frequently at odds with the Moslems.[14] In Portuguese Goa there is a demand for beef in the urban centers, and some smuggling in of cattle from India to supply it. Christian peasants there rarely raise cattle for beef—in this perhaps unwittingly following pre-Christian habit. In Portuguese Damão and Diu, which have predominantly Hindu populations, cattle are never sold for slaughter.[15]

Eating beef has been respectable and fairly common among aboriginal groups. The Dire of Hyderabad, for example, eat it openly at feasts.[16] The Gadaba at every feast sacrifice bulls to the gods and then distribute the flesh among the guests.[17] The Lushai of Assam eat the flesh of the mithan (*Bos frontalis*), which they value more than any other domestic animal.[18*] Several aboriginal groups however reject beef, some of them quite strongly. The Reddi of Hyderabad, for instance, are as strict as any Hindus in their avoidance of the flesh of cattle and water buffalo.[19*] The Kamar of Chhattisgarh in central India not only reject beef as food but expel cattle slaughterers from the tribe.[20] In some cases aborigines' refusal to eat beef may be independent of Hindu influence; in others it is clearly derived from the Hindus.[21*] As aboriginal groups accept Hindu ways or become part of that society, Hindu attitudes continue to spread.

One group, a curious anomaly, remains apart from the struggle on the Indian subcontinent between the traditional views of Hindus and

Moslems. This is the Shin, a nominally Moslem people of Dardistan in northwest India who, unlike all other groups of the subcontinent, treat cattle with abhorrence. They keep cattle for plowing but avoid them as much as possible, touching a newborn calf, for instance, only with the end of a forked stick.[22] They neither drink cows' milk, eat dairy products, nor use cow dung for fuel. This attitude is especially strange in view of the Shin's history, for they are believed to have been an upper caste Hindu tribe which was forced to migrate from Kashmir. They might therefore be expected to share either the normal Hindu or the normal Moslem attitude toward cattle.

The strange thing about beef and cattle in India is that the ancient picture was quite different. It is true that in the Rig Veda, the oldest of the Vedic works, whose material dates from about 1500 to 900 B.C., cattle are regarded as related to certain of the gods,[23*] and that feeling against cattle slaughter is already present.[24*] Nevertheless, numerous allusions occur to the sacrifice of cows, bulls, and water buffaloes, and to the preparation of their flesh.[25]

The feeling about cattle slaughter and beef eating continued inconsistent in the Atharva Veda and the Brāhmaṇas, which look back, for the most part, to the period from 900 to 500 B.C. The Atharva Veda classifies meat with liquor and dice as a bad thing.[26] The Śatapatha Brāhmaṇa contains a religious protest against eating beef.[27] Other statements in the Atharva Veda and Brāhmaṇas reveal, however, that the sacrifice of cattle continued[28] and that cattle were slaughtered when a king or honored guest was received.[29] The sacrifice of cattle had great merit, and when a man sacrificed a thousand or more cows in an oblation ceremony he was believed to "conquer everything."[30] Even the priestly castes of Brahmans ate beef; indeed, there are suggestions that they tried to secure for themselves preferential treatment with respect to cattle and beef. They made strong claims, backed by threats, to exclusive rights to sterile cows and to animals about which there were irregularities in birth.[31] Instructions in the Brāhmaṇas for carving meat and for distributing portions among the priests and others[32] also suggest that the Brahmans were pushing their claims. Yet there was a real difference of opinion in this period about the permissibility of beef, as the Śatapatha Brāhmaṇa shows: "Let him [the priest] therefore not eat the flesh of the cow and the ox. Nevertheless, Yâgñavalkya [the founder of the Śatapatha school] said, 'I, for one, eat it, provided that it is tender.' "[33]

The period from 500 to 100 B.C. was one of great religious turmoil in India. It involved controversy not only between Buddhists and Brahmans but among a swarm of contending sects, and concerned both abstract theological matters and acceptable ways of living. Among the latter was the permissibility of eating various flesh foods. The Hindu writings of this time, in discussing the acceptability of beef, reveal the same pattern that characterized the earlier writings. The Sūtras, for example, show that the cow had considerable status. Foes fleeing from battle "who declare themselves to be cows" might be spared;[34] and for the protection of cows Brahmans and Vaiśyas might take up arms, though ordinarily they were forbidden to do this.[35] At the same time, cows and oxen were slaughtered and cooked at the *arghya* ceremony for the entertainment of honored guests.[36] The Dharma Sūtra of Āpastamba quoted texts that forbade eating beef; yet Āpastamba himself appeared to permit its use.[37] It was apparently not regarded as proper to kill cattle simply for their flesh, for there are statements that it was sinful to eat cows' flesh;[38] and a penance for killing a cow was declared, which included giving cattle to the Brahmans.[39] According to the Institutes of Viṣṇu, the killer of a cow would suffer blindness through divine retribution, and have one hand and one foot lopped off.[40] Yet this work, too, states that it is permissible to slaughter cattle under certain circumstances.[41] The Arthaśāstra of Kauṭilya (fourth century B.C. to A.D. 300), a handbook of government, confirms this statement: a section on the duties of the superintendent of the Slaughter House prohibits the slaughter of cattle, including calves, bulls, and milk cows; yet the work also includes, in a system of classifying cattle, references to "cattle fit only for the supply of flesh," and to the right of herdsmen to "sell either flesh or dried flesh."[42] One can conclude that from 500 to 100 B.C. beef was still eaten in India, although its consumption was regulated and limited.

Buddha, who died about 500 B.C., did not specifically prohibit beef; he did forbid the flesh of man and of certain other animals (including elephant, dog, horse, lion, tiger, panther, bear, hyena, and serpent).[43] Moreover, when King Aśoka made Buddhism the state religion about

250 B.C., he did not specifically prohibit cattle slaughter or beef eating, though he declared in his famous rock edicts that "Not to injure living things is good" and "No animal may be slaughtered for sacrifice."[44] Thus Buddhism took a stand against cruelty and against animal sacrifice[45*] but did not single out cattle for special consideration.

Though the slaughter and eating of cattle by Hindus continued,[46*] the early centuries of the Christian era saw the emergence of the modern pattern. The Institutes of Manu (c. A.D. 100–300), for example, listed the slaying of cattle among the offenses for which penance must be done.[47] By the seventh century the situation was essentially the modern one. The Chinese traveler Hsüang-tsang observed that Indians were forbidden to eat "the flesh of the ox," and that those who did were despised and scorned and lived apart from others.[48] The legend from this period of a Tamil king who decreed the execution of his own son for accidentally killing a calf well illustrates the climate of opinion that prevailed by that time.[49]

Southeast Asia

Although India is the Old World center of the rejection of cattle slaughter and beef eating, similar attitudes, perhaps fostered by Buddhism, were formerly also widespread in Buddhist Southeast Asia.[50*] In Burma it was illegal in pre-British times to slaughter beef animals, or to sell or possess their flesh.[51] In Thailand, though cattle and water buffalo were sometimes slaughtered for food when they were old, it was against Buddhist tradition, and usually against a man's best interests, since work animals were a symbol of wealth.[52] A buffalo was slaughtered for great feasts in ancient times in Indochina, according to Pierre Gourou, but both buffalo and common cattle were too valuable and too useful in agriculture for slaughter on ordinary occasions. Moreover the authorities issued ordinances to prohibit the slaughter of horned animals and trade in horns and hides.[53] Other observers have also indicated that the Indochinese were reluctant to eat beef. John Crawfurd, who was in Cochin China in 1821, reported that people did not use the flesh of either cattle or buffaloes as food.[54] John White noted that in Annam beef consumption was confined to the Chinese population;[55] and Prince Henri d'Orléans noted that chiefs at Thac-By in Annam regarded beef as coolies' food.[56] Lucien de Reinach observed an instinctive repugnance for beef in the Laotians, which he regarded as a vestige from ancient

Fig. 3. Bullfight among the Miao of south China. From the *Ming jen ching hsieh Miao t'u,* a work of unknown authorship possibly deriving from a sixteenth-century source.

Fig. 4. Hathor. (1, 2) "Hathor, lady of the heaven." (3) "Hathor, dwelling in the heart of Uas (Karnak), regent of the west." (4) "Hathor." (5) "Hathor in the land of T'ertut." From J. Gardner Wilkinson.

Fig. 5. The Galla or Sanga ox. From Henry Salt.

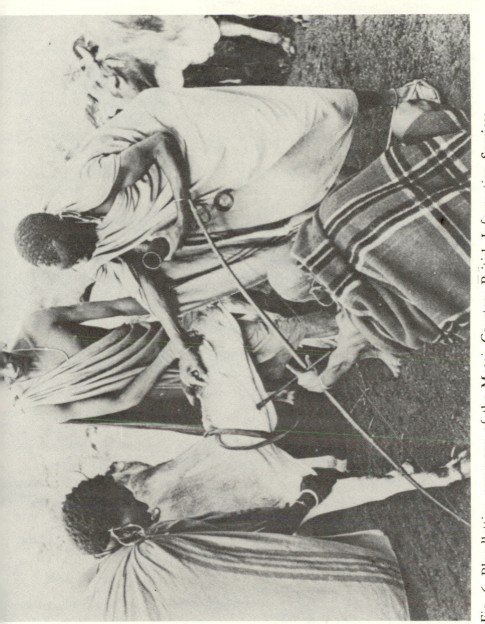

Fig. 6. Bloodletting ceremony of the Masai. Courtesy British Information Services.

Fig. 7. Assyrian human-headed bull statue. Courtesy Metropolitan Museum of Art, Gift of John D. Rockefeller, Jr., 1932.

Fig. 8. Sacrifice of a sacred buffalo among the Toda of India. Courtesy Pierre Rambach.

times when they were a pastoral people and had prohibitions against slaughtering oxen for food.[57]

The spread of Western influence in the Buddhist areas of Southeast Asia has encouraged the use of beef.[58]* Before World War II it was even being shipped from Thailand to Singapore and Hong Kong.[59] But remnants of the old attitudes continue to survive here and there. The people of Thailand, for example, will not slaughter beef animals near their villages because of Buddhist scruples.[60] The Burmese of a generation ago would neither kill cattle nor sell beef, although they would sell pork, fowl, and fish; and all beef butchers in Burmese markets were Indians.[61] Today they are more ready to forego beef than any other common flesh food. When a Burmese Buddhist wishes as an act of piety to give up eating the flesh of one animal, he generally gives up beef.[62] Such acts are encouraged by monks and quasi-religious groups, which from time to time organize campaigns against beef eating.[63]

One departure from strict Buddhist precept is found among the Thai. Despite their reluctance to slaughter common cattle and water buffalo, the Thai love their own form of bullfighting (also found from Madagascar to Japan and in ancient Egypt), in which bulls are pitted against each other rather than against men. In southern Thailand, where bullocks are raised especially for this purpose, the bullfight is a weekly affair, on which the local government collects an admission tax.[64] Though bullfighting used to occur in northern Malaya (it is now banned there) and in south China (Fig. 3) and may still be found in other parts of Southeast Asia, it has not been determined how the practice is reconciled with Buddhist or Moslem belief, or whether it has a historic affinity with the sacredness of cattle in the area.

The widespread acceptance of Islam in Malaya and Indonesia has almost completely counteracted whatever ancient reluctance there may have been to eat beef. In Malaya, for example, people consume beef, though it is expensive and they can afford it only for special occasions; two decades ago many cattle and water buffalo were imported each year from Thailand, both for slaughter and for draft purposes.[65] Indonesians, too, generally eat beef without prejudice, and according to one informant it is one of the cheapest flesh foods available. There are indications however that in the past the reluctance to eat beef was also present in Malaysia. One aboriginal group, for instance, will not touch the flesh of the water buffalo.[66] In the last century the Malays preferred the flesh of water buffalo to that of common cattle, an indication, it has been suggested, that in former times they, like the Hindus, prohibited beef as food.[67]

In the Mentawei Islands off Sumatra, beef is "taboo food" and is refused by the natives.[68] On Bali, a remaining center of Hinduism in Indonesia, in the last century male Brahmans avoided beef.[69] The Dyak tribes of Sarawak, according to one observer, regard the bull and cow as sacred, and will eat neither their flesh nor their dairy products.[70*]

Some groups in the Philippines kept water buffaloes for their flesh in the pre-European period, though common cattle were not known until after the arrival of the Europeans.[71] There is no evidence that people are reluctant to eat the flesh of either animal, but beef is scarce and is generally consumed only a few times a year at important feasts.

Tibet, Mongolia, and the Far East

Just as Southern Buddhism seems to have been the vehicle by which the Indian feeling against cattle slaughter and beef eating was introduced to Southeast Asia, so Lamaism and Northern Buddhism appear to have been the agents by which it penetrated Tibet, Mongolia, and the Far East. In Tibet, where the hardy yak (*Bos grunniens* or *Poephagus grunniens*) replaces the water buffalo and common cattle as the most numerous bovine species,[72*] Lamaist law forbids eating "cow" flesh.[73*] Similarly, in Mongolia, where the numerous herds of bovine animals are composed, on the average, of 70 per cent common cattle and the rest either yaks or crosses between the two,[74] Lamaist priests would not touch "beef."[75] As in Southeast Asia, the Buddhist prohibitions are not strictly followed today. Most Mongols eat beef on rare occasions; Tibetans consume yak flesh, either cooked or raw, in larger quantities than any other meat except mutton, and apparently also eat the flesh of common cattle and the *dzo* (the yak–common cattle crossbreed).[76] The only record of widespread group avoidance of the flesh of a bovine animal in the Tibetan culture area is for the Ladakhi of eastern Kashmir in the region sometimes called "Indian" Tibet or "Western" Tibet; in this case, however, the refusal to eat yak flesh is a direct result of Hindu influence and is accompanied by the belief that the yak is sacred.[77]

Today the pattern of Mongol and Tibetan life is being greatly altered by the Soviet Union and China. Buddhism is clearly on the defensive, and it is likely that the Buddhist-inspired reluctance to eat beef will become even weaker than it is now. At the same time the traditional life of the pastoralist is being modified. Following the Russian model, experimental breeding stations have been set up in Mongolia,[78] and cattle are being raised commercially. This arrangement should greatly increase the export of beef from the region, though it cannot be determined what effect it will have on local consumption.

In China common cattle and water buffalo were already present in Shang times (c. 1520–c. 1030 B.C.),[79*] and they are widespread and fairly numerous today.[80*] Interestingly, there is a traditional reluctance to kill cattle and eat beef similar to that of Buddhist Southeast Asia. Though its origin is not known, some writers have suggested that it developed locally because cattle were useful for plowing and draft purposes. Others point out that the cow was a symbol of agriculture and the object of a sort of veneration, especially in places where Confucian traditions were strong, and that many traditional Confucian scholars had as great a horror of eating beef as Moslems have of eating pork.[81]

Another factor in the reluctance of Chinese to slaughter cattle was that they were symbolic of the social status of the family. From the size of the ox tied near the Chinese farmhouse one could tell how much land the family cultivated and to what social class it belonged; people were proud of their oxen and put their best animals where they would be seen. When marriage arrangements were being made between two families, and the girl's family inquired into the economic position of the prospective husband, the investigators were careful to note the size and quality of the ox. If his family was eager for the marriage but did not have a cow or ox, they might borrow one from a neighbor or friend to display in front of their house.[82] Out of the close tie between the Chinese farmer and his ox grew his reluctance to part with his animal and his tendency to look down on anyone associated with the slaughter of cattle. A farmer who was forced by poverty to sell his animal took as great care in selecting a buyer as if he were finding a husband for his daughter, and was especially concerned that the animal should not fall into the hands of a butcher. The traditional opinion about butchers was that no one could become rich as a professional butcher, that the butcher's soul would be condemned eternally, and that his children, if he had any, would be poor and weak.[83] Thus many Chinese refused to become butchers, and, at least in some places, the slaughter of cattle became the work of Moslems.

The traditional hesitation of Chinese to eat beef has diminished in modern times, and there has been an increasing demand for this meat in both towns and villages. For example, 80 per cent of the families of Ting Hsien in Hopeh Province in north China ate beef, though the sellers were apparently Moslems from another village.[84] It is likely that traditional attitudes toward cattle and beef have been greeted by the Communists with little more tolerance than other traditions, and that the trend toward a wider consumption of beef has been accelerated. The planners in setting a goal of 90,000,000 cattle for 1962 may also envisage the end of the traditional Chinese view of cattle and beef eating.

In the past Koreans, like Chinese, ate very little beef; cattle were too valuable for work to be killed, and their slaughter was regulated by law.[85] Eating beef was permitted only at important festivals, when the slaughtering was done by a butcher who was a sort of government official.[86] Even in modern Korea oxen are too valuable to be killed for food except on rare occasions. Sometimes the oxen, which are regarded as members of the family, appear to be better fed than the people themselves.[87] Elsewhere on the mainland of northeast Asia cattle seem to be recent introductions and are not an important source of flesh food. The Manchu of a generation ago had relatively little knowledge of cattle; they did not milk cows, they killed few cattle, and beef was only a supplementary food.[88] Among the Gold tribe of the lower Sungari cattle also seem to have been introduced recently. Though people used them for plowing, they were in such short supply that on one occasion in the 1930's the authorities around Fuchin forbade their slaughter for meat.[89] In northeast Siberia the Yakut rarely killed their oxen for food, and preferred horsemeat to beef.[90]

Attitudes toward cattle in Japan in the past were similar to those of China and Korea: people did not kill cattle for food, and considered it wrong to eat beef. The Ainu of northern Japan, however, had no reluctance to consume beef and were fond of all parts of bullocks, including the entrails.[91] The traditional attitudes have given way rapidly. When Japan obtained control of Korea, the Japanese began importing cattle for both work and slaughter; by the early years of the century there were few important towns in Japan that did not have beef for sale to the official and merchant classes.[92] Today beef is a very popular though expensive food. Survivals of the ancient attitude occur among some old people who still refuse beef, and in the assignment of slaughtering to a separate slaughterers' and leatherworkers' caste, the Eta.

The Middle East and Mediterranean

The high civilizations west of India may have derived the notion of the sacredness of cattle from inner Asia just as India probably did. Cow, bull, and calf were important in ceremonial life, commonly occupied special positions with respect to the gods, and sometimes were deified themselves (Fig. 4).[93*]

In no case did the exalted status of cattle lead to a general cessation of cattle slaughter and beef eating in this area. It may indeed have encouraged their use as sacrificial animals. But at times a curious prohibition of cows' flesh was found. In ancient Egypt, for example, both cows and bulls were sacred; yet cows were never sacrificed, and their flesh and that of heifers was forbidden, while bulls, bull calves, and oxen were sacrificed and eaten freely.[94] Similar practices were found among the Phoenicians[95] and certain peoples adjoining Egypt. The pastoral tribes of Libya as far as Lake Tritonis, said Herodotus, would not eat cows' flesh, nor would the women of Barce and Cyrene. The feeling against cow slaughter and eating, however, must not have been universal in Libya, for the people of Marea and Apis, on asking priests of the god Ammon for permission to kill and eat heifers, supported their request with the claim that they were Libyans and not Egyptians.[96] From the fifth century B.C., when Herodotus' observations were made, the avoidance of cows' flesh persisted in Egypt for at least several hundred years, for in the third century of the Christian era Porphyry also reported the avoidance for Egypt.[97]

North of the Mediterranean the avoidance of cows' flesh did not occur. There did develop, however, an interesting reluctance to slaughter oxen. The ancient Greeks in Attica and the Peloponnesus so respected the ox that they considered it a capital crime to kill one.[98] The ancient Romans once banished a man as if he had been a murderer for killing an ox for insufficient reason.[99] Unlike the Chinese, however, the ancient Greeks and Romans did not associate their respect for oxen with feeling against eating beef. Indeed, as Varro indicates, oxen were sometimes sold for slaughter.[1]

In the Middle East and Mediterranean today the general factors lim-
iting the eating of beef are its scarcity, high cost, and the prestige value
and usefulness of cattle.[2*] There exist, however, a few strange survivals
in the area. In Mesopotamia "the ox" is regarded as a "taboo animal,"
and in Mosul it is an insult to say that a man eats its flesh.[3] The Mandaeans of Iraq and Iran (if an unclear statement has been properly interpreted) not only regard the killing of water buffalo and common
cattle as a crime but reject the flesh of the latter. A Mandaean is quoted
as saying that cattle were created for plowing, for draft, and for produc-
ing milk, but not for food. Associated with the rejection of cattle flesh
among the Mandaeans is the belief that the bull is sacred to the sun
and to life. Nevertheless the bull does not figure as a Mandaean magical symbol, and the living cow has no special religious importance; nor
are milk, cattle dung, or urine believed to possess magical or other special virtues.[4*]

Africa South of the Sahara

Sub-Saharan Africa can be divided roughly into three large areas in
terms of the position of cattle: a northern belt stretching more than
3,500 miles across the Sudan from Senegal to Ethiopia; a western region consisting of the rain forest and adjacent savannas of West Africa
and the Congo Basin; and an eastern region, including the savannas and
grasslands of East, South, and Southwest Africa.

In the northern belt, which contains both pastoral groups and farmers, cattle are fairly numerous, though they are concentrated in the
hands of such pastoral peoples as the Fulani, who are estimated to own
over 90 per cent of Nigeria's six million cattle.[5] People here commonly
regard cattle as symbols of wealth, and possession of them bestows prestige on a man. They are reluctant to slaughter their cattle and usually
do so only for important feasts and ceremonies. But cattle are not as
much the center of social and ceremonial life as in the eastern region.

In the western region, by contrast, there are few cattle, because of the
presence of tsetse-borne sleeping sickness. It is true that in a few places
resistant strains of cattle exist, such as the Ndama and dwarf breeds of
West Africa; but even these are seldom present in large numbers, and
where infestation by tsetse flies is particularly bad they are absent altogether. Where cattle are present, people commonly know so little about
cattle care that they provide them with no accommodations and permit

them to live in a semiwild state. In the southwest Congo a traveler who was given an ox as a gift had to stalk it and shoot it as if it were a wild beast.[6] The peoples of the western region do not generally rank cattle high in the prestige structure, but tend to regard them simply as another source of meat, though a scarce and expensive one. There are, nevertheless, a few groups in the region who have taken over from peoples of the Sudan or of East Africa the notion that cattle are prestige animals. Among the pagan peoples of the Central Plateau of Nigeria, for example, some wealthy men purchase cattle for prestige purposes and place them in the care of Fulani herdsmen.

The third sub-Saharan region is particularly interesting in terms of the position of cattle in society and economy. In this area, which includes the bulk of East, South, and Southwest Africa, cattle are of such striking importance in the economic, social, and ceremonial life of various native peoples that the phenomenon has been designated the "cattle complex of East Africa," and made the object of special study. Among these peoples, most of whom are pastoral or semipastoral, cattle are the central element of society, around which life revolves. It is said that the life of the Nandi of Kenya would be a meaningless void without cattle, that the Suk of Kenya live for their cattle, that the Masai of Kenya despise anyone who performs work other than tending cattle,[7] and that the Nuer of the Sudan have a profound contempt for people with few cattle or none.[8] Among many peoples it is only through the ownership of cattle, which generally is on an individual basis, that full participation in social life is possible. It has been noted that a man belongs to the lower class if he does not possess cattle, and that without them he cannot court a wife, offer valuable sacrifices, heal diseases, or attend funerals.[9] Among the Bari of the Sudan the man who has no cattle "may not have the proper ceremonies performed when he dies";[10] among the Tswana of southern Africa, a man who owns many cattle is respected and influential in tribal affairs;[11] and among the Kikuyu of Kenya such a man "is given praise-names in songs."[12] Conversation is mostly about cattle; epigrams, riddles, and symbolism center on them; and the languages contain a wealth of descriptive terms for them.

In their economic role, cattle are sometimes used to purchase grain and other goods, and to pay fines and obligations, including those involved in the widespread custom of bride price. This last is in effect a contractual arrangement between the families of the bride and the groom; the groom gives cattle to his in-laws as a guaranty of his good behavior and to recompense them for the loss of their daughter.[13] The bride price has serious implications for a man, for, as Harold Schneider has pointed out for the Pakot (Suk of West Suk District) of Kenya,[14] a man must have a bride to establish a viable economic unit. Another custom, which has perhaps equal economic significance, is "lending" cattle. This lending to neighbors, relatives, or friends gains a man their support and incidentally widens the distribution of dairy products and cattle, since the "borrower" keeps the milk of the loaned animal and in some cases is permitted to keep a calf born of loaned cows.

One of the understandable consequences of the importance of cattle in the social and economic life of the cattle peoples was the encouragement of cattle raiding. As a result, some of the stronger groups, such as the Masai, accumulated enormous numbers of cattle. Even today the Masai, a group of 45,000 people, own about one million cattle, in addition to large numbers of goats and sheep.[15] Weaker groups, on the other hand, suffered serious losses. A century ago the Sejeju, Digo, and Giryama of Kenya and Tanganyika had large herds of cattle, but within thirty or forty years, as a result of raids by the Masai, they had hardly any left. Similarly, the Pokomo of Kenya have no cattle because of raids of the Somali and Galla;[16] and a chief of the Teuso of Kamion, Uganda, many years ago reputedly forced his tribe to give up keeping stock because of raids by stronger neighbors.[17] In other cases, small-scale group abandonment of cattle keeping came about when conquering pastoralists refused subject farmers the right to keep cattle. Also, a number of pastoral groups themselves were forced to give up or decrease cattle keeping when they migrated into tsetse-infested regions and their cattle died of sleeping sickness. This has been particularly common along the eastern margins of the Congo Basin.

A further interesting aspect of the East African cattle complex is that people not only are proud of their animals but display a strong affection for them. The Bari of the Sudan have loving reverence for their cattle;[18] some people among the Hima of Uganda pet and coax their cattle as if they were children and cry over their ailments;[19] and the Turkana of Kenya sing and dance to their cattle in the evening.[20] Some groups go even further, and consider holy certain things associated with cattle. The Nandi of Kenya regard milk, dung, and grass as sacred because of their association with cattle;[21] the Ngoni of the Lake Nyasa region look on the cattle corral as a sacred place and therefore suitable for the grave of a great chief.[22] In many groups a man maintains a special tie with one bull or ox, on which his courage and fortune in battle depend.[23*] When this animal becomes old and feeble, it is not permitted to die but is ceremonially killed. Occasionally the tie between man and beast has been so strong that the man has committed suicide on the death of his animal.

Many Western observers claim that East African cattle peoples are extremely inefficient in their use of cattle for subsistence purposes. They point to the concern with the animals' coloring or size and shape of horns (Fig. 5)[24*] rather than with quality or quantity of milk or flesh; and to the practice of keeping cattle alive regardless of size or state of health, and refusing to slaughter them specifically for flesh or to sell them for market. It is true that the East African cattle groups do not breed animals for their flesh or milk, that they are reluctant to kill them, and that most of them eat beef only when an animal dies naturally or is slaughtered for some important ceremonial occasion.[25*] Among the Tanala of Madagascar, indeed, people associate the eating of beef so closely with funeral ceremonies that a dream of cutting or eating beef is considered a bad omen foretelling a funeral.[26] There are even instances of cattle peoples refusing to slaughter their animals for food when the group is on the verge of starvation.[27*]

The East African cattle peoples, unlike the Hindus, do not have a prejudice against beef; there are numerous references to their eating it.[28*] And in some cases cattle have actually been slaughtered primarily for their flesh. The Zulu king formerly fed his troops from the royal herd of cattle,[29] and chieftains among the Chagga of Tanganyika have sometimes slaughtered cattle to provide food for corvée labor.[30] The Masai, especially the warrior groups, kill large numbers of cattle for eating;[31] and the Mbundu of Angola slaughter cattle when the pasture is poor and food scarce.[32] The Lozi of Northern Rhodesia eat beef when other animal products are in short supply, for to them cattle are primarily a food resource, and only secondarily of prestige value.[33] The Pakot of Kenya say frankly that if it were a question of a person starving or eating his last remaining animal, he would eat the animal.[34] Partly as a result of European influence, there are many groups now who do slaughter or sell their animals commercially.[35*]

Another accusation made against the East African cattle peoples is that they tend to gorge themselves at frequent feasts, thus not using efficiently even the animals they are willing to slaughter. On the other hand, as Harold Schneider has pointed out,[36] the times of ritual slaughter and feasting often coincide with the time of year when the need for flesh is greatest, and the need may in fact determine when the ritual slaughter occurs. Indeed, Schneider and others have argued that the East African cattle people also show marked concern for economic considerations in their slaughtering practices. The extent to which this is true is still debatable, but some cattle people apparently recognize the importance of cows as producers of milk and bearers of young, and for this reason slaughter steers more often. In the Lake Victoria region bull calves are emasculated and reared only for slaughter.[37] Though the Kikuyu kill a bull on important occasions, it is unusual to kill cows, which are kept for breeding.[38] The livestock census figures for 1952 reveal that the Pakot of Kenya have a ratio of one steer to every four or five cows, indicating that more male animals are slaughtered. In trade among the Pakot, cows are worth more than steers, and people assert that while steers with specially trained horns may be most beautiful cows are more valuable because they provide milk and bear calves.[39]

There can be little criticism of the completeness of the use East African cattle peoples make of cattle products. Treated hides are used for sleeping mats, for hut coverings, for making sandals, and for many other things; horns are used as containers; urine serves as hair dressing, face wash, and as an ingredient in softening hides and skins; and dung serves as construction material and fuel. Moreover many groups do not hesitate to eat the flesh of diseased animals as long as the disease is not communicable. They also eat many more parts of the animal than most Westerners will, commonly consuming even the viscera. In addition to using the blood of slaughtered animals, many East African peoples regularly bleed live cattle and use the blood, usually mixed with milk, as food.[40*] The bleeding is done with either a miniature bow and arrow or a knife, which cuts the jugular vein of the animal and provides a flow of blood that is usually caught in a gourd (Fig. 6).

It is probably because of the overwhelming importance of the ritual, social, and affectional aspects of cattle in East Africa that some Westerners have underestimated the extent to which economic factors are considered by the cattle peoples. True, there is much inefficiency in cattle keeping and use. Animals are not bred for milk or meat. Though they eat grass and require care, male and female animals are kept beyond the point of diminishing returns. On the other hand, the end of almost every animal is the pot. When detailed comparative studies are made of the relative efficiency of animal husbandry among the East African cattle peoples and other cattle-herding groups, it may well be found that the former are far more efficient than has generally been acknowledged. In any event, the position of cattle in East Africa has not, as in Hindu India, led men to abandon beef eating. On the contrary, they eat it freely and relish it.

Origin and Diffusion of the Avoidance

We have seen that for millennia in India cattle, and especially cows, were highly regarded; that though feeling existed against their slaughter for food they were sacrificed on ceremonial occasions, and their flesh eaten apparently without prejudice. Why the sacrifice of cattle was discontinued by Hindus and beef eating completely abandoned except by lowly and despised castes remains a mystery.

The least plausible of several suggestions is that the Indians renounced the eating of beef, along with all other meat, as a health measure, either because meat decomposes rapidly in a warm climate and is readily subject to external infection by flies and other insects, or because in a hot climate the organs of the human stomach are so weakened that beef cannot be digested. A second suggestion, perhaps inspired by accounts of large-scale cattle slaughter, is that the early Hindu lawgivers issued their prohibitions to protect animals against improvident destruction.[41]

Another suggestion is that the Aryan conquerors of India, who sacrificed and ate cattle, were forced to give up these practices because they were offensive to the native people who comprised the bulk of the population[42] and who presumably viewed cattle as sacred. Support is claimed for the sacredness of cattle in pre-Aryan India in the observation that among Hindus of south India, where pre-Aryan influences are thought to be stronger, the idea of the sacred cow is most widespread today.[43] If we examine the present-day practices of people who seem to have been little affected by Aryan influences, such as the lower Hindu castes and the aboriginal Indian groups, the evidence is not very convincing that they forced others to give up a practice offensive to them. The low castes are the very ones who persist in eating beef, and when they give up the practice it is usually in an attempt to command more respect from the castes above them. This suggests that the avoidance of beef was introduced from above rather than forced from below. Of the Indian aboriginal groups, many slaughter cattle and eat beef today; those who reject the practices in some cases appear to have done so as a result of Hindu influence, which lends no support to the notion that they originated the avoidance.

A further suggestion is that the final abandonment of beef eating derives from the Buddhist-Brahman struggle for supremacy in India. Ambedkar, champion of the untouchables, follows this line of thought. According to him, the rejection of beef eating had its origin among the Brahmans as a stratagem in their extended, centuries-long struggle against the Buddhists, when Buddhism was a major critic of Brahmanism and of the cattle sacrifice which was an integral part of the Brahman religion. The Brahmans, Ambedkar argues, could improve their position in the struggle for men's minds by giving up cattle sacrifice, and they not only did this but went one step further than most Buddhists and became vegetarians.[44] Ambedkar's suggestion seems to fit with many of the known facts: that the Brahmans as priests sacrificed cattle; that Buddhists objected to animal slaughter and to the cattle sacrifice of the Brahmans; that penalties for cattle slaughter became more severe in the early centuries of the Christian era, a time of struggle between Brahmans and Buddhists; that in India today the rule against beef eating is observed more rigidly by Brahmans and upper-caste groups than by the untouchables; and that certain low castes in trying to raise their status have given up eating beef in imitation of the Brahmans and upper-caste Hindus.

Though Ambedkar's theory has much to recommend it, it does not explain the fact that while animal slaughter in general is disapproved by Buddhists, in some places Buddhist-influenced people place more barriers against slaughter of cattle than of other animals, and against eating beef than against eating most other types of flesh. To the north of India this reluctance occurs, as we have seen, not only in Tibet, where Lamaist law forbids men to eat "the cow," and where ordinary beef is considered inferior to other meat, but in Mongolia, where priests in the last century would not eat beef. In Burma in pre-British days neither Burmese nor foreigners were permitted to kill cattle for beef, and anyone found in possession of beef was punished severely. Even in British times, when there was no law prohibiting the sale of beef, respectable Burmese would not kill cattle or sell beef, although they would sell pigs and fowl. Today a Burmese who wants to give up eating the flesh of one animal to gain merit foregoes beef; and occasionally a quasi-religious group or a body of monks starts an anti-beef campaign. Similar reports of reluctance to slaughter cattle and eat beef occur in Buddhist-influenced Indochina, China, Korea, and Japan. It has not been determined whether these barriers had their origin in Buddhism, were passed on to Buddhism from Hinduism, or developed independently in the various areas for other reasons.

However unsatisfactory it may be, the most likely hypothesis suggested by the evidence is that some Indian groups had feelings against cattle slaughter and beef eating that derived from the sacred character of cattle. But whether the maintenance of herds of sacred cattle, a phenomenon originally found among Indo-Europeans, Africans, and certain other groups, had any special part in the establishment of Indian beef avoidance is not known. The Buddhists may have been sympathetic toward the feelings and early transmitted them to Southeast and East Asia, later to be outdone in India by the Brahmans, who rejected the practices completely and with puritanical fervor in an effort to demonstrate their moral superiority to their Buddhist adversaries. The limited diffusion of the beef avoidance was probably related to the failure of strong Indian influence to spread much beyond South and East Asia, and also to the fact that pastoralists, who were among the most vigorous carriers of food avoidances, did not find the beef avoidance appealing and did not adopt it.

Map 3—Avoidance of Chicken Flesh and Eggs

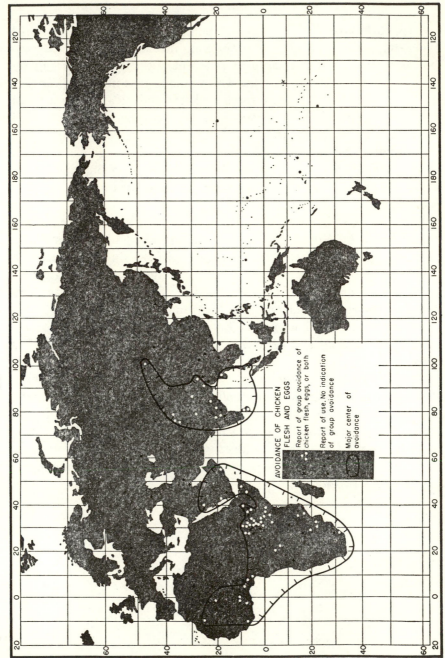

AVOIDANCE OF CHICKEN
FLESH AND EGGS

Report of group avoidance of
chicken flesh, eggs, or both

Report of use. No indication
of group avoidance

Major center of
avoidance

5

CHICKEN AND EGGS

The avoidances of pork and beef are well publicized and their existence is widely recognized by the public, but even well-informed people
are frequently unaware that there is an equally widespread avoidance
of chicken flesh and eggs in the Old World (Map 3). Though the
avoidance is most common in Africa, it has been suggested that it is
an ancient Oriental element which was introduced to Africa. Let us
turn first to Southeast Asia, where the domestication of chickens took
place, to see whether the avoidance is or has been present there, and if
so, to consider how it developed and may have spread to Africa. Since
the chicken has unusual roles in the economy and society of Southeast
Asia, these will be taken up first to determine their relevance to the use
and avoidance of chicken flesh and eggs.

Southeast Asia, the Pacific Islands, India, Tibet, and Mongolia

A striking aspect of the traditional role of chickens in Southeast Asia
is their importance in divination. Though the process of divination may
involve the use of intestines or liver, it more often requires the femora,
or thighbones, which have fine perforations. Bamboo splinters are in-
serted into the perforations; the angle at which they project is the basis
of prophecy. This form of divination was formerly found not only in
Southeast Asia but among the tribal peoples of south China. It is still
practiced among the Lolo, the Karen people of Upper Burma, the

Ahom and other Thai tribes, and the Palaung and other tribes of Mon-Khmer stock.[1] For these groups the cock[2*] plays a basic role in myth, in prayers and rituals, and in stories of tribal migration. It is believed, moreover, to be a sacred bird, a messenger of the gods which is endowed with knowledge of the future and of good and evil. It is primarily for these reasons, and because the cock through its crowing serves as a timepiece, that people keep fowl, and not for their flesh or eggs. The Karen of Burma provide an excellent example of dependence on divination. Traditionalists among them seldom attempt any undertaking, whether great or small, without receiving a favorable omen from chicken bones. Through divination, the Karen believe, they come into direct contact with the powerful unseen forces that dominate the world. If after a favorable omen a venture fails, some other force has interfered, whose favor they must win in order to succeed.[3]

The divination complex in some places extends also to the eggs of chickens. The hill tribes of southern Asia throw eggs on the ground and predict the future from the rings of color.[4] The Khasi of the Assam Hills, though they never eat fowl's eggs,[5] prize them for divination before hunting and at times of misfortune and illness.[6] And the Karen use eggs to ascertain the source of sickness. The Karen diviner rubs the sick person with the egg, then breaks the egg into the palm of his hand and carefully examines the yolk for colored streaks and blood, which indicate the cause of the illness.[7]

A phenomenon that may be related in its origins to the divination complex is cockfighting, which commands a large and enthusiastic following among some South and Southeast Asian groups (Fig. 9). Though its exact distribution in Asia has not been determined, it is found at least from India[8] to Indonesia.[9*] In Indochina the enthusiasm for the sport was so strong in the last century that one writer believed chickens were raised more for this purpose than for their flesh.[10] If a Burmese did not have a specially bred game cock he at least had an ordinary cock which he used for fighting; a cock that was not combative enough was in danger of being killed and eaten in a curry.[11] If the seventeenth-century account of John Fryer is to be trusted, a breed of fighting cocks as large as turkeys was developed in India.

According to Berthold Laufer, cockfighting is a sophisticated offshoot of divination, which developed when communities entered contests with each other to determine which was superior; the question was decided by divine judgment through a fight between sacred roosters.[12]

Fig. 9. Cockfight on Bali. Courtesy Indonesian Information Office.

The strange thing is that the primitive tribes in Southeast Asia who consider the cock sacred do not practice cockfighting.[13] Instead, it is restricted to the so-called "high civilizations," in apparent contradiction to Buddhist and Hindu feeling against cruelty to animals. This suggests that it is older than either of these religions but that it developed after the establishment of the high civilizations.

Whether stimulated by interest in more intricate patterns of thigh-bone perforations or in more combative cocks, many peoples of Southeast Asia have interbred domestic and wild fowl. The Palaung of Burma encourage interbreeding because the bones of the jungle fowl have much more variation in position and number of perforations, and therefore are preferable for divination.[14] The Palaung not only capture wild fowl and cross them with domestic birds but bring home the eggs of jungle fowl and set them under the village hen for hatching. The domestic chickens of the Angami Naga of Assam resemble the local jungle fowl, with which they interbreed occasionally, and must forage like wild fowl, being fed only enough to keep them from straying.[15] And in Burma most domestic fowl fly about freely, are difficult to catch, and in fact are little different from the wild fowl of the nearby forest.[16]

The fact that divination and cockfighting have in some cases outweighed the food use of chickens and eggs, coupled with the fact that wild fowl do not lay eggs in great numbers or propagate much, has led Laufer to suggest that chickens were not domesticated for economic advantage.[17] Instead, it is likely that they were domesticated for their value in divination, and that concern with flesh and eggs was a later development. Though many groups in Southeast Asia have taken up the use of chicken flesh and eggs,[18*] here and there peoples are still indifferent to them. In addition, some groups have strong feelings of rejection which, as will be explained later, may also have derived from the divination complex. The Vedda of Ceylon, for example, have a marked antipathy to the flesh of domestic fowl; the majority do not eat it or that of wild fowl.[19] This rejection is apparently of a magico-religious nature, but it cannot readily be explained as a borrowing from Hinduism because it seems equally strong among all Vedda, even those little influenced by Hinduism. The Sabimba, one group of Orang Laut of Malaya, scrupulously avoid the flesh of fowl as food, though other sections of the tribe relish it.[20] The Batak of Sumatra almost never eat the eggs of their chickens.[21] On Buka and Bougainville in the Solomon Islands domestic fowl seem to be kept only for the tail feathers of the cocks, which are used on ceremonial occasions as hair ornaments; though people regularly gather and eat the eggs of a small bush fowl when they are almost ready for hatching,[22*] they leave the eggs of the domestic fowl alone.[23*]

The justification for the indifference or avoidance is seldom stated by observers; beliefs associated with fertility, childbirth, and sex are known in some cases to be involved.[24*] Most aboriginal Malays do not eat eggs, apparently because of fertility beliefs;[25] among the rural Annamese, pregnant women do not eat chickens, which are believed to be toxic to them;[26] and the Isneg Apayao of the Philippines think women will die if they eat chicken flesh after childbirth.[27] Though both men and women among the Sema Naga eat chicken, women are subject to various restrictions: they must not eat chickens that "lay here and there in different places" lest they become unfaithful; and at harvest time women who eat fowl are not permitted to approach the front of the "fieldhouse" where the grain is stored,[28] an observance which is perhaps also related to fertility beliefs. Though it is not indicated specifically, beliefs involving fertility, childbirth, and sex may also be involved in other cases. Among the aboriginal Kamar of Chhattisgarh in India only men eat fowl;[29] the Ao Naga prohibit eggs to women and to girls after they have been tattooed, which is usually shortly before puberty;[30] the Marquesas Islanders prohibit chicken to women at all times.[31]

A curious thing in Southeast Asia and the Pacific islands is the preference some people show for brooded eggs in which the fetus is well developed. A century ago in Cochin China people regarded such eggs as a delicacy and consumed them mainly at important feasts. When invitations were sent out for a feast, the hens were set to brood, and ten to twelve days later the eggs were considered ripe enough for the epicure.[32] The Tagal of Malaysia share this taste, as do the natives of Brunei.[33] Adult Bontoc Igorot, though they sometimes feed their infants hard-boiled fresh eggs, themselves prefer to eat eggs that have "something in them"; this preference is widespread in the Philippines,[34] where such eggs often are served as a special delicacy.[35] The taste for brooded eggs may have survived from the time before domestication, when people gathered the eggs of wild fowl, many of which contained half-hatched birds, or it may be related to some primitive fear of undeveloped eggs. As eggs are widely considered to be a fertility symbol, primitive man may have been afraid to eat them before they had developed into some recognizable form of life, when their dangerous quality was presumably eliminated.

The avoidances of chickens and eggs mentioned thus far are those developing either out of indifference to them or out of primitive magico-religious beliefs. The major religions are at the root of other cases of chicken and egg rejection in the region. In India, for example, many Hindus, especially members of respectable castes, avoid fowl and eggs. There are regional differences among Hindus in attitudes toward chickens, which deserve study. Thus in one section of the former Central Provinces people do not regard fowl as unclean, and almost all castes that eat goats will also eat fowl; yet in the northern districts people abhor fowl for their dirty eating habits, and a man sometimes takes a purificatory bath after touching one.[36]

It has been suggested that Hindus avoid chickens and eggs as a negative reaction to their use by Moslems;[37] also that the Hindu dislike of chickens originated in a desire to distinguish between their way of life and that of the aboriginal tribes who use fowl in ceremonial pro- pitiation.[38] The evidence suggests, however, that the rejection may derive from Hindu vegetarian beliefs and from the view that the domestic chicken, because of its feeding habits, is an unclean animal. The Kashmiri Pandits, for example, refuse to eat domestic fowl or their eggs because they believe that fowl eat filthy things; but they will eat wild fowl.[39] Hindus in general, moreover, do not have the same objec- tion to the flesh of ducks, geese, and wild birds that they have to domestic fowl.[40] The attempt of some Americans to encourage the use of "vegetarian" (i.e. unfertilized) eggs in India thus overcomes the vegetarian objection to eating living creatures but not the argument that eggs are unclean because of chickens' eating habits. That strong feelings may be involved in the egg avoidance is confirmed by the report of the Brahman who became violently ill from seeing eggs being broken and beaten for an omelette.[41] The Ho of Chota Nagpur are an example of an aboriginal people who have been influenced by the Hindus to give up eating fowl and eggs. Lower class Ho still eat domestic fowl, but members of the upper classes have accepted Hindu ways; they keep domestic fowl for sacrifice but reject them as food.[42]

Buddhism too has spread the avoidance of chickens and eggs. In Ceylon and Southeast Asia the effort has not been very successful; some devout people give up eating one or both, but other Buddhists persist in the practices. Le May suggests that in Thailand even Buddhist priests eat eggs.[43] An early Javanese account (A.D. 1365) written by a Buddhist priest lists "birds" and eggs as acceptable food "according to the holy writings of antiquity."[44] To the north of India Buddhism has been somewhat more effective. In Ladakh District in Kashmir the Brogpa, some of whom are Buddhist and some Moslem, are not permitted to raise fowl or to eat eggs.[45*] In Tibet chickens are prohibited to lamas, are distasteful to other people, and are seldom eaten.[46] Many Tibetans avoid eating eggs, though Lamaist clergy are permitted to eat them and in Lhasa even the great lama has been reported as doing so.[47] The explanation given in Tibet for the avoidance of chickens is that they eat worms, which makes them sinful and their flesh unclean;[48] and that they have claws like those of "vultures which have such a prominent part in the final disposal of the Tibetan dead."[49] Eggs, apparently because they come from fowl, are believed to be unclean and harmful;[50] there is also a curious belief that there is something holy in eggs.[51] The Mongols, like the Tibetans, have a great dislike of fowl.[52] The explorer Przhevalskii reported that one of his Mongol guides nearly turned sick on seeing his European companions eat boiled duck, which like other types of fowl he considered unclean.[53]

China and the Far East

The chicken is believed to have been introduced to China from the south. There is no evidence that it was present in the Neolithic, but by Shang times (c. 1520–c. 1030 B.C.) it had reached north China. Although it was not present in any numbers then, and may have been a recent acquisition, it soon became and has remained an important animal in the Chinese economy.[54] There is no indication of the existence of prejudice against eating chicken. On the contrary, fowl have traditionally been one of the most important sources of animal protein in China, although hens have been so valuable for their eggs that they were generally eaten only when they were too old to lay. Similarly, eggs have been such an expensive food that poor people sold their eggs instead of eating them, and many eggs were exported. The Chinese have developed remarkable techniques of preservation and use of eggs which have eliminated much waste and significantly reduced the costs of handling. It is not known, however, whether the techniques were developed for reasons of economic efficiency or because of the same fear of fresh eggs postulated for various Southeast Asian peoples.[55*]

In the rest of the Far East the Chinese have been instrumental in encouraging the use of chickens and eggs, and most peoples use them freely. Chinese settlers in Inner Mongolia[56] brought chickens with them, and despite Mongol prejudice against fowl have continued to use them. In Formosa people raise chickens for both their eggs and flesh, which now comprise important sources of animal protein for them.[57] The Atayal aborigines of Formosa obtained chickens from the Chinese in fairly recent times, and keep them for their flesh, though they do not eat the eggs.[58] For the Manchu chickens are a sacrificial animal, and both chicken flesh and eggs are important dietary elements.[59] Koreans also keep chickens and eat them and their eggs.[60] The Japanese raise chickens at home and sometimes make pets of them. Because of this, some villagers feel so "cruel if they eat their own chickens" that they frequently let them die of old age.[61] The Japanese have no prejudice against eating chickens that are obtained by purchase or gift; but both chicken flesh and eggs are expensive and ordinary people cannot afford them often. The only evidence uncovered of prejudice against eggs in Japan is for the Ainu, who are said never to eat them.[62]

West of India

The chicken spread westward from India to Iran at an unknown early date. There it became involved with religious belief, with the dichotomy of good and evil and of light and darkness. As in Southeast Asia, the cock was a herald of the dawn who ushered in the new day with his crowing and dispelled the evil spirits of night. In the Kianian Period in ancient Iran (2000 to 700 B.C.) the cock was the most sacred of domestic birds, "the admonisher of mankind to discard sloth, and to wake up early to lead an industrious life," a way of existence encouraged by the prophet Zoroaster.[63] The cock's morning crowing was an important part of the daily ritual of the Zoroastrian, who, wherever he settled, took care to procure a cock.[64] The gift of cocks to the pious was considered a very meritorious act.[65] It is possible that Zoroastrian ideas of the role and position of the cock may have been diffused as far west as the British Isles. *Hamlet,* for example, refers to a cock's crow dispelling the evil forces.[66] In northeast Scotland the cock has been thought to have the power to see evil spirits, and has been viewed as a prophet, its actions being watched for omens of death.[67]

The ancient Iranians did not refuse to eat this sacred animal and herald of dawn, but made chicken flesh part of their daily food.[68] Iranians still eat fowl and eggs without prejudice, as do most Middle

Easterners.[69]* In Arabia, however, the chicken and egg avoidance is present here and there. Eggs are viewed as paupers' food there;[70] and unsophisticated Arabs look down on poultry and their products, though they are generally available to the traveler.[71] Tribesmen in the Medina area do not eat chicken or eggs;[72] and in some villages in the Tihama lowlands along the Red Sea coast of Saudi Arabia people keep chickens but never eat their flesh or eggs, both of which are forbidden food. In the village of Darb in the Tihama a curious crowd gathered to watch eggs being prepared for St. John B. Philby, something they had not seen before.[73] It is interesting that the Tihama has a sizable population of Negroes, who may have brought the avoidances with them from Africa. The people of the Qara Mountains, in Dhufar in the Hadhramaut, also refuse chicken flesh and eggs, and would consider it a personal affront to be served eggs.[74]

The attitudes of the above peoples of south Arabia are matched by those held by certain peoples of the Sahara Desert, where chickens are found in practically all oasis settlements and in many camps as well. One of these Sahara groups is the Ahaggar Haratin, a Negro agricultural folk who keep chickens but as a rule eat only the eggs. The Ahaggar Tuareg do not eat either fowl or their eggs, and even in time of famine give them only to children. The Tuareg's Negro slaves who had recently eaten chickens and eggs were not permitted to use communal drinking vessels. The Moors, the basically white population of the Spanish Sahara and adjacent territory, reject both domestic fowl and their eggs. On the other hand the Chaamba, a nomadic Arab people, and the Teda of the Tibesti, most of whom are nomadic, do eat chicken and eggs.[75]

There have been isolated occurrences of chicken and egg avoidance in Europe. In ancient Greece a cock was consecrated to the goddess Maia, and initiates in her mysteries abstained from eating domestic birds; so did initiates in the Eleusinian mysteries.[76] Julius Caesar reported that the Britons considered it wrong to eat chickens, and kept them for "pastime or pleasure."[77] There may be survivals of the ancient attitude here and there today. On the Aegean island of Chios shepherds keep cocks but not hens, for hens produce eggs, and this, say Argenti and Rose in *The Folk-Lore of Chios,* "according to the belief of the shepherds, causes sickness among the flock."[78]

Inscriptions and drawings prove that chickens were present in Egypt in the fifteenth and fourteenth centuries B.C.[79] It is not known how early they spread into Negro Africa or by what route: whether from Egypt or more directly from Southeast Asia; whether up the Nile, across Arabia, or by sea; whether at the hands of Arabs, Malaysians, or some other group. It is clear from European accounts, however, that not all African groups had chickens even in the last century, and that some who had them kept them not for food but for purposes and with attitudes surprisingly similar to those of Southeast Asia and Iran. The Walamo of Ethiopia, for example, regard fowl as sacred.[80] Pastoralists among the Nyoro keep a cock to wake them in the morning.[81] In the last century the Pondo reared fowl, but only for feathers and head ornaments.[82] The natives of Uzinza in the Nyanza region of Uganda kept fowl only to sell to travelers or for divining purposes through the use of the blood and bones.[83] And the Hangaza of the northern border of Urundi keep chickens for divining purposes but do not eat them or their eggs.[84] The use of chickens in divining has also been reported for the Maji of Ethiopia, the Azande of the Sudan, and the Nyoro. And though the cockfighting complex seems to be absent, the rejection of chickens and eggs as food is found in almost every part of Africa, sometimes applying only to eggs, sometimes to chickens, and sometimes to both.

The feelings associated with the avoidance of chickens and eggs in Africa vary considerably from place to place. Among some groups they are strong, even violent, and are supported by severe sanctions. Among others they simply involve mild disapproval. The Galla and Somali in the nineteenth century disdained the flesh of chickens and today consider eggs the excrement of fowls, as do the Kikuyu, Kamba, Teita, Chagga, Nyamwezi, and Rundi.[85] Many East African tribes have been as disgusted to see a European traveler eat eggs as the traveler would have been to see Africans eat garbage.[86] The German explorer Eduard Vogel may have been killed partly because he offended the local populace by eating eggs.[87] The most severe sanctions were found among the Kafa of Ethiopia, who made slaves of women who broke the rule against eating chicken;[88] and among the Walamo, who put to death anyone who violated the restrictions on eating fowl, which they regarded as sacred.[89] Examples of milder attitudes are the Cape Nguni, who consider poultry women's food,[90] and the Nuer, among whom men think eating eggs effeminate.[91]

The African avoidances of chickens and eggs take a bewildering diversity of forms. In many places the avoidance applies to the entire group,[92]* but elsewhere it varies with the sex, age, and social position of the individual, and in the case of eggs, with their state of decay and method of preparation. Women are more generally subject to prohibitions than men; among many groups they do not taste the avoided food for many years. The prohibitions are commonest, furthermore, for women of childbearing age, and are based on fear of barrenness, injury to the unborn child, or lasciviousness.[93]* Among the Tembu and Fingo, Nguni groups of the Cape region, eggs are believed to have an aphrodisiac effect, driving women who have eaten them to approach men from other kraals. In fact when a woman says to a man, "I shall cook eggs for you," it is recognized as a sexual advance. The Xosa combine two beliefs in their contention that eggs make a woman not only unable to restrain her passions but unable to conceive. And the Yaka of the Congo believe that should a woman eat an egg she would become insane, would rip off her clothes, and run away into the bush.[94]

In some cases the avoidance applies not only to women but also to men during the reproductive years; others are free to eat the food, apparently because infertility and sexual injury would not be problems for them. The Yao of Nyasaland believe that eggs cause sterility, and only people not of childbearing or childbegetting age eat them.[95] Among the Moru of the Sudan only children and aged people eat chickens and eggs.[96] The Mwimbe of Kenya forbid them "to circumcised men and women."[97] The Maji of Ethiopia slaughter chickens solely on ritual occasions, then let only youths eat them.[98] There are but few instances in which males are singled out for an avoidance of chickens or eggs.[99]*

In view of this widespread fear in Africa that eating chickens and eggs will destroy fertility or interfere with sexual functions, it is very interesting to find the belief that eggs can be rendered "safe" by some treatment such as cooking, by allowing them to rot, or by permitting them to develop a recognizable form of life. This recalls the parallel Southeast Asian preferences for brooded eggs.

Origin of the Avoidances

The literature is surprisingly deficient in reasoned general hypotheses for the origin of the chicken and egg avoidance. A few limited explanations have been suggested for Hindu India, which is in the general area where chickens were first domesticated. One of these explanations, by

Nagendranath Gangulee,[1] is that the Hindus wished to distinguish themselves from the aboriginal tribes who used fowl in propitiation ceremonies. The appearance of the avoidances among a few Indian aboriginal groups who do not seem to be strongly influenced by Hinduism, and their scattered occurrence among aboriginal groups in Southeast Asia as well as in the Pacific islands, suggest, however, practices which have their roots deep in antiquity perhaps before the development of Hinduism itself. A second explanation that has been advanced is in terms of Hindu antipathy to Moslems,[2] who eat chickens and eggs freely. This idea finds little support in the present-day situation. If, for example, Hindus did regard the use of chicken flesh and eggs as symbolic of Islamic affiliation, they would probably observe the avoidance more universally than they do. The Hindus themselves commonly explain the avoidances by reference to their vegetarian beliefs or the scavenging habits of chickens. The occurrence of the avoidances in Arabia and northeast Africa shows that in some parts of the Islamic world Moslems have shared them, and suggests that the origin must be sought beyond the Hindu-Moslem conflict.

Lagercrantz has suggested that the African avoidance of chickens and eggs is an ancient Oriental element which was spread in East Africa by East Hamitic cattle herders, who had no chickens and who despised the subject population who kept them.[3] The surprising parallels between African and Southeast Asian attitudes toward chickens and eggs make this view seem worth investigating further, especially through field studies along the avenues of possible introduction to East Africa.

Since the avoidances were present in South and Southeast Asia in ancient times, an adequate hypothesis for their origin must consider attitudes that might have existed among the ancient primitive groups in that area. One striking belief of primitive Southeast Asian peoples today, which may be quite old, is that food is more than simply nutrient matter: it is part of a world that is both mysterious and fraught with danger; if man is not careful the malevolent forces of nature can gain access to his body by way of the food he eats. Group avoidances of chickens and eggs may first have developed from fear that they contained elements harmful to the body. Whether these elements were originally believed to be present in chickens, in eggs, or in both is not known. It is possible that the chicken because of its role in divination assumed certain aspects of the supernatural, and that its flesh was re-

jected through fear of contamination. Or the rejection may have originated because the chicken ate food regarded as unclean or because it
destroyed life and thus violated the sensibilities of the people; Buddhists today often regard the chicken as unclean because it kills and
eats other forms of life, and they avoid eggs because they are its
products.

Another possibility is that the avoidance was based on some quality
in eggs, and then was applied to chickens. The literature reveals that,
above all else, eggs are identified with life and fertility. Indeed, the
Western practice of hunting Easter eggs left by a rabbit is not simply
a children's game but the remnant "of a fertility rite, the eggs and the
rabbit both symbolizing fertility."[4] In France in the seventeenth century
a bride was required to break an egg upon entering her new home to
assure her fecundity; and among the Germans and Slavs a rich harvest
was ensured by smearing a mixture of eggs, bread, and flour on the
plow on the Thursday preceding Easter.[5] In Morocco an egg is used in
magic or medicine to encourage fecundity in a woman, to enhance a
man's virility, and to facilitate childbirth; at weddings it both assures the
happiness of the newlyweds and aids the bridegroom to consummate
the marriage.[6]

These customs are paralleled in Iran by the exchange of eggs between
bride and groom on completion of the marriage contract, and the giving of colored eggs at New Year because, in Henri Massé's words,
eggs mark "the origin and the beginning of things."[7] There is a Chinese
custom of presenting the mother of a newborn child with eggs to eat,[8]
to convey the wish that her fertility continue. The Zigula (Zeguha)
of Africa place eggs in newly planted fields to assure their fertility.[9]
The Yezidi at their spring feast exchange eggs.[10]

In Iraq people are reluctant to present an egg to a friend after sun-
set, for fear of "giving away a life."[11*] The Jews eat eggs after the
death of a relative; the Baghdad Jews, Lady Drower records, used to
give "a bereaved family boiled eggs to eat on their return from the
funeral."[12]

There is a report for the fellahin of Upper Egypt of a divorced
woman who attempted to make her former husband's other wife barren
by magical means which included burying in a tomb an egg and a palm
leaf, both inscribed with spells.[13] If the palm leaf represents virility,
the intended effect of consigning it together with the egg, symbol of

female fertility, to the abode of evil and death is not hard to divine. The account mentions that the spell would no longer be effective if egg and palm leaf were removed from the tomb. The recognition that eggs represent developing life and are a harbinger of what is to come may also have led primitive man to seek signs of the future in them, and contributed to the divination complex of Southeast Asia. Probably related to this is the practice, common in ancient Rome[14] and still found in parts of contemporary America, of divining the sex of the unborn child through the use of eggs.

The Ibibio of Nigeria have a tradition that the first women on earth, who were barren, were given an egg, symbol of fertility, by Eka Abassi, the goddess of heaven, who insisted she would withdraw her gift should human beings eat eggs.[15] Such a tradition against eating the fertility symbol may well have been one of the modes of origin of an avoidance that has been applied by different groups in various ways: for example by prohibiting eggs to everyone or to certain prestigeful persons, or by forbidding them to those who were in particular danger of loss of fertility. This may account for the more widespread and stringent application of the restrictions to women, who since they bear the young are more vulnerable to the evil influences that affect successful reproduction. On the other hand some groups, such as the Beni subtribe of the Nupe of Nigeria,[16] are as afraid that eating eggs will make men sterile as that it will make women barren. If it is not of eggs in themselves but of their fertility-inhibiting quality that people are afraid, it is natural that they should use eggs whenever this quality is dissipated. This would account for some groups rejecting fresh eggs but eating those that are rotten or in which the fetus has begun to develop; or their placing other conditions on the eating of eggs, according to the mode of preparation.[17*] The destruction of life in the egg, or the transformation of the egg into a recognizable form of animal life, the fetus, may have eliminated the fertility-inhibiting quality. The widespread preferance for eggs "with chicken" in Southeast Asia and the Pacific islands, and the desirability of preserved eggs among the Chinese and some neighboring peoples, may have had their origins in just such a fear of inhibiting fertility in humans as we are discussing here.

Though the data presented above are only suggestive, field studies should provide further clues to the possible origin of the avoidances, and indications of whether the avoidance of chickens or that of eggs is basic. The literature favors the claims of eggs.[18*] It is clear that both have been present since antiquity, that they are associated with fertility beliefs in some areas, and that in this context eggs are more significant than chickens. The East rather than Africa seems indicated as the place of origin of the avoidance. Nevertheless, until the regional beliefs of the ancient East are better known and understood, it remains a matter of speculation exactly when and where the avoidances developed, whether they had single or multiple origin, and how they spread over the Old World, coming to be centered today in Africa on the one hand and in South Asia, Tibet, and Mongolia on the other. Their modification is going on rapidly today in Africa, because the avoidance lacks organized religious support; on the contrary, there is religious opposition, for Christians ridicule the avoidance. In South Asia, on the other hand, modification proceeds more slowly since organized religious opposition tends to inhibit the use of chicken flesh and eggs.

6

HORSEFLESH

Inner Asia

The great Old World center of horsemeat eating stretches from Mongolia into easternmost Europe (Map 4). In the heart of the belt in inner Asia lived turbulent pastoralists whose lives centered to an unusual extent on horses, wild and domestic, and who carried the custom of eating horseflesh with them into neighboring areas. The horse served the peoples of inner Asia for riding, for packing, and for food; its hide and hair were used for various manufactures; its milk was made into kumiss and other fermented products. A "Kirghiz" (Kirghiz-Kazakh?) family of five in the nineteenth century was likely to own at least fifteen horses as well as other domestic animals; the Kalmuck (Torgut) of the southern Volga region brought herds of a thousand horses to market in the spring; the Mongols were—and are—dependent on horses, and Mongol shepherds have even tended their flocks on horseback. The practice of setting aside the best pastures for horses—which have exhausted them—has been responsible periodically for the starvation of many cattle.[1]

An extreme example of the importance of horses in inner Asia is the Yakut. According to Yakut tradition the horse was given to man by a benevolent deity, who also saw that man learned how to make kumiss. The Yakut considered it sinful to beat a horse. Their love songs compared the hero to a colt and the heroine to a mare. When a horse died its bones were not permitted to lie on the ground but were placed on a platform. And when a Yakut found a horse's skull he would hang it in a tree out of respect.[2]

The Yakut preferred horseflesh to all other meat, including beef.[3] Their myths pictured kumiss and the flesh of fat mares as food fit for heroes. They slaughtered an animal for food whenever one could be spared from the herd; and at feasts four of them, it is claimed, could handily eat a horse.[4] The favorite dish for the bride to serve to the groom at their wedding, was a boiled horse's head with horseflesh sausages.[5] Their fondness for horseflesh led the Yakut to become adept at stealing horses. Because of this, whenever two convoys with horses camped near each other men were posted to guard the animals. A group that managed to steal a horse would decamp quickly, ride some distance away, slaughter the animal, bury the bones, and hide the flesh in their saddlebags.[6]

In ancient times the Scythians of the Ukraine sacrificed horses and ate their flesh.[7] Ruy Gonzalez de Clavijo, Spanish ambassador to Tamerlane (c. 1336–1405), found horseflesh a favored food in the Emperor's court at Samarkand.[8] In more recent days a group of Samoyed near Archangel has been described as eating the carcasses of horses and having a pile of raw horseflesh in a corner of their tent.[9] The Mongols, who use horses principally for transport and herding, have traditionally sacrificed a man's horse at his grave and buried it with him.[10] They eat horseflesh on special occasions,[11] despite the attempts of Buddhism to abolish the practice. Only pious priests abstain.[12*]

South, East, and Southeast Asia

In present-day India a few untouchable Hindu castes, such as the Mahar of Maharashtra, eat the flesh of dead horses; but other untouchables, like the Gujarati Dhed and Chamar,[13] as well as Hindus generally, refuse altogether to eat horsemeat. There used to be a common belief in India that eating horseflesh caused cramps; and when a Sepoy rifleman missed his target in practice, his fellows jokingly accused him of having eaten horsemeat.[14] Buddha's specific prohibition of horseflesh[15] is paralleled today by its prohibition in Tibet by the northern Buddhists. Tibetan nomads have such strong feelings against eating horseflesh that they shake with nausea when they hear of Chinese and

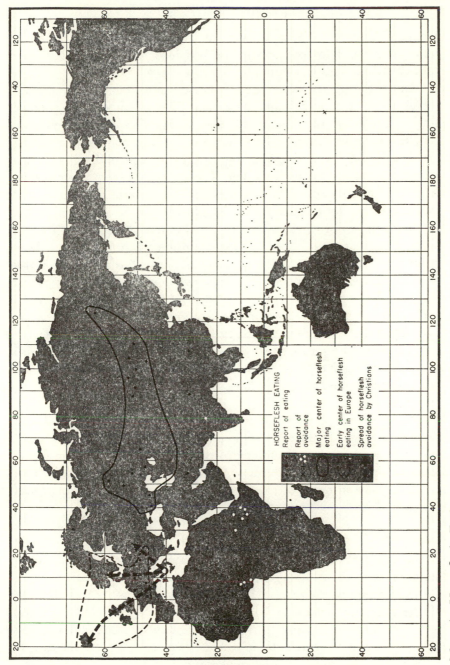

Map 4—Horseflesh Eating

Mongols doing it.[16] Yet even they are sometimes forced by famine to resort to it—and for one group, the people of Bangba Chugdso, the flesh of wild horses is a staple food.[17]

Despite the early occurrence of horses in China,[18*] and the encouragement of horse breeding by various Chinese emperors to counteract the threat of the Hsiung-nu, the Mongols, and other nomadic peoples to the west, horses have not usually been numerous in China. They have played only a minor role in Chinese agriculture,[19] and have provided little for the nation's diet. There are, however, a few specific references to the eating of horseflesh by the people of Shansi, who used horse liver for medicinal purposes; by the people of Yin in Shensi; and by King Mu of Chou, who is reported to have taken three hundred horses along for eating on one of his mythical expeditions to the "Pearl Swamp."[20] There are also some general reports of the practice in the seventeenth century in Robert Burton's *Anatomy of Melancholy,* which relies on observations by a Jesuit who lived in China for many years, and in the nineteenth century in the account of Eduard Hahn.[21]

In Japan the Ainu are very fond of horseflesh,[22] though they have few if any horses. The Japanese eat horsemeat without prejudice, and it is a fairly common ingredient in sukiyaki; the meat is generally obtained from domestic animals which have outlived their usefulness for draft purposes.

Horses are found in small numbers in various parts of Malaysia. They were first introduced at some unknown, moderately remote date; and the early horses were supplemented later by additions from China, from Mexico, and from the Arabs.[23] Though they are not used for food or for sacrifice in much of the region, there are several reports of such practices.[24*]

The Middle East and Africa

The prophet Mohammed himself never ate horseflesh, but he did not declare it unlawful;[25] today there is some doubt among Moslems about the legal status of the practice.[26] Abu Hanifa (A.D. 699–767), founder of the Hanafite school of Islamic jurisprudence, declared it unlawful;[27] but other Moslems, particularly in Central Asia, do not subscribe to this view and continue to eat horsemeat.[28*] Nevertheless, the restrictive view has gradually gained support, even in Central Asia. Thus the Tadjik of Turkestan, strict Moslems who live in the midst of horse eaters, refuse horseflesh and mares' milk because of religious prohibitions,[29] as do most Moslems of the Middle East.

In pre-European times horses were found in many sections of sub-Saharan Africa north of the equator. But the flesh has never been an important food to Africans there, and many groups refuse to eat it, in some cases as a result of Islamic influence and in other cases not. In Ethiopia both predominantly Moslem groups, such as the Galla, and Christian and pagan peoples, such as the Amhara, Kafa, and Mao, refuse it.[30] In the Sudan the tribes of the Nuba Mountains avoid eating it; and when some Nuba tribesmen in Orombe (Otoro) ate their horses after the animals had died, their more conservative fellow tribesmen were disgusted.[31] In the Sudan borderlands the Sokoro, Bua, and Somrai, all mainly pagan groups, will not eat horseflesh, though the Baghirmi will.[32] In Nigeria Moslems strictly forbid horsemeat,[33] and certain pagan or partly Islamized groups there and in nearby areas avoid it. Among the Yoruba of Ife, for example, horseflesh is eaten only by "meaner people," who consume horses which have died of disease.[34] The Katab of northern Nigeria do not eat horsemeat, nor do the people of any of the villages except one in the Bachit area of the Central Plateau.[35] A generation ago the pagan Bassa of central Nigeria ate horsemeat, though the custom was being abandoned.[36] The Warjawa pagans of northern Nigeria, on the other hand, continue to eat it at feasts celebrating the planting and harvesting of crops.[37] In the Cameroons the Kpe people are able to keep horses because their mountain homeland is relatively healthful, but they rarely ride them and do not eat their flesh.[38] The Sotho of South Africa, who first learned of the horse from European settlers, share their prejudice against horseflesh, though a few people eat it.[39]

Europe

Christianity and the Decline in Eating Horesflesh.—The practice of eating horseflesh was widespread in ancient times in northern Europe. According to Hieronymus (c. 347–419?), the Quadi—a Germanic tribe —as well as the Vandals ate wild horses.[40] The context in this instance is not clear, but elsewhere the practice was associated with the worship of pagan deities such as Odin.[41]

With the introduction of Christianity to the region, pressure was exerted to eliminate this along with other pagan customs. In some cases the pressure was subtle: the Penitential of Archbishop Ecbert ruled that horseflesh was not prohibited, but added, in what looks like a hint, that many families will not buy it.[42] In time, however, the strict view prevailed, and the Christian Church made a serious attempt to stamp out the practice. In A.D. 732 Pope Gregory III ordered Boniface, the apostle to the Germans, to forbid the eating of horseflesh, which he had tolerated until that time.[43] Groups that were subsequently converted to Christianity were forced to give up the practice; this made some pagans, such as the Icelanders, reluctant to become Christians.

Despite the influence of the church in bringing about a considerable decline in horsemeat eating in northern Europe,[44] there are indications that it never completely died out. It was apparently eaten even by some Christian monks, for among the benedictions of Monk Ekkehard (c. A.D. 1000–1060) of St. Gall in Switzerland to be given over the food served in the monastery there is one referring to the flesh of wild horses.[45] At the inauguration of the king in one district of Ulster in the twelfth century a white mare was slaughtered, butchered, and boiled, and a bath was prepared of the broth; the king then sat in the bath and ate horseflesh, as did the assembled people, and drank some of the broth in which he bathed.[46] That the Irish at least to some extent continued to eat horseflesh after the introduction of Christianity is further attested by the occurrence, amid the refuse of meals at an archeological site at Ballinderry, of horse bones which were split in the same manner as the bones of domestic animals known to have been eaten.[47] Eating horseflesh persisted elsewhere, too, for in 1520 there was a horsemeat feast in Denmark.[48] Robert Burton noted in *The Anatomy of Melancholy* that young horses were commonly eaten as "red deer" in Spain, and were supplied to the navy for food, especially around Málaga.[49] By that time, however, horseflesh had generally come to be regarded as a low-class food in Europe and not suitable for prestigeful gatherings. It now took starvation to bring many Europeans to eat it; accounts of sieges show that people killed and ate their horses only after first eating grass, oats, and leather jackets.[50]

Attempts to Reintroduce the Meat.—It was in the role of a scarcity food that horsemeat began to assume importance again in northern Europe. In eighteenth-century France a great deal of horsemeat was eaten by the half-starved poor, and its consumption was being urged officially.[51] Baron Larry, surgeon to Napoleon, had such faith in horsemeat bouillon that in all the campaigns he served in he gave it to the wounded. Horseflesh was sold openly at Württemberg in 1841. By the mid-1860's its dietary possibilities had attracted the attention of the European intelligentsia, and serious efforts were made to popularize it. A *banquet hippophagique*, featuring horsemeat dishes, was held at the Grand Hotel in Paris in 1865 and attended by 135 people; the horse soup was good, the boiled horsemeat and cabbage was acclaimed excellent, though certain other horsemeat dishes were not so well received. Soon afterward the first horsemeat butcher shop was opened in Paris. This *Boucherie Hippophagique* was followed by others, and by 1867 there were several. Important men, including the eminent French zoologist Isidore St. Hilaire, joined the cause of *chevaline*, as its enthusiasts called it. St. Hilaire pointed to the widespread eating of horsemeat in other parts of the world, to its importance among the ancient Germans, and to the excellent taste and food value of the meat. He served a variety of horsemeat dishes in his home to help popularize it.

The French campaign stimulated an interest in horsemeat in England;[52]* a rise in meat prices following an epidemic among cattle enhanced this interest and led to the holding of horsemeat banquets in England in 1868. The importance of French inspiration is illustrated by the Falstaff Hotel banquet in Ramsgate: the horsemeat was imported from France and prepared by a French cook.[53] English enthusiasts, like their French counterparts, praised horsemeat in public lectures, served *chevaline* dinners to encourage its use, and even organized a Society for the Propagation of Horse Flesh as an Article of Food.[54]

The campaign to popularize *chevaline* met with some success in Europe, especially in France but also in Belgium, the Netherlands, Switzerland, Germany, and some nearby areas. Its use was adopted, however, only by small segments of the population. Today it is generally regarded as a symbol of low status and poverty, although it may, as among some university groups in the United States, represent a degree of emancipation from societal norms.[55]* The feeling is expressed, too, that it is unhealthy food, perhaps because people commonly believe that the flesh comes from sick old horses. And there is also the sentiment that the horse is a companion of man and therefore should not be eaten. The supply of horseflesh in Europe has been obtained largely from undesirable animals, either domestic or imported from neighboring countries or from North and South America. France also imports corned horsemeat from the United States.[56] How much horsemeat is used in Central and Eastern Europe today is not certain, but it appears to be less important as a food there than in Western Europe. In Czechoslovakia in 1932, nevertheless, it amounted to 1.1 per cent of the meat consumed in the entire country.[57] In Moravia about 1910–35 horseflesh was ordinarily eaten only by some poor people, except in periods of scarcity such as wartime.[58] The Poles, with strong prejudices against it, eat it only in times of dire need.[59] According to a Finnish informant, horseflesh was not eaten in his village a generation ago, and the man responsible for killing aged and crippled horses lived apart from others and was regarded as a pariah. Today, however, horsemeat can be purchased in Finland, and is used by some people, though it is still not fully accepted as a food and is not found in restaurants.

It is certain that the practice of horsemeat eating was more widespread through the Old World in ancient times than today, and that the decline resulted from the spread of Christianity, Islam, and perhaps also Hinduism. Peoples found here and there in Southeast Asia and in Nigeria who eat it represent groups which so far have resisted the pressure, especially of Islam, against the practice.

Origin of the Avoidance

Little is known about the origins of the prejudice against horsemeat. In some cases it probably sprang from the reaction of a world religion, such as Christianity, to the sacrifice and eating of horses in pagan religious rites. In others it may derive from the animal's high status and its supposed holy qualities and association with the deities.[60]* The recent renaissance of horseflesh eating in Europe—a rare example of a counterattack against food prejudice, and one which met with limited success—was possible only at a time when religion was no longer involved in the matter.

7

CAMEL FLESH

The Middle East and Neighboring Areas

The camel is found in the Old World from the Atlantic coast of the Sahara to Mongolia: the dromedary occupies the hot deserts and steppes from North Africa to the Punjab, and the bactrian camel the colder arid lands from the Caspian Sea eastward. Just as the slaughter and eating of horses in Europe was identified with pagan custom, so the slaughter and eating of camels, even though practiced since antiquity, has come to be regarded in the Middle East as almost an Islamic rite, and a sort of profession of the faith. The common Moslem custom of slaughtering camels publicly on ceremonial occasions is based on the belief that the camel has certain holy qualities. In Iran until recent times, for example, a camel was adorned and paraded through the city on one Moslem holiday; then it was slaughtered and butchered and its flesh distributed to the public.[1] People prepared and ate portions of the flesh as an act of devotion, and some smeared the blood on lintels and other places to protect the house against evil spirits. Public camel sacrifice was forbidden in Iran in 1933,[2] but it is still practiced in some other parts of the Middle East.[3]*

The holy qualities of the camel are believed to endow its flesh and other products with medicinal value. Camel urine is drunk in Morocco as a remedy for fever, and the flesh is eaten as a cure for boils as well as for general strength.[4] In Iran some of the flesh of the sacrificial camel was salted and given to sick people as a holy food.[5] That such beliefs have existed since early times is attested by the Spanish Moslem naturalist and traveler Ibn al-Baytar, who in the thirteenth century described the medicinal and magical uses of camel milk, meat, and urine in the Islamic world.[6]

Camel flesh is also widely used in the Middle East simply as food, though it is seldom plentiful enough to be more than a luxury. In Iran, except on occasions of ceremonial slaughter, Moslems ordinarily ate it only when animals had broken their legs or become sick.[7] A few young camels may be killed for their meat in Saudi Arabia,[8] but in ordinary times only injured animals are slaughtered. On the rare occasions when the Rwala Bedouin slaughter a camel, they eat almost every part except the contents of stomach and intestines. The camel's head embellishes the platter at a Rwala feast, much as the boar's head did in royal feasts of northwest Europe. The Rwala apparently regard camel flesh primarily as a food at such feasts; their ravenous manner of eating it seems out of keeping with the notion that this is an act of faith.[9] Egypt imports numbers of camels from the Sudan and Arabia. Though the Egyptian fellahin cannot afford to buy much meat, they are very fond of camel flesh and do manage to purchase an occasional piece of it.[10] At Kharga oasis in Egypt people used to eat diseased camels, slaughtering them before they died, but the government banned the practice.[11] In the Sahara Desert, to kill a camel would be to destroy one's capital; therefore camels are eaten "only in sizable towns or on the occasion of a very big and important feast, or when they are so ill or injured so badly that their lives are despaired of."[12] In spite of this traditional reluctance to part with camels, the Chaamba nomads of the Sahara about 1940 started to raise camels especially for sale to butchers in commercial centers.

This general pattern of consumption prevails among the Moslem peoples living on the fringes of the Middle East, from Central Asia to sub-Saharan Africa: people eat camel flesh as food whenever they can afford it, but commonly obtain it only on ceremonial occasions.[13*] In sub-Saharan Africa it is also eaten without prejudice by some pagan groups.[14*]

The rejection of camel flesh is found chiefly among various non-Moslem peoples of the Middle East but occurs to some extent also on the margins of the area. It goes back far into the past: the prohibition was included in the Levitican code of the Jews;[15] it was observed at ancient Haran in Mesopotamia;[16] and it was enforced by the Syrian Christian hermit St. Simeon Stylites (d. 459?), who forbade camel flesh to his Saracen converts in an effort to rid them of their heathen ways.[17] In modern times the meat is rejected as food by the Zoroastrians of Iran,[18] the Mandaeans of Iraq and Iran,[19] the Nosairis of Syria,[20] the Christian Copts of Egypt,[21] and the Saharan Jews.[22] In Ethiopia, where camel flesh is an important food for the Moslem pastoral peoples, the Christians of the highland will not eat it; they regard it as unclean and consider its use a Moslem habit.[23] Some Christian highlanders have maintained their prejudices against the products of the camel even after conquering and settling in areas where camel flesh and milk were the mainstays of the local diet. A century ago the ruling class of the Mansa, a tribe of cultivators living thirty miles northwest of Massawa, kept the prohibition against using camel meat and milk as long as they were Christians, but dropped them when they abandoned Christianity.[24]

Though the Moslems themselves have adopted many Jewish food observances, they claim that the Jewish prohibition of camel flesh was abrogated by Jesus, whom they recognize as a prophet. Former feeling against eating camel flesh has been almost entirely eliminated among converts to Islam, though a few survivals are found even among Moslems. R. Campbell Thompson reported that at Mosul in Iraq it was an insult to say that a man eats camel flesh.[25] Robert Graves observed that one group of Indian Moslem soldiers who served with T. E. Lawrence in Arabia during World War I refused camel flesh as "against their principles."[26] This attitude, though not characteristic of Moslem practice, is in keeping with Hindu Indian practice; even members of the Chamar caste, who eat carrion and the flesh of many types of animals, will not usually touch the carcasses of camels.[27]

In Mongolia, too, there is some reluctance to accept camel flesh. Though Chinese traders in Mongolia eat it, and the Mongols themselves drink camel milk, they do not usually eat the flesh of domestic camels.[28] The status of camel meat is illustrated by the observation that when Mongol caravan drivers are not given enough meat they "will bring camel flesh into the tent, scorch it at the fire, and pretend to eat it, to shame the caravan master."[29] The Mongol reluctance to eat the flesh of domestic camels is said by Lattimore to derive from the feeling that it would be an insult to the souls of those who have provided men with a living. The fact that the Mongols have no prejudice against eating the flesh of feral camels seems to support this suggestion.

Origin of the Avoidance

The origin of the avoidance of camel flesh is not known, and does not seem likely now to be determined. We know only that in the Middle East it dates back to pre-Islamic times; and that for some non-Moslem groups it has been reinforced by negative reaction to Moslem ways. Camel flesh is another interesting example of a flesh food which, like pork, beef, and horseflesh, became embroiled in religious controversy. In this case, however, the use of the flesh became symbolic of membership in a major religious group which was active in propagating it.

8

DOGFLESH

Many Westerners are surprised or shocked to hear that anyone eats dogflesh. Some think of it as a tough, unpalatable meat. Others regard eating dogs as little different from cannibalism. A good illustration is the recent case of Andrew O'Meara, a United States Army officer, who killed, skinned, and put a stray dog on a spit in Peoria, Illinois, to demonstrate means of military survival to some friends.[1] He was prosecuted under an Illinois statute against cruelty to animals, pleaded guilty, and was fined the maximum $200 permitted by the statute. An interesting aspect of the case is that though Lieutenant O'Meara killed the dog with a sudden blow, and could have pleaded innocent, he felt public pressure sufficiently to plead guilty and to accept by agreement the maximum fine. The judge in the case received crank letters and threatening phone calls, one from as far away as Washington, D.C., to make certain that he "did his duty."[2]

The fact is, of course, that there are many areas of the Old World where dogflesh is or has been eaten—chiefly in (1) tropical West and Central Africa and (2) Southeast and East Asia and the Pacific islands (Map 5).[3*] It may be interesting to determine whether the people of these regions eat dogmeat because they like it, or are forced to it by starvation. In pursuing this inquiry we can examine the context of the practice and the methods of keeping dogs. It is fortunate that focus on centers of dog *eating* is desirable: the literature contains scant material

91

on avoidance, since most of it is written by Westerners, who commonly record a practice which shocks them, but accept avoidance as normal and seldom note it.

Centers of Dogflesh Eating

Africa South of the Sahara.—Dogs, generally of a lean, ill-tempered, mongrel type, are found among almost all African peoples. They serve a few groups as a herding animal, and more groups as a companion and aid in hunting. Their primary function, however, is as scavenger and guardian who consumes the refuse of the village and protects it from predators.

The center of dogflesh eating in Africa is in the rain forest and adjacent savannas of West Africa and the Congo Basin. Here some peoples prefer it to other types of food. The Tallensi of Ghana and the Poto of the Congo, for example, consider dogmeat a delicacy.[4] The Mittu of the southern Sudan used to like dogflesh so much that soldiers of a slave trader's encampment in Mittu country bred dogs to barter to the Mittu for slaves.[5] When a dog stole a piece of meat from the market place of some Ngala people of the Congo, they seized the animal, cut it open, and thus had not only the stolen meat but the dog itself, which they prized more.[6*]

Outside this center of dog eating, most of the groups in Africa eating dogflesh do so under extenuating circumstances.[7*] The Gogo and Rangi of Tanganyika eat it only in time of need.[8] The Mandanda pointed out that their enemies the Zulu did not like dogflesh and would not steal Mandanda dogs, though they would steal other animals.[9] The Lango of Uganda prescribe eating dogflesh in ordeals or tests of guilt, but only because they consider the dog an unclean animal.[10] The people of Fazogli, along the Blue Nile in the Sudan, sacrificed and ate dogs, but on a special occasion when the dog was a substitute for the king.[11] The Koma of southern Ethiopia, at an annual celebration of the New Moon, sacrificed a dog and presented its tail to their ruler to eat; his position was thereby extended until the next celebration.[12] This practice may be related to the veneration of reddish-colored dogs among the Koma; they reared these dogs carefully and believed that misfortune would befall any person who mistreated one.[13*]

Liking for dogflesh has not led Africans in the center of dog eating to develop special breeds of dogs for their flesh,[14*] but they employ

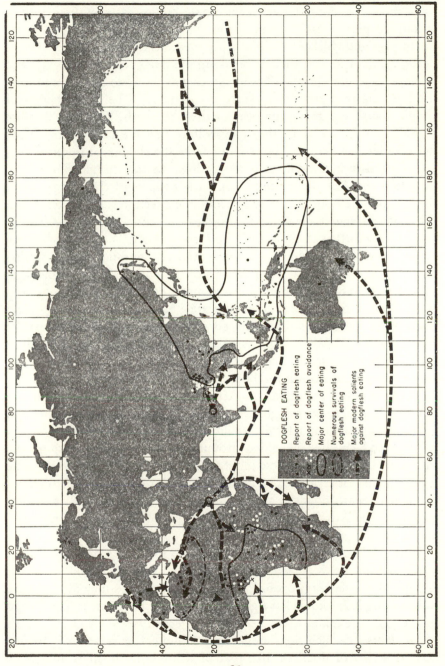

Map 5—Dogflesh Eating

DOGFLESH EATING
Report of dogflesh eating
Report of dogflesh avoidance
Major center of eating
Numerous survivals of
dogflesh eating
Major modern salients
against dogflesh eating

other means to assure tender meat. Some groups castrate their dogs to encourage plumpness.[15*] Some fatten them for slaughter much as we fatten pigs and chickens.[16*] Others use methods of slaughter believed to make the flesh tender, such as breaking the dog's legs and leaving it to whimper and cry (many tribes in the Congo Basin do this), or turning the live dog over the fire to singe off its hair.[17] There are reports of people slaughtering dogs by beating them to death;[18*] though it is not so stated in the accounts, they may believe that the beating makes the flesh tender. It should not be assumed from the above that these peoples are necessarily indifferent or cruel to dogs. In fact certain dog eaters, including the Azande of the Sudan,[19] the peoples of the Congo,[20] and the Mbundu of Angola,[21] have considerable affection for their dogs. But it has not lessened their liking for dogflesh any more than East Africans' affection for cattle has diminished their love of beef.

Dog sacrifice is common in tropical Africa,[22*] and not limited to dog eaters. It is done to make it rain or stop raining, to bind alliances, to make peace, to develop friendships, to make a funerary offering, to keep away disease[23] or to cure it, to inaugurate a blacksmith, or to celebrate a festival. In some cases the sacrificed dog is eaten for its medicinal or spiritual value, in others more as a food. In still others the body is given away or thrown into the bush for wild animals to devour.

Mention of discarding the body brings us to the restrictions on eating dogflesh that are found in Africa. Some, like the restrictions on other flesh food, have the goal of preventing ritual contamination, and are directed at individuals who are in particular danger, such as officials, women, and children. The Ibo around Awka in Nigeria require the Priest of the Earth to avoid dogflesh; should a dog even enter the priest's house, it is immediately killed and thrown out.[24] The Tallensi of Ghana regard dogflesh as the food of men; women neither eat nor cook it.[25] The Afusare of Bauchi in Nigeria prohibit dogflesh to everyone except the senile.[26]

Some African groups prohibit dogflesh to everyone. Such groups are found within the West and Central African center[27*] as well as in the regions of dogflesh rejection.[28*] Though some groups may always have rejected dogflesh, others have given up the practice recently. The Bango of the Congo explain their decision to reject dogmeat by citing a rash of incidents in which dogs ate wounded hunters or travelers.[29] In fact their rejection of dogflesh, like that of many other peoples, may have resulted from Christian or Moslem influences, which have acted strongly against the practice. In one curious case, that of the pagan Warjawa of Nigeria, the group has come to regard the eating of dogflesh as a symbol and rallying point for its ancient way of life.[30]

The feelings against eating dogs range from indifference to disgust. The Badjo of the northeast Congo regard the dog as an inferior animal, and only poor people eat its flesh; the Yaka of the Congo fear the meat will cause illness.[31] The Zulu consider dogflesh repulsive;[32] the Bongo and Dinka both say that they would rather die of hunger than eat it[33]—attitudes which recall those of Westerners.

The East Asian–Pacific Area.—There are indications, both from present-day distribution and from the historical record, that in the East Asian–Pacific area dog-eating groups were formerly found over an enormous expanse. The area extended from China north into Korea and eastern Siberia, south and southwest through Southeast Asia as far as Assam, and east across the Pacific to the Hawaiian Islands. As in Africa, the dog-eating peoples have been under long-continued pressure to abandon the practice, first from the Buddhists and subsequently from Moslems and Westerners. Though many groups have succumbed to these influences, others persist in eating dogs.

In China, where dogs traditionally served as guards and vied with pigs as village scavengers, dogflesh has been used for food since antiquity. In Neolithic times dogs were second only to pigs as food animals, and in Shang times they were sacrificed and eaten in considerable numbers. There was a noble named the "Dog Marquis" who was a vassal or ally of the Shang peoples.[34] In later days the Chinese sometimes called the barbarians by names which included "dog"; but it is not clear whether the term denoted contempt or depicted fierceness. One writer has argued that not only were the early Chinese dog lovers but they "were pre-eminent as a dog-loving nation until about a hundred years ago."[35] This affection did not deter the Chinese from sacrificing and eating dogs. At one period, indeed, dogmeat was the *pièce de résistance* at ceremonial banquets. A special breed, the chow, was developed for culinary purposes.[36] Because its flesh toughens as the dog matures, and because dogs eat all manner of filth, the Chinese came to prefer the flesh of suckling pups, and to regard puppy hams as a delicacy.

As with pork eating, the Chinese carried the habit of dog eating with them when they left the mainland: to Southeast Asia, the Philippines, Formosa, and elsewhere. They have been under pressure in these places, however, to abandon the practice, and many have given it up. The police of Taipeh, on Formosa, have recently promulgated stringent regulations for the slaughter of dogs and selling of dogflesh—ostensibly "to suppress the stealing of dogs" for sale to restaurants,[37] but prejudice was probably involved too. Those Chinese in foreign areas who persist in eating dogflesh do so surreptitiously in some cases, and in others adopt various expedients to avoid drawing attention to it. Because the British authorities look on dog eating with disfavor, gourmets in Hong Kong eat it only in private.[38] It is called "fragrant meat" in Formosan restaurants.[39]

In mainland China there has been a tremendous decline recently in the use of dogflesh, the result not of prejudice but of a government campaign to reduce the number of dogs. The killing of dogs was begun during the germ warfare scare at the time of the Korean War, because, according to official Communist pronouncements, dogs had become infected. Actually the campaign may have been an attempt, in a country that is chronically short of food, to get rid of an animal that consumes food.[40] Since 1952 teams of executioners have killed large numbers of dogs in every city of China. By 1957 William Kinmond, who traveled extensively in the country, saw evidence of dog life in only one Chinese city, Lanchow, though there were still a few dogs in the countryside which had evaded the national dragnet. In a few years one member of the ancient Chinese scavenging triumvirate of pig, chicken, and dog has been virtually eliminated.

Though some Koreans abroad deny that their people eat dogflesh, there are many references to the practice there.[41] Hulbert asserts that dogmeat consumption is confined to the lower classes in Korea, but Griffis and Kang imply that it has had fairly general use. Griffis' description of "canine sirloins served up in great trenchers" to guests does not suggest that the Koreans were ashamed to use it. Some Koreans today look on dogmeat as a healthful food appropriate to the warm part of the year, and raise dogs for eating at that season. Some Korean families have too much affection for their household dogs to eat them at home, yet will sell them for slaughter. Western influence, it is true, has long been making inroads against eating dogs in Korea: one Christian Korean considered it wrong to eat dogflesh because dogs are so intelligent and faithful.

The Japanese keep dogs as guards and pets, and the average person would be shocked at the idea of eating them. There is, however, a report that in 1953 one group of Eta, members of the slaughterers' caste, ate dogs when food was scarce. They did not consider dogflesh very different from other kinds of meat; they distributed pieces of cooked meat to family and guests and considered it a good day when dogflesh was available because all members of the family could eat meat. In 1960, when the living standard was appreciably higher, the same group of Eta ate dogs only rarely; at that time pork, beef, and horseflesh were the principal meats consumed.[42] In addition, the Ainu aboriginals both ate dogs and used their skins for winter clothing.[43] All of this suggests that dog eating was once more widespread in Japan.

There are groups in northeast Asia who eat dogflesh. In a time of need in 1901 the Chukchee living near the mouth of Anadyr River on the Mariinsky coast ate almost all their dogs. Even in times of plenty, however, a Chukchee family at the beginning of this century would slaughter a fat dog and eat its head and intestines; because Russians, Cossacks, and American whalers scoffed at them for this, they tended to conceal the fact.[44] The Gilyak like dogflesh and eat it whenever possible. They not only eat their own dogs that become too old for draft purposes but sometimes beg Russian settlers for their fat house dogs.[45] The attitudes of other northeast Asian peoples toward dogflesh contrast sharply with these. The Tungus reject dogmeat and despise both the Gilyak and the Orochon for eating it.[46] The Koryak sacrifice dogs but deny that their people have ever eaten them.[47*]

To the southwest of China a considerable area of dog eating exists in aboriginal Burma and Assam, and there is even a small-scale trade in dogs from China to northern Burma.[48*] Among the Angami Naga[49] dogs are scavengers, like pigs, but they are probably better fed. They are slaughtered and eaten in large numbers at religious rites, probably, as Hutton says, because people believe the flesh has medicinal value. But he adds that dogs "are eaten much as turkeys are eaten at Christmas in England, as a matter of custom." The Angami "antidote for poison is to pluck out the eyes of a living dog and swallow them," and their remedy for dog bite is to apply burnt dog hair and ashes. Besides ordinary village dogs, some Angami men own hunting dogs which they treat better and which they bury with honors. Though such dogs may be killed and eaten when they are too old to hunt, they are never eaten by the man who has trained or kept them. The Sema Naga[50] have similar beliefs and practices regarding dogflesh and dogs. They think the meat an excellent tonic. Although a man will not eat his hunting dog, he will sell it for food when it is past usefulness. When a Sema dies, his favorite dog is usually slaughtered as its master's body is being lowered into the grave, so that its soul may accompany his and guard him on the trip to the village of the dead. On the death of a great hunter a dog must be killed, for his soul is in danger from those of the numerous animals he has killed. Among some Sema the flesh of dogs killed at a man's grave is eaten by the person who buries the body; others divide it among those who attend the funeral. The position of dogflesh among the Sema Naga is illustrated by the story of one Sema clan, the Awomi, which amalgamated with some Sangtam, who claimed to belong to the same clan. One Sema Awomi pointed out that if the Sangtam were really fellow clansmen they would eat dogflesh. Many of the group did then adopt the practice, though others did not. Today, as a result, the Awomi clan is divided into two groups, those who do and those who do not eat dogmeat.

Not only do Moslems and Hindus in South Asia reject dogflesh, but so do certain aboriginal groups.[51*] Some of these have quite a strong feeling against it, the Dafla, for example, abhorring it as food.[52] Some of the tribes of the Assam Hills believe they would die of boils if they ate it.[53] Buddhists of Burma base their rejection[54] on Buddha's specific prohibition[55] and will not even kill unwanted puppies. Around Burmese villages there have traditionally been large packs of seemingly unattached dogs, which served no function except as guards and scavengers. Like the scavenger dogs around African villages, these obtained food wherever they could; but they were in a favored position compared to other scavengers, for they consumed some of the food given to the Buddhist monks during their daily round of begging, as well as the offerings left at the pagoda.[56] In Vientiane, Laos, packs of dogs, many of them crippled, rabid, or mangy, wander unmolested in the streets because the law in that Buddhist land also forbids their destruction.[57]

Dogs were so numerous and troublesome in Burma that the British, on taking control, tried to reduce the number by poisoning and clubbing them. One can imagine how abhorrent this campaign was to the Burmese from the story of the British assistant resident who, apparently while protecting himself, killed a dog with a swift blow of his stick; he was forced to flee for his life from an incensed mob.[58] In recent times, however, the independent Burmese government under General Ne Win started a similar effort in Rangoon to reduce the size of the scavenger packs of dogs by leaving poisoned meat out every night for them; however, the carcasses were removed before daybreak in order not to offend Buddhist feelings.[59] The Burmese are motivated by a desire to clean up their city rather than to save food, and the effort has not, as in China, brought about a decline in the consumption of dog-flesh.

Another interesting rejection of dogflesh in Southeast Asia is that of groups who, like the aboriginal Yao, or Man, of Indochina, believe that the dog is their ancestor. According to a generally accepted Man legend, about 525 B.C. Pen Hung, ruler of the Chinese province of Su, was attacked by a marauder, Cu Hung. Unable to contain the enemy forces, he offered his daughter's hand and half his kingdom to anyone who would eliminate Cu Hung. A dog named Phan Hu killed Cu Hung, married the ruler's daughter, and their offspring were the ancestors of the Man people.[60] Legends involving the marriage of a princess and a dog to develop a new tribe occur among many groups in Southeast and East Asia (though not all the groups involved reject dogflesh); and somewhat similar stories are found in North America and in Europe.[61] There are a few reports of groups in Southeast Asia simulating the appearance of dogs. The men of the Nicobar Islands wear ears attached to a fillet tied around the head, and conceal their genital organs "in a blue bag with a long red point to it, ... the waist-band ... arranged to fall down behind in a tail."[62] It is quite conceivable that the beliefs in dog ancestry originally developed from totemic observances; various other groups of Southeast Asia regard the dog as a totemic animal and therefore reject its flesh. Thus the Ao Naga have a dog clan whose members assert that they have canine characteristics and who until recently rejected dogflesh (they now use it as a medicinal).[63] On Sumatra one clan of Batak regards the dog as its totemic animal and forbids dogflesh,[64] though other Batak eat it. The Bauri of Bengal reject dog-flesh for a slightly different reason. The dog is their sacred animal; they will neither kill one nor touch its carcass. They claim that they chose the dog as their sacred animal as a counterpart to the Brahmans' reverence of cattle.[65] They may, however, simply have adjusted earlier totemic ideas to the necessities of the Hindu environment.

In Annam many dogs are kept as guards and scavengers, but people also regard them as a source of food. Dogflesh is eaten in the country districts, particularly in Tonkin and northern Annam.[66] Pierre Gourou has pointed out that few dogs live to grow old among the Annamese of the Tonkin Delta; they are boiled or roasted for food as they reach full growth.[67] The Annamese peasants, indeed, have preferences about types of dogs to eat: they regard red-haired dogs and black-tongued dogs as tastier than other kinds. Though considerable dogflesh is consumed fresh, and a peasant considers a dog chop and a cup of rice wine a treat, dogflesh is also made into sausages, some of which are sold. When officials meet for deliberations in a Tonkinese village and must be provided with a light meal, dogflesh is one of the dishes commonly given them. It is customary, when a dog bites someone, for the officials who arbitrate between victim and owner to eat the offending beast. If the dispute is not settled promptly they eat other dogs as well, which are provided, of course, by the disputants. When a controversy between villagers seems difficult of solution, peasants remark that "things are going ill for the dogs."

In Malaya and the Malay Archipelago, as in much of Southeast Asia, there has been a decline in dog eating, encouraged in recent times in the south by Islam and in the north by Christianity. It is clear, however, that feeling against eating dogflesh existed at least two centuries before serious Islamic penetration of the area. In the *Nāgarakṛtāgama,* a panegyric written in A.D. 1365 to King Hayam Wuruk of Majapahit in Java, the Buddhist clergyman Prapañca mentions that the holy writings of antiquity forbid dogflesh and decree punishments for violations.[68] Despite the antiquity and strength of religious antipathy, dog eating still survives in the region today on Sumatra, Java, Celebes, Borneo, and the Moluccas.[69]* In the Philippines pressure from Christians has been strong, and it is said[70] that dogmeat feasts are illegal today. A decade ago dogs were no longer allowed to be sold in the public market at Baguio in Luzon, which was frequented by Igorot who came in from the hills to trade. Nevertheless the dog market continued outside of town,[71] and various people have persisted in dog eating. The Bontoc Igorot eat dogs on ceremonial occasions, such as funerals and marriages; the animal is slaughtered, its tail cut off, its hair singed in the fire and sheared, and then its body cut up and boiled. Since people feed them sparingly and give them little attention, Igorot dogs are seldom fat when eaten.[72] Apayao men eat dogs on ceremonial occasions, though the women refuse dogmeat.[73] In imitation of the Lepanto-Benguet Igorot, a few Ifugao have taken over the custom of eating dogmeat;[74] apparently others of that group, as well as the Ibilao of Luzon,[75] do not eat dogs.

In Melanesia, Micronesia, and Australia dog eating was formerly widespread.[76*] The Australian aborigines, for example, were "passionately devoted to dog meat" and hunted wild dogs to obtain their flesh.[77] They kept tame dogs around their camps just for their company, and these they apparently did not eat. Among both the Australian aborigines and the Tasmanians[78*] it was not uncommon for a woman to suckle a puppy.[79*] Both this practice and the petting and pampering of tame dogs seemed unreasonable to European observers.

In Polynesia, where the dog was formerly present in most places,[80*] widely scattered groups ate dogflesh.[81*] Captain James Cook, on the voyage of the *Endeavour* in 1769, observed that it was a common food on Tahiti, as did Spanish voyagers a few years later.[82] When the Cook expedition arrived in Tahiti, they were so short of flesh food that some of the Europeans tried dogflesh. Cook himself liked it, and claimed that it was sweet and almost as good as English lamb; others were not so enthusiastic about it, and still others strongly opposed eating it. Eventually, in the Pacific, the latter view prevailed and encouraged a decline in the practice. Thus the Maori abandoned dog eating after European contact.[83] Present-day Samoans are unwilling to admit to the practice, which they consider a disgrace, though there are reports that dogs were eaten and even regarded as a delicacy in Samoa in earlier times.[84]

Dog Eating Outside the African and East Asian–Pacific Centers

Outside the centers of dog eating there have been many instances of dog sacrifice, and occasional cases of eating dogflesh during times of scarcity. Dogmeat was resorted to in Russia and the Ukraine during the famine after World War I,[85] and in World War II during the Warsaw rebellion against the Germans, and in Vienna.[86*] Europeans overseas have sometimes eaten it, usually out of curiosity or acute hunger, as Captain Cook's party did in their Pacific explorations, and as Oviedo and De Soto did in the New World.[87]

Dogmeat has been a regular food, however, only in the Mediterranean region.[88*] Hippocrates commented on the qualities of dog and puppy flesh,[89] and the physician Diocles in the fourth century B.C. prescribed dogflesh to certain patients.[90] Pliny says the Romans regarded the flesh of suckling pups so highly that they used them as sacrifices to the gods, and ate them at feasts inaugurating priests or honoring the gods.[91] The flesh and blood were also used for medicinal purposes, the blood serving as an antidote for narcotic poisons. In later times in Greece and Rome dogflesh fell into disrepute; Sextus Empiricus about A.D. 200 indicated that eating it was sinful (in Greece?), though some Thracians persisted in the practice. The only instance of dog eating today on the north shores of the Mediterranean that I have learned of is in Extremadura in Spain, where the meat is a delicacy.[92*] Though it is not certain this is a survival from ancient times, it fits in so well with the classical pattern that it quite likely is.

That dogmeat was eaten in classical times in North Africa we know because Darius, King of the Persians, sent an edict to the Carthaginians ordering them to abandon the practice of human sacrifice and the use of dogflesh.[93] It has been suggested that the island Gran Canaria may have been so named because its people formerly ate dogs, or because the dog was a cult animal there—though there is no evidence that they ate dogs at the time of first European contact.[94] There is, however, convincing evidence from Arab and Western sources of the existence of dog eating elsewhere in North Africa. The tenth-century Arab geographer El Mokaddasi related that the people of Castilia (Tozeur) and Nafta (Nefta) in Tunisia sold dogmeat publicly in butcher shops; Aboulfeda in 1189 and Edrisi in 1207 also reported dog eating in the south of Algeria.[95] The practice has continued in North Africa, largely among Berbers, into modern times, though people generally try to conceal it. Dogs have even been sold for slaughter in North African markets, such as those in coastal Libya around Tripoli, in Misurata, and in Bengasi. In the interior, dog eating has been reported in the northern and central Sahara, including the oases of Gadames and Ghat in Libya; Tolga, Souf, Mzab, and Touat in Algeria; and the Djerid region of Tunisia.[96] The practice has been reported for Morocco, and for Siwah in Egypt.[97] The natives of the Kharga Oasis of Egypt also probably ate dogs.[98*]

There are indications that some North African peoples regard dogflesh simply as another meat. Thus some sell it in the market place like other commodities. Others claim that they eat it only because they like its taste. On the other hand, the consumption of dogflesh in the region often has magico-religious and medicinal significance. On the island of Djerba and in the Mzab, for example, eating dogflesh was formerly "and perhaps still is associated particularly with an autumn festival."[99] At Siwah and on Djerba it has been eaten by people who wished to become fat;[1] and in Morocco it has been given to small children to strengthen them.[2] It has also widely served as a therapeutic to cure syphilis, to prevent and cure fever,[3] to counteract poison or witchcraft, to cure barrenness in women, and to assure the birth of a son. This medicinal use of dogflesh and the fact that in some places dogs are slaughtered at specified times and by strange methods suggest that the original purpose in eating dogs in North Africa may have been ceremonial or religious. There is the curious case in Morocco of one Moslem religious order, the Isowa, who assembled annually at the shrine of their founder, where they danced and devoured live goats which they tore to pieces. Occasionally the dancers seized a dog wandering about during the affair, tore it to pieces, and ate or pretended to eat it in rage.[4]

Groups Opposed to Dog Eating

Various groups have taken a stand against the eating of dogflesh. Perhaps the most interesting of these was the ancient Zoroastrians of Iran, who regarded the dog as the most holy of all the animals associated with their god Ahura-Mazda. They considered it a serious offense to fail to feed dogs, to mistreat them, or to kill them. Should his dog go mad, the Zoroastrian was required to care for and heal the beast.[5] Naturally the Zoroastrians took what action they could to stamp out the practice of dog eating, as for instance Darius did among the Carthaginians.[6*]

A similar rejection occurred at Haran in ancient Mesopotamia, center of a syncretic pagan sect, where a deity was referred to as "the Lord with the dogs."[7] The Haranians regarded the dog as a sacred animal and made sacrificial gifts to it.[8] The people of Cynopolis, in Egypt, who venerated the dog,[9] fought a civil war with the people of Oxyrhynchus, because the latter had killed and eaten dogs.[10*] Though some other groups in the ancient Middle East also regarded dogs highly, there is nothing in the record to indicate whether they rejected dogflesh, or, if they did, how active a part they took in spreading the avoidance.[11*]

The Moslems, in spite of the absence of a specific Koranic prohibition against dogflesh, have been active in eliminating dog eating in the areas they have converted, especially in North Africa, along the fringes of the West African area of dog eating, and in Indonesia. This campaign, in contrast to those of the Zoroastrians and Cynopolites, has been based on the belief that the dog is unclean, an attitude reputedly incorporated into the Islamic faith because Mohammed disliked dogs. According to one tradition he said that "when a dog drinks in a vessel, it must be washed seven times, and that the first cleansing should be with earth."[12*]

Rejection of dogflesh in the West is associated with the idea that the dog is the companion of man, guardian of the homestead, aid of the hunter; with what Carl Sauer aptly called the "Rover complex." Only famine will drive Europeans to feed on dogs. Other groups, including many African peoples, and of course Hindus and Buddhists, disapprove of the eating of dogflesh. As a result of the action of many powerful groups there has been a considerable decrease in the number of dog-eating peoples in the Old World and a reduction of the area in which the practice is common. The forces arrayed against it are so numerous and their influence so pervasive that unless a new champion appears dog eating is likely to continue its precipitous decline.

Origin of the Avoidance

It has been argued that man domesticated the dog to obtain its flesh for food, and that at first this was the only use made of it.[13] From the information available at present, it is impossible to determine whether this argument is valid, or how or when avoidance of dogflesh came about. Was it the result of familiarity? Did it arise because the dog was the companion of early hunters, intimately associated with him in the chase and serving as camp guard and fireside companion; or did it develop because the dog worked closely with the pastoralist in herding? The Old World areas of dogflesh rejection indeed correspond roughly to areas of pastoral tradition, where a strong functional intimacy often exists between man and dog; and the areas of dog eating are roughly those where agriculture is the basis of subsistence and dog-man relationships are not so strong.

These arguments remain distinct possibilities and warrant more detailed consideration. It should be pointed out, however, that intimacy between a man and an individual dog does not necessarily lead him or his group to avoid all dogflesh. Though a man in a dog-eating group will not ordinarily eat an animal with which he has been closely associated, he may sell it or give it away for slaughter when its period of usefulness is over. Moreover, the largest area of pastoral tradition where dogflesh is rejected is also Islamic in faith. The rejection there may stem not from pastoral tradition but from the widespread Moslem belief that the dog is unclean. In Hindu and Buddhist areas a major influence in bringing about the rejection of dogflesh quite likely was a combination of the attitude that the dog is a scavenger who eats dirty food and the feeling against taking life and eating flesh of any sort. Among the Zoroastrians of Persia a contributing factor may have been the dog's being a holy animal, the favorite of their god Ahura-Mazda.

9

CONCLUSION

Nature and Manifestations of Group Avoidances of Flesh Food

Many people, if they consider the eating habits of mankind at all, tend to assume that man's selection of food is determined by instinct or by reasonable consideration of the material available for human consumption. What the preceding chapters have shown about the complex patterns of use and avoidance of certain foods in the Old World exposes the inadequacy of this assumption. The foods used by a group are chosen in accordance with cultural attitudes and patterns of behavior toward food—the group foodways. The Nambikwara Indians of Brazil present a curious illustration of this. They have many domesticated animals suitable for eating, yet keep them simply as pets, sharing their food with them, and playing and talking to them; they do not even eat the eggs their hens lay. Western man, despite his frequent temptation to claim that *his* foodways are based on rational considerations, is no more rational in this than other men, for it makes no better sense to reject nutritious dogflesh, horseflesh, grasshoppers, and termites as food than to reject beef or chicken flesh.

Some group attitudes toward food are explicit, like the attitude toward pork in the Islamic world: everyone is aware of a loathing for it. Other group attitudes are implicit, and people may even be unaware of having them. An implicit attitude usually becomes explicit

106

when violations of the foodways are threatened or carried out. In such cases the group may pass over the violation or it may avoid trouble by pretending that the food is some more acceptable item. Commonly, however, strong feelings are displayed about the acceptability of the food in question. An illustration of this is the story told by Mark Graubard of two young biologists who were engaged to be married. On a field trip a caterpillar fell on the young woman's blouse and frightened her. Her fiancé removed it, laughed at her fright, and apparently to show her that her fear was groundless, swallowed the larva. Far from soothing the young woman, his act so shocked her that she broke their engagement.

Of all the group food avoidances, those which pertain to foods of animal origin, particularly flesh, are accompanied by the strongest feelings, are most frequently incorporated into religious observance, and are supported by the most severe sanctions. The strength of feeling associated with animal food is superbly demonstrated in the "blunder" that set off the Sepoy Rebellion of 1857–58, which rocked British rule in India. An already precarious situation involving the Indian regiments was fanned into violent mutiny by the rumor (later shown to have some foundation) that the new Enfield rifle cartridges, which Hindu and Moslem sepoys would have to put into their mouths to uncap, were greased with fat from cows and pigs, the one animal sacred to Hindus and the other defiling to Moslems. Examples of strong feeling abound in the Western world as well. Marston Bates tells of a French lady who, at a dinner party in South America, ate a dish which she found delicious. From the subsequent talk she suddenly realized that the "iguana" she had eaten was a lizard and she became violently ill.[1] In the case of Przhevalskii's Mongol guide who saw his European companions eat boiled duck, which he regarded as unclean, observation of others committing the act was enough to produce a reaction. As Shakespeare's Julius Caesar reminds Antony:

> On the Alps
> It is reported thou didst eat strange flesh,
> Which some did die to look on.[2]

Mere mention can sometimes have an effect.

It is interesting that animal and not plant foods should be the frequent objects of disgust. Angyal[3] offers an hypothesis about the nature of disgust which may provide insight into this question. He says that disgust derives from a primitive dread of being contaminated or debased, and is generated principally by the waste products of the human and animal body, which in a broad sense include anything coming from the body. Involved also is a fear of coming into contact with the object of disgust and, even more, of ingesting it. To remove the disgust associated with flesh it must go through a process—which usually involves cooking, smoking, or similar action—to change it and its meaning from "waste product" to "food." He sees support for this hypothesis in the more general acceptability of the flesh of herbivorous animals than of carnivores—the latter eat material that is itself disgusting. A survey of university students in the United States revealed, one notes, that of all categories of food the most disliked was animal organs.[4]

In many societies conformity to the group restrictions on eating particular flesh foods, far from being a matter of individual whim, is of utmost gravity, and strong sanctions are applied to violators. The Ethiopian Christian who eats camel flesh, which is regarded as a Moslem food, is subject to excommunication; the orthodox Moslem or Jew who eats pork is summarily ruled out of his group; and the upper caste Hindu who eats beef is despised by his brethren and deprived of his caste affiliation. Such severe sanctions are rarely associated with group avoidances of foods of vegetable origin. Transgression of custom here is ordinarily greeted only with mild feelings of disapproval, though in some cases the violator is considered strange or effeminate, and his social status may be affected. The Amhara of northern Ethiopia have traditionally associated eating the false stems and young shoots of the banana-like *Ensete* with ethnic groups whom they look down upon, but an Amhara simply loses status in his group by eating it, nothing worse.

Because feelings associated with group avoidances of flesh food commonly are strong and institutionalized in religious and ceremonial observance, the avoidances are often difficult to modify. As Porphyry noted about the Syrian avoidance of fish, the Hebrew avoidance of swine, and the Phoenician and Egyptian avoidance of cows, "though many kings have endeavoured to change these customs, yet those that adopt them would rather suffer death, than a transgression of the law [which forbids them to eat these animals]."[5] Indeed, in these and certain other cases the modification of the avoidance could be accomplished only through major changes in the culture. Yet individuals and groups do violate the group avoidances, especially at times of hunger and famine. Moreover, like other folkways, food avoidances can change in a culture with the passage of time; and they can be diffused to other cultures and reinterpreted by them, sometimes, then, serving quite different functions in society. The existence in the Old World of large contiguous areas in which peoples have similar biases against pork and beef suggests that diffusion has been a major means by which avoidances became established over wide areas. It is certain that Islam was the principal agent in spreading the pork avoidance widely across the Old World, and that Hinduism, perhaps aided by Buddhism, has encouraged the spread of the beef avoidance. However, avoidances also can and do develop independently in different places.

Food avoidances, besides differing in the strength of feeling associated with them, the severity of the sanctions supporting them, their persistence, and the extent of their diffusion, vary in the forms in which they are observed. Thus, prohibition of a food may not pertain throughout the year but only at certain times, as during mourning, illness, on religious fast days, or other specific occasions of limited duration. It may involve only cooking or eating a food together with other particular foods. Some peoples of East Africa must not eat meat mixed with milk, a custom curiously similar to Orthodox Jewish observance. Among the Masai warriors, who traditionally ate only meat and milk, the prohibition against eating the two together was nevertheless very strong. Before starting on a meat diet the warriors would take a powerful purgative to make certain their stomachs contained no trace of milk.[6] Another aspect of this avoidance is the custom of not mixing foods belonging to different broad categories; certain Eskimo groups, for example, will not mix sea foods with land foods.

The food avoidance may apply only to particular age, sex, or status groups. Persons whose services are vital to the successful functioning of the group, especially shamans and priests, are most often singled out. Malinowski notes a Trobriand belief that if the magician breaks the food avoidances associated with his magic a crop failure will follow. Other avoidances apply to all men, or to all infants and youths. Among the Australian aborigines these food restrictions are gradually removed as they grow older. The Binbinga forbid the newly initiated boy to eat snake, female kangaroo, wallaby, and a considerable list of other flesh foods. When his whiskers are grown, and he has made certain formal offerings of the foods to some old men who have a special connection with them, he is free to eat them. A Warramunga tribesman is usually middle-aged before he is permitted to eat "wild turkey" and emu.[7]

Restrictions are perhaps more commonly applied to women as a group than to youths. In aboriginal Hawaii and other Pacific islands, as we have seen, women were forbidden the flesh of pigs and chickens as well as certain other foods; and the Tallensi of Ghana forbid the flesh of chickens and dogs to women though not to men. The Ngongo, a subtribe of the Kuba (Bushongo) of the Congo, go so far as to prohibit the flesh of all domestic animals to women. Even where women are not prohibited a flesh food, they may be discriminated against in the division of the meat. The Chukchee of Siberia carry this to great lengths: the Chukchee woman skins the slaughtered reindeer, cuts up the flesh and prepares it, and in return receives the leftovers and the bones after her husband has selected and eaten the choice parts himself. The Chukchee have a saying, "Being women, eat crumbs," which portrays the position not only of their women but of women among many other Old World peoples.

In addition to the restrictions on eating flesh food that apply to women generally, others apply under certain circumstances, as during pregnancy, nursing, menstruating, or the age of childbearing. Though these proscriptions may derive in part from the desire of men to reserve the available flesh food for themselves, it is also probable that some were motivated by intent to prevent contamination of the women and to assure normal, healthy offspring. This is the common explanation given in Africa for the avoidance of chickens and eggs by women.

Other special groups very commonly affected by restrictions on flesh food include hunters or particular castes, classes, clans, or other sections of the tribe.

The opposite situation also occurs. Instead of a particular age, sex, or status group being singled out for a restriction, they may be free of it. This freedom is usually accorded persons of high status, such as priests or headmen, old men, or members of secret societies or other prestigeful social, political, religious, or ethnic groups. Among the Lele of the Congo each of the three cult groups enjoys privileges to certain flesh foods forbidden to outsiders; members of the Pangolin cult group, for example, are the only persons allowed to eat the flesh of the pangolin, the scaly anteater.

The manner in which an animal dies often determines whether its flesh is acceptable. Thus, for some peoples the flesh of animals that die a natural death constitutes the bulk of the meat consumed; other groups reject such flesh. Many groups prohibit the flesh of animals killed by predators. The Chukchee used to refuse the flesh of reindeer killed by wolves, for fear they would become easy marks for their enemies. Other groups go still further, prohibiting the flesh of all animals not killed according to ritual observances. Prohibitions of this sort are found among Orthodox Jews; but the strictest forms occur among Moslems, some of whom refuse locusts as food if they have not been killed with the appropriate Moslem benediction. Observance of the group's traditional means of slaughter is necessary to assure not only the well-being of the persons who will eat the meat but the continued success or survival of the group. In one New Guinea village, when the traditional way of sacrificing pigs by deliberately cruel methods was forbidden, the people begged for permission to kill one pig by the traditional method: unless the mango trees heard the squeals they would not bear fruit.

Some restrictions against flesh food concern the condition of the flesh. Decayed flesh or that of diseased animals is often rejected—although there are numerous groups who do not hesitate to eat such meat, and some even prefer flesh in a putrid state. Other restrictions apply only to certain parts of animals or certain organs which are believed harmful to man. There are restrictions, too, which apply to the flesh of all wild animals, that of all domestic animals, or that of domestic animals raised by members of other ethnic groups, or other clans or villages. We have seen an example in the Murut of Borneo, who will eat only home-raised pigs and not those raised in neighboring villages. Finally, some peoples put restrictions on use of the flesh of particular species of wild or domestic animals, the question with which this study has been mainly concerned.

Origin and Diffusion

In discussing the origins of their own group flesh avoidances, people often claim that they were determined solely by reason. The supposed origin of the avoidance of pork as a health measure is a good example. Despite the attractiveness of such "rational" explanations one must be wary of accepting them too readily; not only are they usually presented with little or no supporting evidence but they conform suspiciously well to the Western bias in favor of the rational. The social scientist con-

sidering the origin and diffusion of avoidances of flesh food must take
into account the possible roles of totemism, magic and religion, fear of
ritual contamination, and the social structure. In the evolution of foodways, it is true, some of the factors contributing to the origin of an
avoidance may become obscured or lost, but the mechanisms of origin,
spread, and change often can be worked out with some assurance. With
this in mind, then, let us first evaluate some of the explanations that
have been advanced for the origin of the group avoidances considered
in this book, and then outline the mechanisms by which the avoidances
become accepted and spread.

The suggestion that unfamiliarity with an animal may contribute to
the rejection of its flesh appears to have considerable merit. An
"emancipated" Westerner will often refuse the flesh of strange animals, partly perhaps from fear that it will cause illness but also from
reluctance to partake of something new. An interesting illustration is
the story of a man and woman who saw fields of artichokes in California for the first time. They were invited to try the artichokes, but
answered with finality, "Oh, no! We never eat strange foods."[8] Primitive man views the flesh of unfamiliar animals with even greater trepi-
dation, for it may be the means by which harmful spirits or other mysterious elements enter his body. Before accepting a strange meat the
group commonly establishes a satisfactory spiritual relationship with the
animal. The fear of eating an unfamiliar animal is frequently increased
through its introduction by a disliked and feared donor group, who
might do serious harm or might be regarded as unclean. In any event,
rejection of the flesh of unfamiliar animals is common throughout the
world, sometimes covering entire species, sometimes only individual
animals. An example is certain Andaman Islanders who will not eat
particular foods when they are away from their own sections of the
islands, perhaps from fear that in a strange place the chances of illness
are greater and the spirits are more dangerous. And the Guiana Indians
reject the flesh of certain animals such as oxen, sheep, goats, and fowl,
which were not native to their country but were introduced from
abroad. When there is no other food available, they eat these animals,
but only after a medicine man or old woman has blown on the flesh,
apparently to expel the spirit of the animal.

Two avoidances in which unfamiliarity may have played a role are those of pork and fish in the Middle East. As we have seen, the avoidance of pork may have come about because of the unsuitability of the pig to the pastoral way of life common to so much of the area. According to this view, the pastoralists were relatively unfamiliar with the domestic pig, came to look on it as symbolic of their despised antagonists, the settled people, and thus rejected it. The same factors may have been involved in the widespread rejection of fish among pastoral groups of the Middle East. The fish, too, may have been symbolic of the settled people, whether of farmers living along streams or of fishermen living along rivers or by the sea. Numerous observations support this idea: the importance of fishing among settled groups in the Hadhramaut and along the Red Sea and Persian Gulf margins of Arabia, together with the rejection of fish by many bedouins except as feed for their animals; the contempt many pastoral Somali of northeast Africa have for fish, for the Negro farmers who fish in the rivers, and for the coastal groups who fish in the sea; the rejection of fish by many East African cattle herders, who use fish only after they have lost their cattle and with them their self-respect; the concentration of prejudice against fish in arid sections of the Indian subcontinent, where pastoral traditions are stronger; and the case of Piankhi, the pastoral conqueror of Egypt, who refused to admit to his presence those delta princes who were fish eaters.

The opposite explanation is also advanced to account for the origins of some avoidances: that man rejects the flesh of animals with which he is particularly familiar. In our society children often cannot bear to eat the flesh of a chicken that has been raised for the pot but has become a pet; the young Clarence Darrow was so shocked at the "murder" of his pet that he refused from then on to taste chicken. This reluctance to slaughter or eat familiar animals exists in many parts of the world. Among the Bari of the Sudan, when a man's favorite ox grows old and is ceremonially killed, his friends eat the flesh, but the owner himself sits grief-stricken in his hut. This old notion that the ox which tills the ground should not be slaughtered is still found in modern Greece, China, and Korea; and though it may derive in part from a desire to preserve useful animals, it is also motivated by affection for a companion and friend. Among cannibal tribes, such as those of the Congo Basin, the same trait appears, in the restriction against eating the flesh of members of the immediate family; and those cannibals of desperation, the Donner party, wrestled with this problem in the snows of the Sierra Nevada in 1846–47.

Two types of rejection are present in the above examples: that by an individual of the flesh of a particular animal associated with him, and that by the group of the flesh of an entire class of animals, such as plow oxen, because of close contact in daily activities. Such association, it should be noted, does not necessarily lead either the individual or the group to reject the flesh of all animals of a species. A person or group may suffer feelings of guilt at permitting the slaughter of such animals, and then seek ways to assuage its conscience. It is common, for example, for an individual who refuses to kill or eat an animal himself to sell it to others for slaughter. Or he may be freed of the necessity of killing and simply grieve when the act is done. Indian women of the Quito area of Ecuador are so fond of their fowls that they neither sell nor slaughter them; yet, when a traveler staying with them finds it necessary to kill a chicken for food, the landlady, despite shrieks, tears, and wringing of hands, will afterwards quietly accept payment for the animal. A group, by similar stratagems, including assigning the slaughter to professional butchers or justifying the sacrifice in supernatural terms, will also avoid responsibility for killing and eating animals that serve it in a close relationship. Sometimes, of course, conflicts are brought about by differences of opinion regarding the rights of ceremonial slaughter: at Tenedos in ancient Greece a priest who offered a calf to Dionysius was set upon by a crowd and had to flee for his life.

However, it is possible that familiarity with animals, particularly in functional relationships and as pets, led to the rejection of the flesh of entire species of domestic animals. Avoidance of dogflesh in the Western world may have come about because the dog was the friend of the family and eating it seemed an act akin to cannibalism.

The explanation that some flesh avoidances were introduced to prevent the destruction of animals useful to man has occurred most frequently for horseflesh and beef. In the case of horses, however, most Asian horse peoples, who are more dependent on horses than anyone else, have not prohibited horseflesh; on the contrary, they use it extensively. Moreover, there is little support elsewhere for the view that the avoidance stems from the utility of the horse. Prohibitions and restrictions on the slaughter of cattle, in order to preserve them for work or for milk, have been claimed for the early Hindus, and for the ancient Egyptians, Phoenicians, and Romans among others. Whatever the merit of these claims, there are a few substantiated recent cases: among the Gold tribe of Manchuria in the 1930's, and for the Burmese after World War II. But peoples who restrict slaughter did not necessarily give up eating beef. And there is no convincing evidence that the avoidance of cows' flesh in Egypt and Phoenicia derived from the usefulness of cows; it was more probably related to their sacred position. In India, too, the rejection of beef was closely tied to religious belief and controversy. And in Southeast and East Asia where beef is avoided or where beef and beef eating are not highly regarded, religious belief and the notion that the ox is a member of the family are involved. Though the possibility remains that utility contributed to the development of the horseflesh and beef avoidances, the case is far from proved.

Still another explanation suggested for the origin of particular avoidances is that they were developed by a favored group in an effort to keep the best foods for themselves. It is true that the mechanism for such a development exists in many places. In parts of Oceania village headmen, priests, and other prestigeful people have first claim on certain flesh foods, and women and children either get the smallest share or are forbidden to partake at all. Some authorities on the Australian aborigines are convinced that the primary object of their food avoidances is to maintain a plentiful and superior supply of food for the elders; it may well be, therefore, that the elders, who are respected and feared for their knowledge of the natural and supernatural worlds and for their skill in manipulating them, originally introduced prohibitions for selfish reasons. Certain groups of pastoral conquerors in East Africa have forbidden milk and the keeping of cattle to subject agriculturalists, apparently for similar reasons. Elsewhere in Africa secret societies or other masculine organizations in some cases have the primary claim on flesh food. Thus it is quite possible that the self-interest of a favored group, whether of old or prestigeful men, members of particular societies or age classes, persons politically dominant, or whatever else, has led to the institution of a food avoidance which at first applied to other members of the society but gradually came to apply even to the self-designated elite.

Another group of explanations, currently in favor, may be termed hygienic explanations, for they are couched in terms of present-day concepts of disease: the avoidance comes about because people fear pathogenic organisms. A specific organism may be involved or a host of them. Though hygienic explanations have been used to account for the rejection of several flesh foods, the best-known ones are applied to the rejection of pork by the Jews. We have found, however, no strong evidence that the Jews or any other Middle Eastern group gave up eating pork either because it decays rapidly in that climate, because the pig is a scavenger that eats all kinds of filth, or from fear of trichinosis. Among many Middle Eastern peoples, including even some Semites, the pig was a sacred animal, usually associated with agricultural gods. In some cults pigs were sacrificed and eaten ceremonially; in others both pig sacrifice and pork eating were rejected altogether. Though certain writers believe that out of this situation alone, with the complex factors inherent in it, the avoidance evolved among various Middle Eastern groups, it is probable that external factors, particularly the conflict between agriculturalists and pastoralists, were also involved. It is a curious fact that today in the Middle East, though Moslems and Ethiopian Christians consider pigs and pork unclean, some of them eat the flesh of wild pigs for its medicinal value. This belief that pork will cure disease rather than cause it may well be a survival from ancient times.

Despite the questionable applicability of hygienic expanations to the pork avoidance of the Middle East, it is possible that other group food avoidances did develop for hygienic reasons. It should be noted, however, that hygienic beliefs are often tied to other deep-seated and unadmitted factors, such as fear of magical contamination or ritual impurity. Most modern hygienic explanations, in fact, seem to be secondary rather than primary reasons, and more in the nature of rationalizations. The establishment of group avoidances of a widely used flesh commonly requires the generation of strong group emotions and the support of powerful institutions. The failure of modern Americans to give up tobacco despite the clear evidence of its danger is a case in point.

Somewhat related to fear of disease, as a factor encouraging the avoidance of flesh food, is the belief that eating forbidden food will bring about human infertility. We have seen in this book how the rejection of eggs and chickens as food, which is especially widespread in Africa, may first have developed from just such a fear. In support of this suggestion, we noted that the avoidance of eggs is primary and that of chickens secondary; that the avoidance of eggs in Africa appears to be more widespread than that of chickens; that in Africa and elsewhere eggs are sometimes regarded as symbols of fertility and as such, on occasion, play a role in magical and ceremonial life; and that the avoidance of eggs and chickens in Africa is associated most closely with women of childbearing age, who are believed to be most in danger of a loss of fertility.

This brings us to the idea that the origins of various avoidances we are dealing with were in the magical, totemistic, and religious life of man. Though the origins of most of them lie far back in prehistoric times, it is possible to conjecture how supernatural factors may have operated in bringing them about. Primitive man is greatly concerned about the flesh food he eats: in consuming a fellow creature he exposes himself to all sorts of physical and spiritual influences, many of which are dangerous and can lead to ritual impurity, disease, and even death. A factor in his concern is that to obtain flesh an animal has to be killed, an act which has fearful potentialities for retribution both for the person who kills the animal and for the one who eats it. It is for this reason then when a great Sema Naga hunter dies a dog is slain to protect him, as he journeys to the land of the dead, from the spirits of the animals he has killed. Somewhat related to this belief is the notion that food touched by a murderer is contaminated, that the spirit of death is in it. Samuel Hearne, observing in 1771 a group of Copper Indians, noted that those who had killed some Eskimos were regarded as unclean, were prohibited from cooking food either for others or for themselves, and ate only from their own dishes.[9]

Another factor influencing primitive man may be his belief that through eating the flesh of an animal one gains its physical or personality characteristics. James Adair noted among American Indians, particularly of the South and near the Mississippi, the belief that a person who eats venison is swifter and more sagacious than one who eats "the flesh of the clumsy bear, or helpless dunghill fowls, the slow-footed tame cattle, or the heavy wallowing swine."[10] The Malay of Singapore, one recalls, eat tiger and the Hottentots eat lion flesh, to acquire the wisdom, strength, and courage of these animals. Warriors and young men among the Dyak of northwest Borneo avoid venison lest they become timid like the deer; Zulu girls avoid pork lest their children resemble pigs, and Caribs avoid it lest their eyes become small like a pig's. These beliefs, as E. M. Loeb points out, call to mind the German proverb, "A person is what he eats" (Man ist was man isst).

In some places a flesh avoidance is associated with the belief that human souls transmigrate to animals. Along the Malabar coast of India people abstain from fishing after the death of a ruler, for fear of eating the fish inhabited by his soul.[11] On Tamara, an island off New Guinea, people reject pork as food because they believe that souls sometimes pass into pigs.

Thus primitive man sees many possibilities in partaking of flesh food, some of them safe and leading to desirable ends, others filled with danger, unknown terror, and destruction. It is not difficult to imagine how, once eating an animal had become associated with particular consequences, this association would influence man in his acceptance or avoidance of its flesh.

The totemic relationship, which may exist between an animal and a group, whether tribe, clan, lineage, or other unit, is commonly said to have arisen because in the past the animal helped the group in some way. The observances connected with the totemic animal take a great variety of forms, but usually the group shows honor and affection for the totem and places restrictions on killing it. Though some groups permit unrestricted use of the totemic animal's flesh, most of them have strong restrictions on this, either forbidding it entirely or permitting only sacramental consumption. The Selkup Samoyed, for example, never kill or eat their totemic animal, however predatory it may be; this would be the equivalent of cannibalism. Among the northern tribes of central Australia a man is not permitted to kill or eat his totem or that of his father or his father's father. Instead he is responsible for increasing its number: the Aruntas perform special ceremonies in which the men eat the flesh of their totem in order to bring about such an increase.[12] Though some groups do not insist that a wife follow her husband's totemic avoidances, others expect her to observe them at all times or at least on particular occasions. In the Northern Territories of Ghana a wife customarily observes her husband's totemic food avoidances either when nursing her infants or throughout her childbearing period. This is because people believe that food is transformed into milk, and that the child would be violating the avoidance if the mother ate flesh forbidden to her husband's group.

A still stronger relationship with the totemic animal has developed among peoples who believe they are descended from it. Members of the dog clan of the Ao Naga claim that they have canine characteristics, such as speed and doglike features; and the men of the Nicobar Islands intend their dress to simulate the appearance of a dog.

The process of identification which may have contributed to rejection of the flesh of a totemic animal may among more advanced peoples have led to rejecting the flesh of an animal associated with a god or goddess, or, in more complex situations, of an animal viewed as the embodiment of the deity or regarded as a deity in its own right. These circumstances provide broad opportunities for the development of an avoidance; and explanations have been made in terms of them, both by groups practicing the avoidance and by investigators seeking understanding. Thus the Zoroastrians divided all animals into two classes: those which belong to Ahura-Mazda and those which belong to Ahriman. To kill an animal belonging to Ahura-Mazda was regarded as a sin, and to kill one of Ahriman's was a pious act. For example, severe penalties were imposed on anyone who killed a dog, the most sacred of all the animals belonging to Ahura-Mazda. These observances were so important to the Zoroastrians that they tried to introduce them among the peoples with whom they came into contact.

The origin of some flesh avoidances may lie hidden in the dualism of man's attitude toward certain animals, in his considering them at the same time both sacred and unclean. This dualism stems from the undifferentiated feelings of awe and fear, in which, as Frazer says, "reverence and abhorrence are almost equally blended,"[13] with which man often regards his religious symbols. In this connection the Latin word *sacer* is of interest. On the one hand it means "sacred," "devoted to the divinity for destruction," and "forfeited"; on the other, "accursed," "criminal," "impious," and "wicked." The French word *sacré* carries the same duality; and to some extent so does the English "sacred." The many groups who prescribe purification rites, such as ritual washing or bathing for persons who have had contact with a religious symbol, illustrate this mixed attitude. As a society and its institutions evolve, one feeling may triumph over the other, and the object emerge as "sacred," regarded with awe and reverence, or as "unclean," feared and despised for its contaminating qualities. Even after such an evolution, remnants of the early duality often persist and are manifested in various ways. Thus the pig, after its fall from grace in Egypt, was a lowly and abhorred animal but still retained elements of its former exalted position.

The triumph of one of two feelings may have occurred among the Shin in northwest India, that Hindu caste with a veneer of Islam, whose attitudes toward cattle we have noted differ from those of both religions. They regard the cow with abhorrence, much as Moslems regard the pig, and not only refuse to eat its flesh but avoid its milk and milk products. Thus they reject the flesh of the "fallen animal" completely. Among other peoples such flesh may continue to be used generally—or by lowly groups, with people in general continuing to eat it on ceremonial occasions or for medicinal purposes.

Because so many flesh food avoidances are closely tied to religious practices, the prophet or founder of a religion may play a critical role in fostering their introduction and acceptance. The most notable example of this is Mohammed, whose prohibitions of pork in the Koran led to the considerable recession of pork eating that accompanied the spread of Islam. Malelaka, a prophet of Alor, came near to instituting a food avoidance among his followers. In 1929 he predicted that upon the imminent arrival of supernatural beings people would be healed of their illnesses and death would be eliminated. Meanwhile people must abstain from such food as eels, crayfish, crabs, and fish.[14] Malelaka's influence was cut short by government action, and apparently the fish avoidance did not persist. Had he been thought successful in prediction, the avoidance might have become permanently established among the group. Religious leaders other than prophets and founders have also had a great effect in introducing food avoidances and in enforcing them. It may be that because they are usually required to follow the strictest avoidances themselves they are tempted to insist that others also do so. One of the most interesting lines for investigation is the role of the mentally disturbed—for they more commonly develop strong food avoidances than do normal persons—in instituting food avoidances by means of a religious affiliation. In many societies such persons have assumed influential roles in religious cults; they are to be found in primitive societies among the shamans, in more advanced groups among ascetics, dervishes, other clergy, or laymen. It is likely that such individuals have had a part in fostering food avoidances that is out of keeping with their numbers in society.

After an avoidance custom about an animal and its flesh has developed, the further possibility, of extending the avoidance to similar animals, appears, and often is effectively exploited. In some places in Africa Moslems have extended avoidance of the flesh of the domestic pig to related animals. In Hindu India the ban on beef, which was originally associated with common cattle, now extends to the flesh of water buffalo.

Moreover the use or avoidance of a particular flesh food sometimes becomes identified with, or symbolic of, the group, and serves to strengthen group ties. The converse also occurs, and the use or avoidance is used to distinguish out-groups, such as other classes or castes, other clans, tribes, or ethnic groups, or members of other religions. This is related to the need for what Gordon Allport has called "visibility and identifiability."[15] We have seen how the western Lange of the Congo are called "Baschilambua," or "dog people," because, unlike other sections of the tribe, they eat dogmeat. The Dhor, a subdivision of the Katkari caste of Bombay, were given their name because they eat beef. Moslems regard the eating of camel flesh as a profession of the faith; and in Morocco the Prophet is quoted as saying, "He who does not eat of my camels does not belong to my people." Avoidance of camel flesh by some other Middle Eastern religious groups is in negative reaction to Islamic custom.

The attempt of an out-group to change its status with respect to the in-group or to affiliate itself with it commonly involves conforming to the food customs of the in-group, either adopting, or more usually abandoning, the use of particular kinds of flesh. We recall how a Sema Awomi pointed out that if the Sangtam were really fellow clansmen they would eat dogflesh. Many of the Sangtam did adopt the practice, though others did not; thus the Awomi clan today is divided into those who eat dogflesh and those who do not. Two other well-known instances are the abandonment of pork eating by peoples converted to Islam, and the abandonment of various types of flesh food by Indian castes trying to improve their status in the caste structure. Though avoidances of flesh foods about which there are strong group feelings of rejection, such as pork in the Islamic world, tend to be adopted readily and without question by those seeking affiliation with the group, avoidances of flesh foods that evoke less feeling, such as horseflesh in Europe, may be evaded completely or adopted only after considerable effort by reformers and others who are concerned that the group patterns be followed. The decline in the use of horseflesh in northern

Europe after the acceptance of Christianity was brought about only by means of papal decrees and long-continued action by the clergy, nobility, and others; its use still has not been given up completely.

The diffusion of group avoidances of flesh food has been accomplished by many agents. Some have spread them by gradual means from one local area to another; others carried them rapidly and with great force across large areas of the Old World. Perhaps the most effective diffusion occurred after the beginning of the Neolithic, with the rise of pastoralists and farmers, whose goals and ways of life sharply contrasted. The individualistic, restless pastoralist pitied and despised the farmer for his drudgery, his servility, and his lack of courage and daring in battle. It is reasonable, then, that the pastoralist, his own life centered on his domestic herds, should, when seeking symbolic expression of his contempt for another's way of life, turn to the farmer's strange animals as symbols. Thus we find the Mongols, who, as has been noted, speak of pigs as "black cattle," calling the Chinese "keepers of black cattle" and the Emperor of Cathay "the pig emperor." From this identification of animals, such as the pig, with an alien way of life, it is a simple step to the rejection of their flesh as food. Once this was done, large possibilities arose for the diffusion of the avoidance, for pastoralists frequently take great pride in their avoidances of flesh food, they are mobile, and they have often conquered settled people. They also exert a subtle moral influence on farmers. The Tibetan nomads of the Kansu border refer frequently to the disgusting food habits of the settled Tibetans. The latter delight in the taste of a fat marmot, but confess it with shame, for in their hearts they feel that the nomad is right.

With the rise of the world religions, such as Buddhism, Islam, and Christianity, ancient avoidances of flesh food found another effective vehicle for diffusion. These religions commonly incorporated into their observances some of the old avoidances, and usually insisted that new adherents observe them. Thus the Middle Eastern avoidance of pork was spread rapidly by Islam across huge areas of the Old World, and the Mediterranean avoidance of the horse was carried to northern Europe. Today, as the world religions, especially Islam, continue to expand, they urge on their converts acceptance of their restrictions on the use of flesh food.

In modern times great changes in the pattern of food avoidance have resulted from the extension of Western foodways over the world. In many instances this has been achieved in conscious effort by Western-ers, through missions, the United Nations, or other agencies, to incul-cate their own foodways among peoples with whom they are working. Sometimes it has brought more restrictions to bear on an already limited use of the local food resources; in other cases it has encouraged the abandonment of native avoidances of flesh food—as by introducing "vegetarian" (unfertilized) eggs to India, and encouraging pig keep-ing and pork eating in East Africa. Though non-Western peoples have been more willing to accept Western avoidances than to shake off their own, some progress is taking place. It is appropriate to consider briefly the agents and means by which the abandonment of avoidances is brought about.

Traditional group foodways tend to be maintained unless modified by disruptive factors of some sort. Perhaps the most common mode of change, as Jitsuichi Masuoka has pointed out,[16] is through the disorgani-zation of traditional institutions that generally follows culture contact and culture change, and which is more pronounced in urban than in rural areas. Differences in the availability of food, changes in the tra-ditional taste for food, disruption of customary sanctions, and shifts in the social status of individuals are often involved in the process. Be-cause change everywhere follows similar patterns, certain types of indi-viduals are more likely to be found among the agents of change and others among the agents of conservation. Older people, for example, are more thoroughly indoctrinated in the foodways of the group and tend to resist change, as do country people and those in the group who benefit in status or in some other way from maintaining an avoidance.

Among those active in bringing about abandonment of traditional foodways are persons of broad experience with food, such as traders and teachers. That experience is an important factor is supported by Stefansson's observation that among both dogs and men individuals ac-customed to a variety of foods take more readily to a new food than those used to a restricted diet. Men of an intellectual bent, he asserts, are more willing to try new foods because of a sense of adventure[17]—a statement perhaps borne out by the tradition of experimentation with strange foods on American college campuses.

The role children play in changing family food habits by introducing attitudes learned at school has long been recognized by American nutritionists. It is less generally recognized that children tend to be permitted greater deviation from the group foodways and are therefore in an ideal position to act as innovators. In some cases they are actually forced into such deviation by the food shortage and by the discrimination they so commonly experience in gaining access to the food supply. Cora DuBois has pointed out that the child of Alor, who is given no food between morning and evening meals, soon learns to forage for himself by scraping remnants from the cooking pot, collecting insects which are spurned by the adults, and raiding the fields for fruit and vegetables.[18] Their resourcefulness is duplicated in many groups. Indeed, any study of food would be incomplete without considering the myriad of tidbits obtained and eaten by children away from home. In East Africa little girls, who are permitted great liberty in eating when they are young, are gradually subjected to the food avoidances of the group; the beginning of these restrictions is a sad time for them, when some of their favorite foods may be forbidden.[19] The willingness of the young to try new foods is also to be noted. Stefansson, after trying to get different dog teams to eat types of flesh that were unfamiliar to them, concluded that the older the dog the longer it persisted in refusing such meat, and the stronger its food prejudices presumably were. He found the same pattern among his human companions, both whites and Eskimos. Among the Coronation Gulf Eskimos he had no difficulty in getting children to eat the edible "salmon berry," except when the mother objected; some adults refused them.[20]

Though the role of mothers and of other women in changing foodways needs more careful study, the general pattern is that women side with the forces of tradition in resisting change. Among the Yukaghir of Siberia contact with the Yakut has led some people to eat new flesh foods, including beef and horseflesh. The women, however, display aversion to this "alien food"; when horsemeat is cooking, some Yukaghir women leave the house because "they cannot endure the odor."[21] Though most of the Japanese of Hawaii have begun to eat beef and pork, many old women among them still abhor the idea, which in Japan was discouraged by Buddhist teachings.[22] Surveys show that in the United States, too, food dislikes "are more common among women than among men"; Richard Wallen explains this in terms of the more permissive attitude our society takes toward food avoidances of girls and women than of boys and men.[23] Biological factors offer a distinct possibility to account at least partially for the difference in readiness to accept new foods.

It is clear that many powerful and complex agents play a part in the establishment and abandonment of food restrictions. Great opportunities exist here for the cultural geographer, the historian, the student of culture change, and the nutritionist to extend our knowledge of a little-understood problem that is of much importance in the effort to feed the world's peoples.

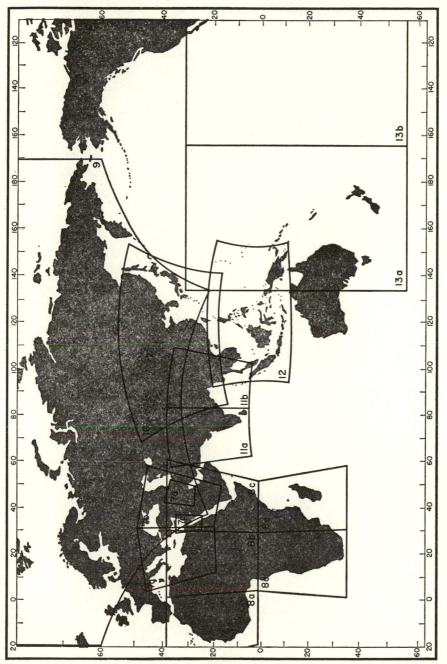

Map 6—Location Map Index

127

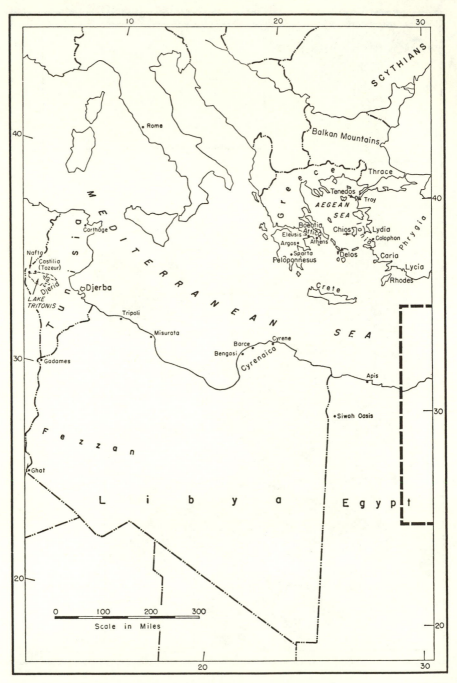

Map 7a—Mediterranean and Middle East. Continued on pages 129–131.

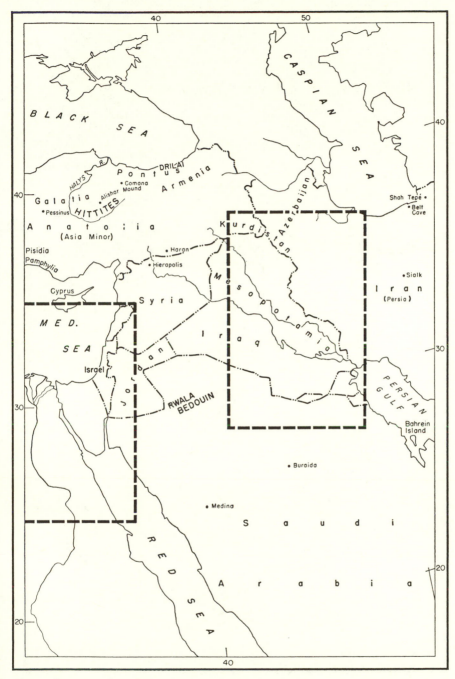

Map 7b

129

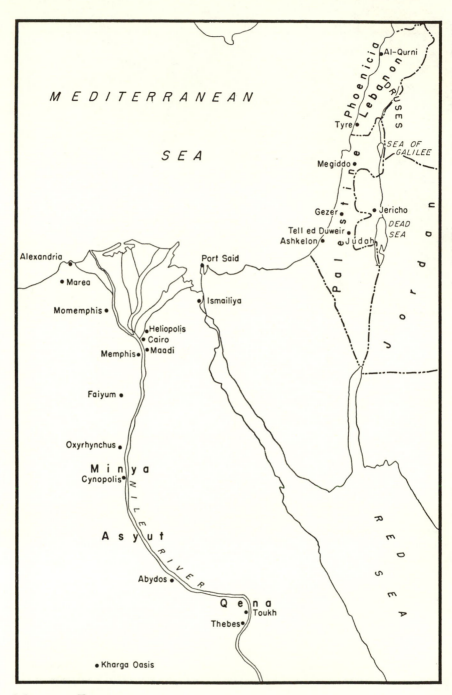

Map 7c—Egypt

130

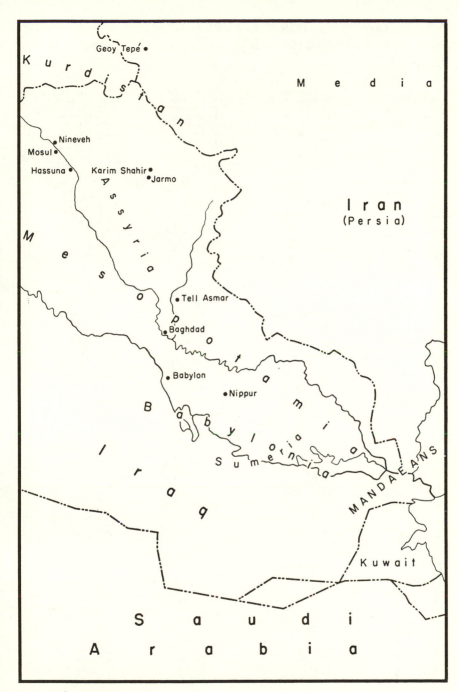

Map 7d—Mesopotamia

131

AFRICAN GROUPS MENTIONED IN TEXT. Indicated by number on Maps 8a through 8e, which follow on pages 133–137. Map number follows group name.

1 Ababua 8b
2 Adele 8a
3 Afusare 8b
4 Agow 8c
5 Ait Waryager 8a
6 Ambo 8d
7 Amhara 8c
8 Antandroy 8e
9 Anuak 8c
10 Anyanja 8e
11 Ashanti 8a
12 Aten 8b
13 Attakka 8b
14 Azande 8b, 8c
15 Badjo 8c
16 Baghirmi 8b
17 Baka 8c
18 Balante 8a
19 Bango-Bango 8e
20 Banjangi 8b
21 Banyum 8a
22 Banziri 8b
23 Barabaig 8e
24 Bari 8c
25 Bassa 8b
26 Batom 8b
27 Bedde 8b
28 Bemba 8e
29 Bena 8e
30 Berbers 8a, 8b
31 Berta 8c
32 Besom 8b
33 Biafada 8a
34 Bidjuk 8b
35 Bijogo 8a
36 Birom 8b
37 Bodi 8c
38 Bolewa 8b
39 Bomam 8b
40 Bongo 8c
41 Bua 8b
42 Bubi 8b
43 Budu 8c
44 Bunda 8d
45 Busa 8a
46 Chaamba 8c
47 Chagga 8e
48 Chamba 8b
49 Chewa 8e
50 Chokwe 8d
51 Chopi 8e
52 Chuka 8e
53 Cilenge 8d
54 Comendi 8a
55 Dagu 8b
56 Danakil 8c
57 Didina 8c
58 Digo 8e
59 Dinga 8d
60 Dinka 8c
61 Diola 8a
62 Dodos 8c
63 Doko 8c
64 Ekiti 8b
65 Ekoi 8b
66 Elgeyo 8e
67 Emberre 8e
68 Embu 8e
69 Ewe 8a
70 Fan 8b, 8d
71 Fanti 8a
72 Fia 8b

73 Fingo 8d
74 Fulani 8a, 8b
75 Ga 8a
76 Galla 8c
77 Ganda 8e
78 Gbande 8a
79 Gimira 8c
80 Giryama 8e
81 Gogo 8e
82 Gumis 8c
83 Gussii 8e
84 Ha 8e
85 Hadzapi 8e
86 Hangaza 8e
87 Haruro 8c
88 Hausa 8b
89 Haya 8e
90 Hehe 8e
91 Herero 8d
92 Hima 8e
93 Holo 8d
94 Hottentot 8d
95 Huana 8d
96 Ibibio 8b
97 Ibo 8b
98 Igara 8b
99 Ila 8d
100 Ingassana 8c
101 Iraqw 8e
102 Janjero 8c
103 Jie 8c
104 Kababish 8c
105 Kabere 8b
106 Kadullu 8c
107 Kafa 8c
108 Kagoro 8b
109 Kakwa 8c
110 Kalai 8d
111 Kaliko 8c
112 Kamba 8e
113 Karamojon 8c
114 Katab 8b
115 Kebu 8a
116 Kenga 8b
117 Khasonke 8a
118 Kikuyu 8e
119 Kimbundu 8d
120 Kissi 8a
121 Koma 8c
122 Kongo 8d
123 Konso 8c
124 Konta 8c
125 Kossi 8b
126 Kpe 8b
127 Kru 8a
128 Kuba 8d
129 Kuku 8c
130 Kullo 8c
131 Kunabembe 8b
132 Kundu 8b
133 Kwafi
     (Wakuafi) 8e
134 Kwangari 8d
135 Kwotto 8b
136 Lakka 8b
137 Lala 8e
138 Lamba 8d
139 Lange 8d
140 Lango 8c
141 Lele 8d
142 Lemba 8e

143 Lendu 8c
144 Lenge 8e
145 Lissel 8b
146 Lokko 8a
147 Lokoiya 8c
148 Lotuko 8c
149 Lovedu 8e
150 Lozi 8d
151 Luapula 8e
152 Luba 8d
153 Luchazi 8d
154 Luena 8d
155 Lugbara 8c
156 Luluba 8c
157 Lumbwa
     (Kipsiki) 8e
158 Lunda 8d
159 Maban 8c
160 Mabum 8b
161 Macha 8c
162 Madi 8c
163 Maji 8c
164 Maka 8b
165 Makaraka 8c
166 Mambwe 8e
167 Mandanda 8e
168 Manganja 8e
169 Mangbetu 8c
170 Mansa 8c
171 Mao 8c
172 Marille 8c
173 Masai 8e
174 Mbala 8d
175 Mbundu
     (Ovimbundu) 8d
176 Mekan 8c
177 Mende 8a
178 Mittu 8c
179 Mondari 8c
180 Mongo 8d
181 Moru 8c
182 Murle 8c
183 Mwimbe 8e
184 Nandi 8e
185 Ndali 8e
186 Ndebele 8e
187 Ndzimu 8b
188 Ngala 8b
189 Ngamo
     (Gamawa) 8b
190 Ngombe 8d
191 Ngonde 8e
192 Ngongo 8d
193 Ngoni 8e
194 Nimadi 8a
195 Nkole 8e
196 Nuba 8c
197 Nuer 8c
198 Nupe 8b
199 Nyamwanga 8e
200 Nyamwezi 8e
201 Nyangbara 8c
202 Nyaturu 8e
203 Nyema 8d
204 Nyika 8e
205 Nyima 8c
206 Nyoro 8e
207 Nzakara 8b
208 Paämway 8d
209 Pabir 8b
210 Pare 8e

211 Pepel 8a
212 Pojulu 8c
213 Pokomo 8e
214 Pondo 8e
215 Poto 8b
216 Pyem 8b
217 Rangi 8e
218 Rega 8e
219 Reshiat 8c
220 Ruanda 8e
221 Rukuba 8b
222 Rundi 8e
223 Safwa 8e
224 Sakalava 8e
225 Sandawe 8e
226 Sango 8e
227 Sejeju 8e
228 Sena 8e
229 Shashi 8e
230 Shilluk 8c
231 Shona 8e
232 Sidama 8c
233 Soga 8e
234 Soko 8b
235 Sokoro 8b
236 Somali 8c
237 Somrai 8b
238 Songo 8d
239 Southern
     Sotho 8d
240 Suk 8c
241 Sukuma 8e
242 Surma 8c
243 Swazi 8e
244 Tallensi 8a
245 Tanala 8e
246 Teda 8b
247 Teita 8e
248 Teke 8d
249 Tembu 8d
250 Teso 8e
251 Tetela 8d
252 Teuso 8c
253 Tharaka 8e
254 Thonga 8e
255 Tikar 8b
256 Tiv 8b
257 Toma 8a
258 Toposa 8c
259 Tsamai 8c
260 Tswana 8d
261 Tuareg 8a, 8b
262 Turkana 8c
263 Twa
     (Batwa) 8d, 8e
264 Venda 8e
265 Vende 8e
266 Vili 8d
267 Walamo 8c
268 Warjawa 8b
269 Xosa 8d
270 Yaka 8d
271 Yalunka 8a
272 Yambasa 8b
273 Yanzi 8d
274 Yao 8e
275 Yaunde 8b
276 Yoruba 8a
277 Zigula
     (Zeguha) 8e
278 Zulu 8e

132

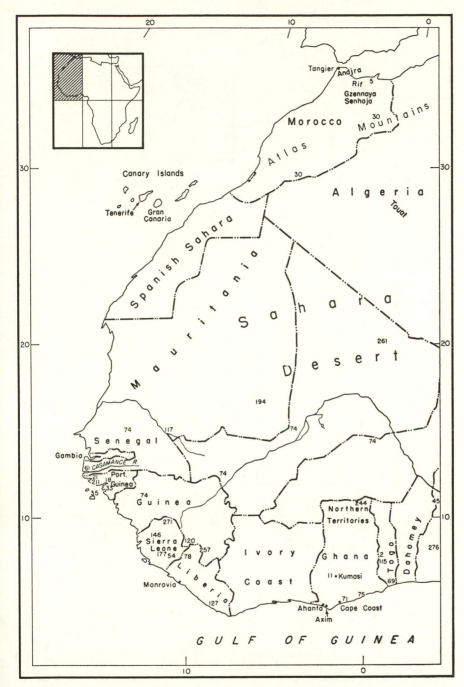

Map 8a—Northwest Africa. Continued on pages 134–137. See key to groups mentioned in text on the facing page.

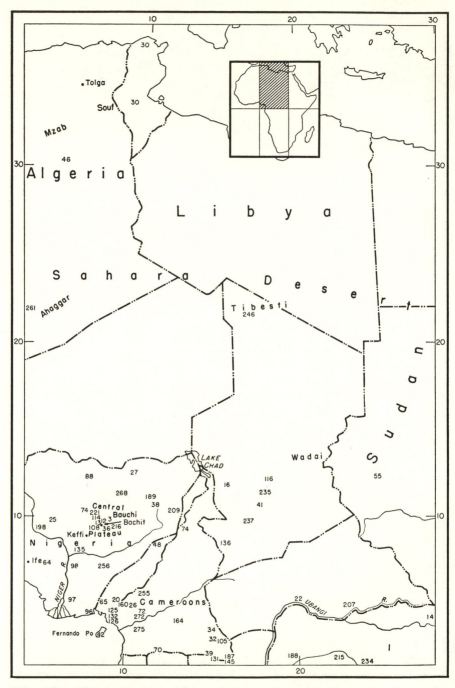

Map 8b—North Central Africa. See key to groups mentioned in text
on page 132.

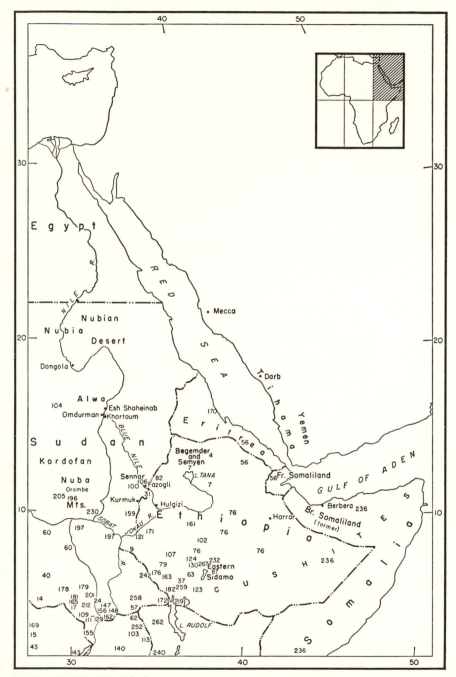

Map 8c—Northeast Africa. See key to groups mentioned in text on page 132.

135

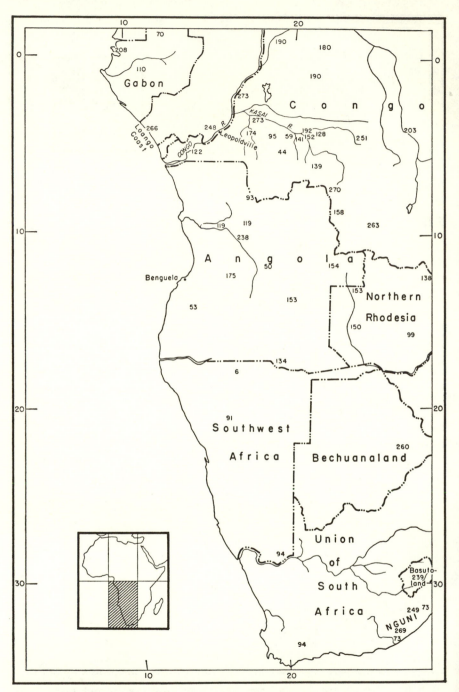

Map 8d—Southwest Africa. See key to groups mentioned in text on page 132.

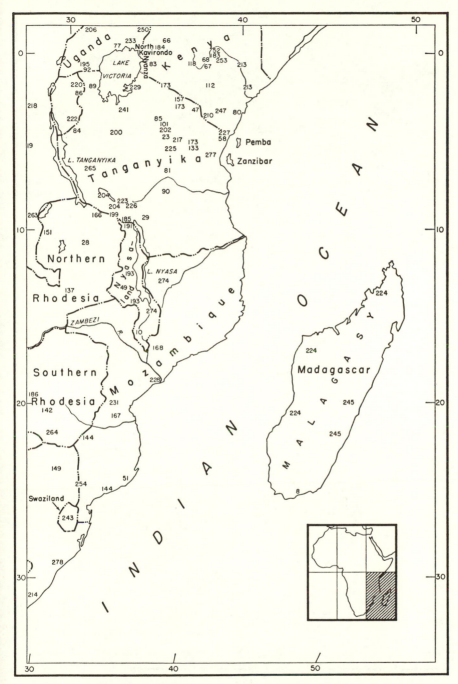

Map 8e—Southeast Africa. See key to groups mentioned in text on page 132.

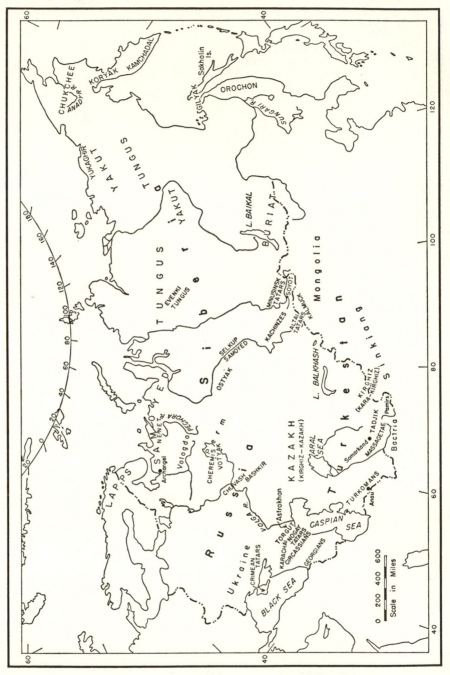

Map 9—Soviet Union

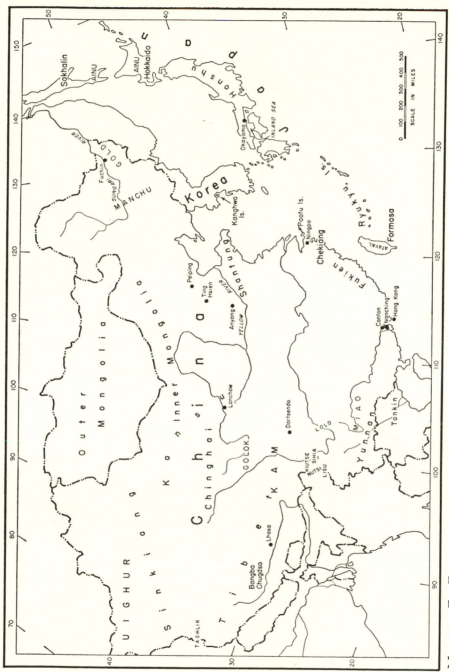

Map 10—Far East

139

GROUPS OF INDIA AND BURMA MENTIONED IN TEXT. Indicated by number on Maps 11a and 11b, which follow on pages 142 and 143. Map number follows group name.

 1 Abor 11b
 2 Agaria (of Mandla District) 11a
 3 Ahom 11b
 4 Aka (Hrusso) 11b
 5 Angami Naga 11b
 6 Ao Naga 11b
 7 Baiga 11a, 11b
 8 Bhil 11a
 9 Burusho of Hunza 11a
10 Chenchu 11a
11 Chin 11b
12 Dafla 11b
13 Dhimal 11b
14 Dire 11b
15 Gadaba 11a
16 Garo 11b
17 Gond 11a, 11b
18 Ho 11b
19 Irula 11a
20 Kachari 11b
21 Kachin (of Lajung Village) 11b
22 Kamar 11b
23 Karen 11b
24 Khasi 11b
25 Khond 11b
26 Kiutse 11b
27 Kocchi 11b

28 Kota 11a
29 Koya 11a
30 Kuki 11b
31 Kurumba 11a
32 Lhota Naga 11b
33 Lisu 11b
34 Lushai 11b
35 Lynngam 11b
36 Mon 11b
37 Munda 11b
38 Nutsi 11b
39 Oraon 11b
40 Paharia 11b
41 Palaung 11b
42 Poraja 11a, 11b
43 Reddi 11a
44 Sangtam 11b
45 Santal 11b
46 Sema Naga 11b
47 Shan 11b
48 Sihia 11b
49 Sikhs 11a
50 Synteng 11b
51 Taghlik (of Pilal) 11a
52 Tangkhul Naga 11b
53 Toda 11a
54 Vedda 11a

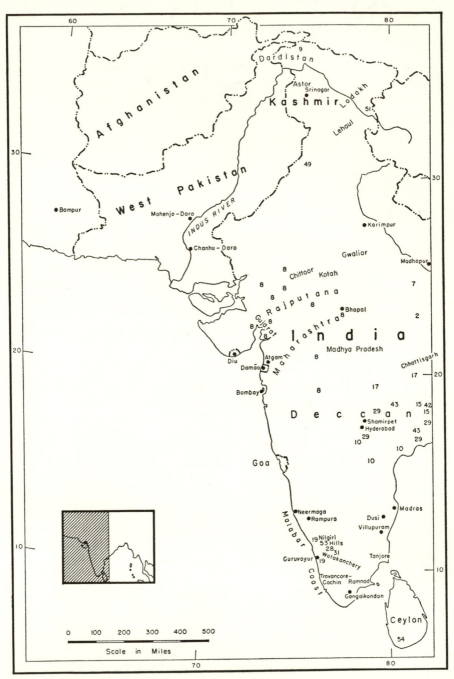

Map 11a—India and Burma. Continued on facing page. See key to groups mentioned in text on page 141.

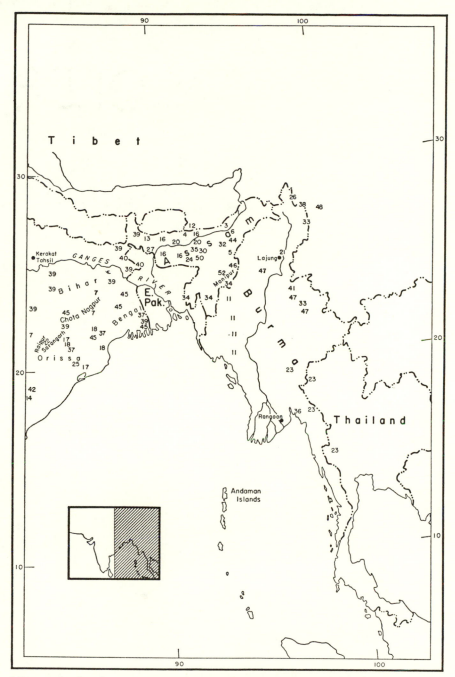

Map 11b. See key to groups mentioned in text on page 141.

143

SOUTHEAST ASIAN GROUPS MENTIONED IN TEXT. Indicated by number on Map 12, following below on the facing page.

1 Achinese	11 Ifugao	21 Lubu
2 Apayao	12 Igorot	22 Massim
3 Batak	13 Jakun	23 Minahasa
4 Bisayans	14 Kai	24 Moi
5 Bugi	15 Kaunje	25 Moro
6 Bukidnon	16 Kayan	26 Murut
7 Cham	17 Kenyah	27 Orang Laut
8 Dusun	18 Klemantan	28 Punan
9 Gambadi	19 Koita	29 Roro
10 Ibilao	20 Land Dyak	30 Sadang

31 Sakai
32 Sea Dyak
33 Semang
34 Tagal
35 Thai
36 Tinguian
37 Toradja
38 Yao

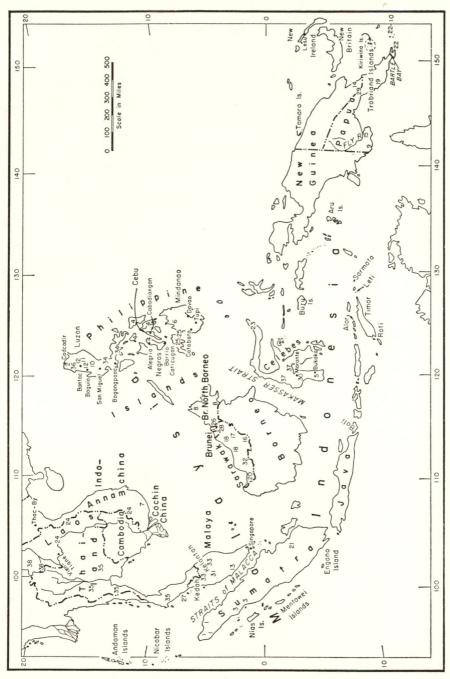

Map 12—Southeast Asia. See key to groups mentioned in text on the facing page.

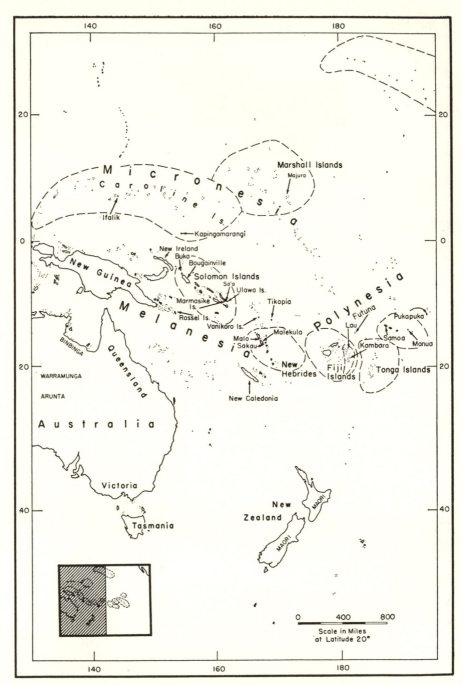

Map 13a—The Pacific. Continued on facing page.

146

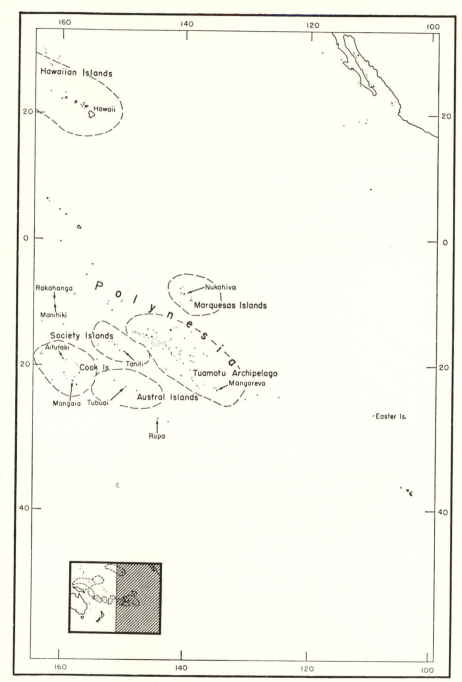

Map 13b

Reference Matter

NOTES

Chapter 1—INTRODUCTION

1 Bennett, 1943: 561–63; A. I. Richards, 1948: 162–63.
2 Macbeth, IV.1.4–38.

Chapter 2—USE AND POTENTIALITIES

1 Stefansson, 1946: 10–13, 102, 108–9.
2 *Ibid.*, 60–89.
3 A. I. Richards, 1939: 42, 57–58, 63, 65.
4 M. Douglas, 1955: 5.
5 Hahn, 1896: 78; Simoons, 1954: 61–62.
6 Gandhi, 1949: 3–4.
7 Westermarck, 1924, 2: 498–99.
8 *Ibid.*, 497–98.
9 Liu En-lan, 1937: 134–35.
10 Porphyry, "On Abstinence from Animal Food," IV.16.
11 Bliss, 1912: 80.
12 Harnack and Conybeare, 1911: 574; Burkitt, 1925: 45.
13 Porphyry, "On Abstinence from Animal Food," IV.2.
14 Ritson, 1802: 52–53.
15 *Ibid.*, 3, 57, 86, 102, 124, 146.
16 Drower, 1937: 48, 50.
17 A. I. Richards, 1939: 64–65.
18 Westermarck, 1924, 2: 493.
19 Ratzel, 1896–98, 3: 455; Donoghue, 1957: 1003.
20 Waddell, 1895: 567–68; Bell, 1928: 218; MacDonald, 1929: 177.
21 M. Douglas, 1955: 23–26.
22 Nadel, 1947: 518.
23 DuBois, 1944: 57–58.

Chapter 3—PIGS AND PORK

1 Among the sites in which pig bones have been reported are Mohenjo-Daro (J. Marshall, 1931, 1: 348, 352; 2: 661, 669) and Chanhu-Daro (Mackay, 1943: 248) in the Indus Valley; Geoy Tepé in Persian Azerbaijan (T. B. Brown, 1951: 81); Anau (Pumpelly, 1908, 1: 38, 41; 2: 356–57); Shah Tepé on the Turkoman steppe of Iran (Amschler, 1939: 65); Belt Cave, four miles south of the Caspian Sea in Iran (Coon, 1951a: 49–50); Sialk (Childe, 1952: 193); Troy (Gejvall, 1937–38: 53); Alishar Mound in Anatolia (Von der Osten, 1937: 294–95, 302, 309, 411); Amouq in Syria (Reed, 1959: 1631, 1636); Jarmo (Braidwood, 1952: 30–31); Karim Shahir (*ibid.*, 26), Hassuna (Childe, 1952: 110), and Tell Asmar (Hilzheimer, 1941: 27, 41, 48) in Iraq; Jericho (Kenyon, 1956: 191), Tell ed Duweir, the ancient city of Lachish (Tufnell, 1953: 63–64, 410–11), Megiddo (Bate, 1938: 212), and Gezer (Baikie, 1923: 431) in Palestine; and Maadi (Childe, 1952: 74), Faiyum (*ibid.*, 35–36), Kau (Sandford, 1934: 86), Merimde (Butzer, 1960: 1619), and Toukh (Gaillard, 1934: 66–72, 116) in Egypt.

For many of these sites there are

claims that the pig bones were from domesticated animals. In most cases convincing proof is lacking; and Charles A. Reed, a zoologist who has considered the osteological evidence, regards most of the claims as unacceptable. The only certain osteological evidence of domestic pigs in the *prehistoric* (pre-2500 B.C.) Near East (Egypt through Iran) that he finds is for Anau and nearby Iran. He assumes, in the absence of convincing argument to the contrary, that for Egypt "the numerous bones of pigs found in the remains of prehistoric villages represent wild pigs from the adjacent Nile marshes." By 3800 B.C. or before, he asserts, "the pig was quite probably an important food animal in southern Mesopotamia"—though his conclusion is based on slight cultural evidence. He does not doubt the importance of pigs in Sumeria in early historic times (Reed, 1959: 1635–36); he does not raise the question of their presence at that time in other parts of the Near East.

2 Espinosa, 1907: 33.
3 Newberry, 1928: 211. Dating for Egypt is based on tables prepared by W. C. Hayes and M. B. Rowton for the forthcoming *Cambridge Ancient History,* Revised Edition.
4 Northampton et al., 1908: 13–14; Newberry, 212; Gaillard, 1934: 115.
5 Newberry, 211.
6 Herodotus, *History,* II.47.
7 *Isis and Osiris,* 5, 8.
8 Wilkinson, 1878, 3: 298; Newberry, 213.
9 Paton, 1925: 17, 19.
10 Wilkinson, 3: 298–99; Gaillard, 1934: 115.
11 Wilkinson, 3: 143, 298–99.
12 Frazer, 1935, 8: 29–30.
13 Lev. 11: 7–8; Deut. 14: 8.
14 Prov. 11: 22.
15 Isaiah 65: 3–4; 66: 3, 17.
16 Plutarch, *Symposiacs,* IV.5.
17 I Macc. 1: 44–48, 50; II Macc. 7: 1–40; Diodorus Siculus, *The Library of History,* XXXIV.1.3–4.
18 II Macc. 6: 18–30; IV Macc. 5: 1–30.
19 W. Smith, 1893, 3: 1393; Davis, 1944: 585.
20 Matt. 8: 28–34; Mark 5: 1–20; Luke 8: 26–33.
21 Jensen, 1886: 306–12; Maspero, 1901: 560; Handcock, 1912: 19.

22 Hilzheimer, 1941: 48.
23 Ungnad, 1908: 534.
24 Goetze, 1938: 5, 11, 17, 99, 101.
25 Xenophon, *Anabasis,* II.2.
26 *Ibid.,* IV.4, 6; V.2.
27 Peters, 1897–98, 2: 131.
28 Jastrow, 1898: 662.
29 Chwolsohn, 1856, 2: 42, 445.
30 Lucian, *The Syrian Goddess,* 54.
31 Strabo, *Geography,* XII.8.9.
32 Diodorus Siculus, *The Library of History,* V.62.5.
33 Foucart, 1873: 119, 123.
34 Julianus, *Orations,* 177 B–C.
35 Pausanias, *Description of Greece,* VII.17.5.
36 Frazer, 1935, 5: 264–65.
37 W. M. Ramsay, 1890: 32–33.
38 Vickery, 1936: 61.
39 Hippocrates, "Regimen," II.46.
40 Paulus Aegineta, *Seven Books,* I.84.
41 Pliny, *Natural History,* VIII.77–78; XXVIII.37.
42 Martialis, *Epigrams,* XIII.41.
43 Paulus Aegineta, *Seven Books,* I.84.
44 Varro, *On Farming,* II.9; Ovid, *Metamorphoses,* XV.111.
45 Frazer, 1935, 7: 74.
46 Epictetus' reference (*Discourses,* I.22.4–5) to the conflict among Jews, Syrians, Egyptians, and Romans over whether the act of eating swine's flesh is holy or unholy suggests that there was indeed a general difference in attitude between East and West.
47 Cato, *On Agriculture,* 139.
48 Frazer, 1935, 8: 16, 19–20.
49 Athenaeus, *The Deipnosophists,* IX.18.
50 The worship of Cybele was introduced to Rome in 204 B.C., and with it, Frazer believes, the worship of Attis. This was a direct adoption in fulfillment of a prophecy that if the Phrygian goddess were brought to Italy the foreign invader (Hannibal) would be expelled. The Romans sent emissaries to Phrygia to the sacred city of Pessinus where they received from the Phrygians themselves the black stone which embodied the goddess and carried it back to Rome. It was received with awe and enthusiasm (Frazer, 1935, 5: 265–66; Julianus, *Orations,* 159 C—161 B). The cult of Cybele and Attis flourished under the Roman Empire, and inscriptions

show that they were worshiped not only in Rome but in various provinces from Portugal to Bulgaria (Frazer, 5: 298).

51 Koran, 2: 172; 5: 3; 6: 146; 16: 115.

52 Rushdy, 1911: 163.

53 Dussaud, 1900: 94.

54 Layard, 1849, 1: 301.

55 Drower, 1937: 47.

56 Simmons et al., 1954: 113, 151.

57 Guys, 1863: 167.

58 Rushdy, 1911: 163; Newberry, 1928: 212; Platt and Hefny, 1958: 188.

The small numbers of pigs that are raised in Egypt are concentrated in areas where Copts are numerous, such as the provinces of Qena, Asyut, and Minya, and within town and city limits, especially Cairo, Alexandria, Port Said, and Ismailiya. The domestic production of pork, however, is too small to supply the demand, and considerable additional pork must be imported (Platt and Hefny, 1958: 188).

59 Moslem groups that have been reported as eating the flesh of wild pigs include the Nimadi hunters of southeastern Mauritania (Marty, 1930: 121–23), the Rwala Bedouin (Musil, 1928: 395), the Baluchi of Bampur (Phillott, 1907: 341), and the Moro of Mindanao. Other Moslem groups, such as the people of Pemba (Craster, 1913: 283–84), the Iranians (E. C. Sykes, 1910: 241), and the Afghans (Fox, 1943: 118), have refused such flesh, considering it unclean.

60 Gruner, 1930: 220.

61 Paulus Aegineta, *Seven Books,* I.84.

62 de Planhol, 1959: 58.

63 Coon, 1931: 41.

64 *Ibid.,* 60.

65 Westermarck, 1926, 2: 312–13.

66 *Ibid.,* 2: 314–15.

67 G. Clark, 1947: 128.

68 In certain Balkan areas some Christians did reject pork as food (de Planhol, 1959: 57), apparently following Islamic example. Curious and mixed attitudes toward the pig are reported for northeast Scotland: it was regarded as unclean; its bite was believed to cause cancer—yet soup made of fresh pork was considered a remedy for many diseases; at sea, the men of several villages would not pronounce the word "swine," which was a word of ill omen;

and despite all this, the people ate pork (Gregor, 1881: 129–30).

69 Thus there is nothing in the Mesolithic site at Khartoum to suggest any knowledge of domestic animals (Arkell, 1949: 27, 107), including pigs; nor did the Neolithic site at Esh Shaheinab (about 3300 B.C.) north of Omdurman yield any remains of pigs, though the people did have sheep and goats (Bate, 1953: 15, 18).

70 These statements are confirmed by several observations: (1) Pigs were kept in the Nubian kingdoms which bordered Egypt on its southern marches and which were strongly influenced by Egyptian civilization. (2) Today pigs of types apparently unrelated to those of modern Europe are found in the steppe region of the Sudan: in Sennar (Bruce, 1790, 4: 421; Hartmann, 1883: 31; Hahn, 1896: 217; Seligman and Seligman, 1932: 413), among the Kadullu, Ingassana, and Berta (Cerulli, 1956: 17, 18), and among the pagan people of the southern Nuba Mountains (Seligman and Seligman, 1932: 368). (3) In the case of Sennar, pigs were present for almost two centuries before intimate contact with Europeans developed. (4) There is a tradition among one group in the Nuba Mountains that when their ancestor emerged onto the earth from a rock he was accompanied by pigs (*ibid.,* 393), which suggests that the pig may indeed be an ancient domesticate among them. (5) Pigs have also been reported among pagan groups farther south along the Sudan-Ethiopia border: among the Gumis living around Hulgizi near the Blue Nile (R. E. Cheesman, 1936: 371); among the Maban, who live south of the Gumis near Kurmuk; and in many villages of the Koma, a group of border tribes living still farther south and not far from the Jokau River, a tributary of the Sobat (Corfield, 1938: 151; Cerulli, 1956: 18).

71 Budge, 1928, 1: 105.

72 Crowfoot, 1925: 125; Nadel, 1947: 60.

73 In the 1880's, it is said, the Gumis tribe of the Sudan-Ethiopia border possessed many pigs (Cerulli, 1956: 18). Though some members of the group in the south may still keep pigs, the people living in

the border region west of Lake Tana—
who have considerable contact with
both Islam and Ethiopian Christianity—
have none at all today (personal observation).

74 It is generally accepted today that Europeans introduced the domestic pig into
both West and Central Africa and East
and South Africa. This is supported
not only by European tradition and the
unquestioned present-day role of Europeans in diffusing pig keeping, but by
the spotty distribution of domestic pigs
in tropical Africa and by the fact that
many peoples use the same name for
both the domestic pig and the wild bush
pig (*Potamochoerus*), which suggests
that they simply applied the name for a
familiar wild animal to a newly introduced domestic one.

75 Because of Islamic influence either pigs
are absent or pork is rejected, or both,
among many West African groups, such
as the Nupe (Nadel, 1951: 203), the
Yoruba (Forde, 1949: 156), the Bolewa
of Bauchi (Temple, 1922: 68), and
others. Moslem influence was also evi-
dent among the Ashanti of the Gold
Coast a century ago, for William Hutchinson, British Resident at Kumasi, reported that a "Moorish Shereef" made a
great fuss when he discovered pork in
a boy's room (Bowdich, 1819: 412).

76 In the Nubian provinces of the Sudan,
for example, "Arab hunters" ate the
flesh of the "wild boar" when food was
scarce (S. W. Baker, 1867: 166). Unfortunately we cannot be certain whether
the "wild boar" was the bush pig or
wart hog. In Ethiopia, Mansfield Parkyns
noted, some Moslems ate the flesh of the
"wild boar" (1868: 208). Nathaniel
Pearce reported that an Ethiopian ate
with him the meat of a wild hog, apparently a wart hog, because he was
ill and the meat had medicinal value
(1831, 2: 253). In Begemder and
Semyen in northwestern Ethiopia people
say that they never use the blood or
flesh of the bush pig for medicinal
purposes; but here and there the flesh
of the wart hog is so used (personal
observation). The Kafa of southwest
Ethiopia consider the flesh of the "wild
pig" unclean, whereas their neighbors

the Janjero eat it (Huntingford, 1955:
109, 138). The Xosa (Kafir) of South
Africa also eat "the wild hog," though
they refuse domestic swine (Westermarck, 1924, 2: 327–28).

77 Among the groups reported in this century as still not eating pork are the
Barabaig of Tanganyika (Huntingford,
1953a: 96), the Yao of Nyasaland
(Stannus, 1922: 347), and the Lemba of
southern Africa (Stayt, 1931: 44).

Of other tribes of southern Africa: (1)
The Zulu formerly did not regard pigs
as fit for human consumption, but today
pigsties are frequent in their kraals
(Bryant, 1949: 290, 343). (2) In
former times the Ngoni did not eat
pork, though they may do so now
(Earthy, 1933: 38). (3) Though pigs
are kept by the Southern Sotho (Basuto), and their flesh and fat are prized,
some still refuse to eat them because of
their dirty scavenging habits (Ashton,
1952: 135). (4) Some Thonga refuse
to eat pork, apparently because it is a
recent introduction which they are not
used to (Junod, 1913, 2: 52, 66).

In Madagascar some groups keep pigs
and others do not. Thus the Hova, who
have strong Malaysian elements in their
culture, keep them; the Sakalava do not
(Keller, 1901: 130). Many groups
among the Tanala consider the pig unclean because it eats excrement and other
filth; they not only refuse to kill or eat
pigs but will not permit pork to be
cooked in their pots or allow it in the
village. Some Tanala explain their avoidance of pork by pointing out that the pig
in the past did a good deed to their group
(Linton, 1933: 230–31), an explanation
which seems to be totemic in nature.

78 WEST AFRICA: Here pigs are found
principally in the southern sections of
Nigeria and Dahomey, in the southern
and central Ivory Coast, in the Casa-
mance region of Senegal, and around
various towns elsewhere (Church, 1957:
135). In Dahomey pork is considered
a delicacy, and the pig is the most
common domestic animal except for the
chicken (Herskovits, 1938, 1: 40). The
keeping of pigs or eating of pork, or
both, have been reported for Monrovia,
Liberia, where pigs serve as scavengers

(Johnston, 1906, 1: 447–48); for Ghana, where the dedication of pork to the fetish has been reported for Ahanta, on the coast near Axim (Bowdich, 1819: 279), and the keeping of pigs for the Cape Coast region (Cruickshank, 1853, 2: 133, 275); for the Tiv of Nigeria, who relish pork (East, 1939: 97–98); for the Bedde of northern Nigeria, who eat pork (Temple, 1922: 61); for the pagan Bassa people of Nigeria, who keep pigs and kill them for sacrificial purposes (*ibid.,* 46); and for the Tikar of the central Cameroons, who rear pigs (McCulloch, 1954: 27).

CONGO: Pigs are kept and their flesh is eaten by many groups. Mentioned specifically as pig-keeping groups are the Kongo (Baumann, 1887: 163), the Teke (Johnston, 1910, 2: 616), and the Lunda (*ibid.,* 1: 197). The Lele of the Kasai do not generally raise domestic pigs for food, for they consider them dirty, though they will eat wild pigs killed in the forest, and a few progressive Lele men raise domestic pigs to sell to their neighbors, the Luba and Dinga (M. Douglas, 1955: 5).

ANGOLA: Pigs are found widely in Benguela and in Kimbundu country (Ratzel, 1896–98, 3: 114). Among the Mbundu (Ovimbundu) every family owns a pig, which wanders about eating the village refuse as well as the daily ration of water and food usually given him (Hambly, 1934: 154; Childs, 1949: 14, 31, 109), and eventually ends in the pot. Among the Luena of Angola and Northern Rhodesia there are a few pigs, as there are among the Luchazi of Angola (McCulloch, 1951: 61, 62).

TANGANYIKA: Pig keeping is not universal, though many tribes keep pigs for consumption and even for market. In the past the Chagga kept sizable numbers of pigs, though this has been abandoned (Hill and Moffett, 1955: 573).

SOUTHERN AFRICA: Aside from the reluctance of some groups to keep pigs and eat pork, which has already been described, the Eastern Tswana keep pigs (Schapera, 1953: 23); the Venda regard pork as a delicacy, though pigs were still scarce in 1931 (Stayt, 1931: 44); the Chokwe keep pigs (McCulloch, 1951:

38); and so do some of the more wealthy Lenge (Earthy, 1933: 25).

SOUTHWEST AFRICA: Kuanyama Ambo Christians keep pigs, though pagans do not (Loeb, n.d.: 220).

It is true that some pig-keeping groups of Africa have restrictions on eating pork, but they are the same sorts of restrictions that apply to all flesh foods. Thus, pork is forbidden to chiefs or rulers among the Holo, the Bondo branch of the Kimbundu, and the Lunda and Luba peoples, because it is considered unclean. Similarly, some groups of the Tiv forbid pork to women; among the Banjangi, pregnant women avoid it lest their children's speech be affected; and among the Vili some people are not permitted to eat pork (Kroll, 1928: 187). In addition, pork is rejected by certain families, clans, or tribes that regard the pig as their totemic animal.

79 Herodotus, *History,* IV.68.
80 Minns, 1913: 49.
81 Nweeya, 1910: 241.
82 E. C. Sykes, 1910: 72, 240–41.
83 This belief was also recorded among the Turkomans along the eastern shores of the Caspian Sea just north of Iran (Vámbéry, 1864: 72–73).
84 Phillott, 1907: 341; E. C. Sykes, 1910: 241.
   In Baghdad, too, a wild boar is sometimes kept in the stable (Phillott, 1907: 341).
85 Featherman, 1885–91, 4: 537.
86 Westermarck, 1924, 2: 326–27.
87 Donner, 1926: 26.
88 Great Britain Admiralty, n.d.: 169.
89 Lattimore, 1941: 220.
90 Combe, 1926: 128; Bell, 1928: 233–34.
91 Combe: 126–27.
92 Bell, 1946: 181.
93 Rockhill reported that Tibetan nomads never ate pork (1895: 705); and Ekvall, in considering the Kansu-Tibetan border of China, says that though Tibetan farmers eat pork some nomadic tribes farthest away from the sedentary peoples refuse it (1939: 78).
94 Rockhill, 1895: 705.
95 Combe, 128.
96 MacDonald, 1929: 168.
97 Krader, 1955: 312, 315.
98 The one record I have found of the

failure of a non-Moslem Chinese community to keep pigs is that referred to in Chapter 2: Pootu (Puto Shan), the island near Ningpo in Chekiang where over half the population was vegetarian Buddhist monks, and meat could not be bought anywhere (Liu En-lan, 1937: 134–35).

99 Gibson, 1935: 342, 346–47; Sowerby, 1935: 234–37; Creel, 1937: 182–83, 242–43; Creel, 1937a: 43, 78–79, 81, 200; Li, 1957: 21–23.

1 Various aboriginal groups of south China have been reported as either keeping pigs or eating pork or both. These include the Sihia, Kiutse, Nutsi, Lisu, Kachin (Bernatzik, 1954, 2: 124, 126–28), Miao (Moninger, 1921: 46; D. C. Graham, 1937: 20; Mickey, 1947: 23–24), and the Lolo (Legendre, 1909: 343; Pollard, 1921: 123–24; Lin Yueh-wha, 1944: 54; Bernatzik, 1954, 2: 127). There is, however, one curious suggestion of pork avoidance for the Lolo: a traveler reported that a deculturated Hua Lolo living among Shan people regarded the pig as unclean and claimed that in his tribe, though men ate pork, women were forbidden to (Bourne, 1889: 122).

2 Winfield, 1948: 72–73.

3 Ekvall, 1939: 23.

4 Gerard, 1952: 260–61.

5 Winfield, 64–66.

6 Ekvall, 23.

7 L. Buxton, 1929: 51–52.

8 Broomhall, 1910: 225–26.

9 Lattimore, 1929: 227–28.

10 Broomhall, 226, 244–45, 281.

11 Bell, 1928: 53.

12 Cammann, 1951: 35.

13 Yamasaki, 1900: 233; Stanford University, 1956: 259.

14 Shirokogoroff, 1924: 132–33.

15 Griffis, 1882: 267; Hulbert, 1906: 20; Heydrich, 1931: 42; Osgood, 1951: 31, 77.

16 Groot, 1951: 75.

17 Beardsley, Hall, and Ward, 1959: 107.

18 Bernatzik, 1954, 2: 154–55.

19 That the keeping of pigs and eating of pork by members of some low castes is the pattern throughout Hindu India is attested by numerous specific and general references in the literature—G. W. Briggs, 1920: 45; Blunt, 1931: 94–96; Singh, 1947: 91; Hutton, 1951: 77; Marriott, 1955: 73; Dube, 1955: 176; Wiser, 1955: 318, 346; University of California, 1956, 1: 149–50. The practices also occur among the Syrian Christians of Watakanchery in south India (Slater, 1918: 131).

20 Marriott, 1955: 9, 21, 26.

21 *Ibid.*, 73.

22 Gondal, 1948: 22.

23 Some of the aboriginal Indian groups reported as keeping pigs or eating pork or both are (1) the Kamar tribe of Chhattisgarh (Dube, 1951: 49); (2) the Oraon, who occupy a large part of northern and western Chota Nagpur, and who consider pork their favorite food and keep pigs in almost all their villages (Featherman, 1885–91, 4: 96); (3) the Santal (*ibid.*, 4: 52); (4) the Ho of Chota Nagpur (Majumdar, 1937: 26); (5) the Kachari or Bodo (Featherman, 4: 26; Endle, 1911: 15); (6) the Dhimal (Featherman, 4: 26); (7) the Garo (*ibid.*, 4: 82); (8) the Kocchi (*ibid.*, 4: 21); (9) the Khasi (Gurdon, 1907: 35); (10) the Lushai (Shakespear, 1912: 32, 70, 74, 77); and (11) the Ao, Angami, and Sema Naga (Hutton, 1921: 81; Hutton, 1921a: 71, 223; W. C. Smith, 1925: 32).

24 Hutton, 1921a: 71, 223.

25 Cornell University, 1956, 1: 123.

26 Fürer-Haimendorf, 1943, 2: 97–98, 100.

27 Among these are (1) the Bhil, who are said not to eat pork (Featherman, 1885–91, 4: 138); (2) the Tangkhul Naga of Manipur, who believe that the pork eater would become insane, prematurely gray, and then would die, often suffering a horrible death from boils (Hutton Webster, 1942: 333); (3) the Khasi, most of whom, as mentioned above, do eat pork, though certain clans avoid it (Gurdon, 1907: 52); (4) the Kamar of Chhattisgarh, among whom pork is eaten by men but not by women (Dube, 1951: 49); and (5) the Vedda of Ceylon. Though ordinary Vedda do not hesitate to eat pork, shamans are not permitted to touch or eat it; if a shaman ate it they believe he would become sick and

shiver for four or five days (Seligman and Seligman, 1911: 179–80).

28 Fürer-Haimendorf, 2: 97–98.

29 Majumdar, 1937: 26.

30 Sopher, 1959: 7.

31 Sauer, 1952: 31–38.

32 Groups known to eat pork include the Karen (H. I. Marshall, 1922: 69), the Kachin of Lajung village (Huke, 1954: 18), and certain peoples of the Assam border of Burma; and in Indochina the Miao of the China border (Reinach, 1901, 2: 108) and the Moi, or Kha (*ibid.,* 1: 406; N. Lewis, 1951: 97). On the Nicobar Islands pork is a favorite food eaten on feast days (Featherman, 1885–91, 2: 241). On the Andaman Islands, though the natives have no domestic animals but dogs, they hunt and eat wild pigs, and occasionally keep young wild pigs in captivity to slaughter when they are grown (Man, 1932: 122, 142; Radcliffe-Brown, 1933: 36–38, 417). Though some aboriginal Malay groups, apparently under Moslem influence, will not touch wild pigs (Williams-Hunt, 1952: 94), others continue to eat them much as the Malays did before their conversion to Islam (Dennys, 1894: 224). The Jakun hunters and gatherers of Johore consider the flesh of the wild hog their favorite meat; the Blanda, a Jakun group, occasionally cage wild pigs for future consumption (Skeat and Blagden, 1906, 1: 215, 220). And certain aboriginal Malays suckle wild pigs whose mothers have died (Williams-Hunt, 1952: 94).

In Indonesia pig keeping and pork eating have been reported for (1) the pagan and Christian Niasese (Loeb, 1935: 132–33); (2) the Batak of Sumatra (*ibid.,* 24–25); (3) the people of Engano Island southwest of Sumatra (*ibid.,* 210–11); (4) those of Alor, who regard pigs as currency, and hence seldom eat their flesh except at feasts (DuBois, 1944: 22); (5) the pagan Sadang of Celebes, who carry their pigs to market trussed on shoulder poles, and consider pork their best food; some Sadang pagans, indeed, have preferred Christianity to Islam because it permits eating pork; other Sadang, when they

married Moslems or when they were converted to or influenced by Islam, gave up eating pork (Kennedy, 1953: 128, 166, 176); (6) the Minahasa of Celebes (Featherman, 1885–91, 2: 63); (7) the non-Moslems of Timor (*ibid.,* 2: 458); (8) most groups in Borneo, where all non-Moslem peoples eat wild pigs, and where domestic pigs also are kept and eaten by some groups (Roth, 1896, 1: 379–81, 389, 424), such as the Sea Dyak (Hose and McDougall, 1912, 2: 90, 107) and the Dusun of British North Borneo (Roth, 1896, 1: 424–25). On the other hand, the Murut of Borneo have a curious prejudice against eating the flesh of domestic pigs not raised at home; thus they refuse not only European bacon but the flesh of pigs raised in neighboring villages (*ibid.,* 1: 424). In addition, the Punan of Sarawak, a group of pagan hunters and gatherers, reject domestic pigs as food and for sacrifice because the animal is strange to them (Hose and McDougall, 2: 84).

In the Philippines pigs are widely kept, except by Moslem groups, and their flesh is relished. On Mindanao, pork eating has been reported for the wild tribes of the Davao District (Cole, 1913: 68), the Bukidnon (Cole, 1956: 56), and the people of Tupi village, Cotabato (Rivera and McMillan, 1952: 213). Elsewhere in the Philippines, too, pig keeping and pork eating are carried on without prejudice: (1) In Barrio Caticugan on Negros Island, for example, pork is the most prized meat. Most families have several pigs, which are permitted to forage freely except when crops are in the field; then they are either tied or penned and fed (Hart, 1954: 338, 427–28). (2) Among the Tinguian of Luzon the pigs run loose around the villages and in the nearby countryside, apparently interbreeding with wild pigs (Cole, 1922: 412). (3) The Bontoc Igorot pamper their pigs and confine them in pens, feeding them three time a day, in some places carefully washing and cooking their food but in others feeding them garbage and human excreta (Jenks, 1905: 109; Keesing, 1949: 586).

33 On Alor, however, pigs are controlled by the men, for they are regarded as currency (DuBois, 1944: 22) and figure in the prestige structure, as they do in the Pacific islands.
34 H. I. Marshall, 1922: 64–65.
35 de Young, 1955: 98.
36 Ferrars, 1901: 150.
37 Frazer, 1935, 2: 107.
    There are several other examples of the use of pigs as sacrificial animals. On Alor pigs are sometimes sacrificed on ceremonial occasions, especially those associated with cultivation (DuBois, 1944: 23–24). The people of Timor sacrifice a black pig to the Earth Goddess for rain, and a white or red one to the Sun God for sunshine (Frazer, 1935, 1: 291). On Borneo the Sea Dyak sacrifice pigs, and at an earlier date sometimes substituted them for human sacrifices (Hose and McDougall, 1912, 2: 90, 107). The Maanjan sacrifice pigs at the time of planting and when the first grain is ripe (Ratzel, 1896–98, 1: 430). The Klemantan, Kenyah, and Kayan also use pigs as sacrificial animals. In one religious rite of the Kenyah the men, before leaving on an expedition, sprinkle the blood of young pigs on the altar of their god, then fix the carcasses on tall poles nearby and leave them there; at other times, although they may assure the pig before slaughter that it will not be eaten, they do prepare and eat the flesh (Hose and McDougall, 2: 60, 64–66, 80).
38 H. I. Marshall, 1922: 284.
39 Lévy-Bruhl, 1923: 186.
40 Frazer, 1935, 1: 382.
41 References for this paragraph:
    Bali: Featherman, 1885–91, 2: 402; Burkill, 1935, 2: 1724; personal communication, Mr. Dyatmoko, Jogjakarta.
    Burma and *Thailand:* Young, 1898: 111; W. A. Graham, 1924, 1: 156–57; V. Thompson, 1941: 333–34; Andrus, 1947: 54; de Young, 1955: 98.
    Indochina: Reinach, 1901, 1: 406; League of Nations, 1937: 78; Andrus, 1943: 31.
42 Linton, 1955: 221.
43 Burkill, 1935, 2: 1725. Maxwell, 1881: 22; Wheeler, 1928: 255; V. Thompson, 1943: 59; Cole, 1945: 121.

44 Cole, 1945: 196–97.
45 In addition to the violations by Javanese Moslems mentioned below, there are suspicions of laxity among Moslems in the Philippines (Spencer, 1954: 68) and among the Lubu of central Sumatra (Loeb, 1935: 296).
46 Grist, 1936: 325.
47 Chen, 1940: 93.
48 Personal communication, Mr. Dyatmoko, Jogjakarta.
49 Gourou, 1936: 427.
50 Best, 1924, 2: 354; P. H. Buck, 1932: 83; P. H. Buck, 1938: 310–12; Beaglehole and Beaglehole, 1938: 106; P. H. Buck, 1944: 15–16.
51 P. H. Buck, 1938: 194–95.
52 Curiously, the Maori word for pig, *poaka,* which is derived from the English work "pork," is very similar to the original Polynesian word for pig, *puaka* (P. H. Buck, 1950a: 110–11).
53 Rivers, 1914: 333; Raymond Firth, 1930: 107.
54 Smyth, 1878, 1: 237.
55 Frazer, 1935, 8: 296.
56 *Ibid.,* 33.
57 Seligman, 1910: 680.
58 *Ibid.,* 681.
59 A. B. Lewis, 1932: 52.
60 E. G. Burrows, [1949]: 18; Spiro, [1949]: 7; Forde, 1949: 209.
61 Mead, 1930: 48–49.
62 P. H. Buck, 1930: 119, 323; Grattan, 1948: 55.
63 In some places the killing of pigs is restricted to such occasions: Ratzel, 1896–98, 1: 306; Seligman, 1910: 730; Lévy-Bruhl, 1923: 390; Ivens, 1927: 36–37, 54, 241, 407–8; Armstrong, 1928: 19; Aitken, 1930: 37; P. H. Buck, 1930: 119; Powdermaker, 1933: 183–84, 202; Deacon, 1934: 16–17; Frazer, 1935, 2: 98–99 and 10: 9; Malinowski, 1935, 1: 31-32, 52; Blackwood, 1935: 281; E. G. Burrows, 1936: 134; Beaglehole and Beaglehole, 1938: 106; L. Thompson, 1940: 138; P. H. Buck, 1944: 15–16; Spoehr, 1949: 150; P. H. Buck, 1950: 48.
64 Malinowski, 1935, 1: 46–47.
65 Herskovits, 1952: 429–30.
66 P. H. Buck, 1944: 15–16.
67 Beaglehole and Beaglehole, 1938: 106.
68 Buck, 1944: 15–16.

At Nukahiva in the Marquesas Islands a stone image of a pig's head was found buried with some human bodies (Ratzel, 1896–98, 1: 306); it may have been a symbol of rank of a chief or other important person. On Nias Island off Sumatra the "head of the pig goes to the foremost chief present" (Loeb, 1935: 133).

In the southeast Solomons pigs are associated with chiefs because of the latter's right to hold feasts (Ivens, 1927: 241–42). In the Marquesas Islands the chief could taboo the slaughter of pigs to guarantee an adequate supply for a future feast (Herskovits, 1952: 275). The people of Vanikoro, or La Pérouse Island, eat pork mainly at the homes of the chiefs, who apparently consider its use a privilege of their rank (Featherman, 1885–91, 2: 94).

69 Featherman, 1885–91, 2: 47.
70 Hutton Webster, 1942: 118.
71 Lowie, 1940: 441.
72 Webster, 1942: 118.
73 Steiner, 1956: 88.
74 In Sa'a in the southeast Solomons younger children are never permitted to touch pork (Ivens, 1927: 36–37).
75 Seligman, 1910: 88.
76 Powdermaker, 1933: 202–4.
77 Seligman, 1910: 513.
78 J. R. Baker, 1929: 30–31.
79 Harrisson, 1937: 24–35.
80 Frazer, 1935, 1: 339.
81 J. R. Baker, 1929: 30; Deacon, 1934: 16–17; Harrisson, 1937: 25.
82 Harrisson, 25.
83 Linton, 1926: 31.
84 Williams, 1936: 224–25.
85 Seligman, 1910: 681–82.
86 J. R. Baker, 1929: 30; E. G. Burrows, [1949]: 7, 18; Spiro, [1949]: 18.
87 Best, 1924, 2: 4.
88 Ratzel, 1896–98, 2: 306.
89 Though Buddha is reputed to have died from eating pork, early references to pigs being forbidden in India appear in the Āpastamba Dharma Sūtra (c. 500–100 B.C.) (Āpastamba, I, 5, 17, 29; trans. in Bühler, 1896: 64) and in the Baudhāyana Dharma Sūtra (Baudhāyana, I, 5, 12, 3; trans. in Bühler, 1882: 184) and the Gautama Dharma Sūtra (Gautama, XVII, 29; trans. in Bühler, 1896: 269).

90 Cheyne and Black, 1899–1903, 1: 842.
91 Virchow, n.d.: 30, 39; Gould, 1945: 14.
92 Virchow, 30–31.
93 Belding, 1958: 145.
94 Gould, 237–38.
95 In the United States the situation is approximately as follows: in areas of high incidence of trichinosis, 25% incidence in humans, 2.5% in swine; in areas of intermediate incidence, 15% incidence in humans, 1.5% in swine; in areas of low incidence, 4.3% incidence in humans, 0.43% in swine (M. C. Hall, 1938: 1100–1102).
96 In the United States during 1949–1952 hogs fed on grain or forage were found to have considerably less than 1% infection, with an average of only 5 and a maximum of 7 or 8 viable trichina cysts per gram of muscle tissue..., whereas hogs fattened on uncooked municipal garbage from Boston, New York and Philadelphia had an incidence of 11.21 per cent with recovery of 100 to 2,741 larvas per gram" (Faust, 1955: 266). In former times offal-fed swine showed up to 18% infestation (M. C. Hall, 1938: 1099–1100). As a result of differences in feeding habits of swine, there are striking regional differences today in the incidence of trichinosis in both pigs and humans: the Southern United States, where pigs "run at large and are not fed garbage or swill," has a very low incidence of trichinae in humans and animals; but California, Massachusetts, and New York, where garbage- and swill-fed hogs are common, have very high incidences (Hall, 1101-2; see also Sawitz, 1938: 376). Recent experiments (Spindler, 1953: 34) have also proved that trichinosis can be transmitted through eating feces in which the parasite is present. It is not clear, however, whether sty pigs, which have greater access to the feces of their fellows, or free-ranging pigs, which may have greater access to the feces of dogs, men, and other infected animals, would be more subject to infection by this means.
97 It is estimated that the United States contains three-fourths of all infected people in the world. Studies from 1931 to 1942 have disclosed an average in-

cidence of human trichinosis at autopsy of 16% in the United States (Gould, 1945: 19, 56) ; with better detection techniques, the percentage of infection may run as high as 25–30% (Belding, 1958: 145).

98 Gould, 1945: 15–16, 19, 56, 284–85.

99 Morrison, 1935: 531.

1 Virchow, n.d.: 39

2 *Ibid.,* 6.

3 In Europe, from 1860 to 1877, 140 epidemics of trichinosis occurred; a total of 3,044 persons were known to have become ill and 231 to have died (Gould, 1945: 14).

4 Chandler, 1955: 396.

5 Harmer, n.d.: 181–83.

6 Coon, 1951: 346.

7 de Planhol, 1959: 58–59.

8 Ekvall, 1939: 60.

9 Lattimore, 1941: 220.

10 *Ibid.*

11 Clavijo, 1859: 134.

Chapter 4—BEEF

1 Although many writers on India speak of "sacred cows" and prohibitions against "cow killing," they generally use "cow" in a generic sense to refer to common and zebu cattle of whatever sex but not to the yak (*Poephagus grunniens*) or water buffalo (the *carabao; Bubalus*). In the India section "cattle" will be used in a generic sense to refer to both common cattle and zebu cattle; "beef" will be used for the flesh of these animals only; "cows" will refer to female cattle; and water buffalo, yak, and crossbred animals will be indicated by name. The prohibition against eating beef is generally applied to the flesh of water buffalo too, though apparently not as stringently. The water buffalo is less highly regarded than cattle; indeed, Hindus sacrifice buffaloes to Kali, goddess of death, and pretend to despise them (Kipling, 1891: 171–72, 175).

2 S. K. Das, 1953: 234–36.

3 Among the many organizations active in protecting cattle in India are the Cow-Preservation League of Calcutta and the All-India Cow-Protection Society. The Islami Gorakshan Office at Sitapore is a Moslem cow-protection agency (Sundara Ram, 1927: 196).

4 *New York Times,* Aug. 20, 1957: 8.

5 Crooke, 1896, 2: 235.

6 Mukerjee, 1938: 144–45.

7 O'Malley, 1941: 26.

8 Kipling, 1891: 119; Crooke, 1896, 2: 235.

9 E. A. H. Blunt, 1931: 95–96; Hutton, 1946: 67; Marriott, 1955: 37.

10 Gondal, 1948: 22, 25.

11 Sundara Ram, 1927: 122–23.

12 Dube, 1955: 67, 176.

13 Durand, 1900: 160.

14 Sundara Ram, 1927: 96–97, 100–101, 103, 119; Gangulee, 1939: 207.

15 Sopher, 1959: 7.

16 Fürer-Haimendorf, 1943, 2: 329.

17 Golish, 1954: 49.

18 Shakespear, 1912: 31–32, 36.

     The Sema Naga keep hybrids of common cattle and mithan specifically for their flesh (Hutton, 1921a: 69). The Ao Naga consume beef as a common food, and when they kill an ox eat everything except the hair, hoofs, and horns (W. C. Smith, 1925: 32). The Khasi of Assam are reported to be fond of beef (Gurdon, 1907: 51). And the Ho of Chota Nagpur eat it whenever it is available (Majumdar, 1937: 26).

     Groups that are reported to slaughter cattle or water buffalo include the Koya, Gond, and Poraja (Fürer-Haimendorf, 1943, 2: 97), and the Oraon of Bihar and Orissa (Cornell University, 1956, 1: 123).

19 Fürer-Haimendorf, 1943, 2: 96.

     The Kurumba of the Nilgiri Hills in south India avoid the flesh of cattle but eat buffalo calf on ceremonial occasions. Their neighbors the Irula eat neither (Featherman, 1885–91, 4: 150–51). The Vedda of Ceylon, too, abstain from both (Seligman and Seligman, 1911: 178, 180).

20 Dube, 1951: vi, 48, 134.

21 The Munda of Chota Nagpur (Majumdar, 1937: 26) and some of the Synteng of Assam (Gurdon, 1904: 58) have given up eating beef, apparently as a result of Hindu influence. The Toda, a small south Indian group of pastoralists, maintain buffalo herds, and in the past slaughtered and ate buffalo calves, if only ceremonially. Though there is one report of their slaughtering buffaloes

ceremonially a few years ago (Fig. 8), they have adopted the idea from their Hindu neighbors that slaughtering and eating buffalo is disgraceful (Breeks, 1873: 9–10; W. E. Marshall, 1873: 130; Rivers, 1906: 274–75, 290; Golish, 1954: 16–17).

22 Drew, 1875: 428; Leitner, [1893], App. 6: 1.

23 In the Rig Veda the god Indra was "constantly designated a bull," a term which was "applied much less frequently to Agni, and occasionally to other gods"; the cow was addressed as Aditi and a goddess (Macdonell, 1897: 150–51; Hopkins, 1915: 16).

24 In one place in the Rig Veda the poet urged that "the sinless inviolate cow" not be killed (Rig Veda, VIII, 101: 15–16; trans. in H. H. Wilson, 1866–88, 5: 210); in 16 different places the cow is designated as *aghnyā*, "not to be slain," and the corresponding masculine form *aghnya* occurs three times (Macdonell, 1897: 151). Some writers have argued that "not to be killed" simply reflects the economic importance of cattle (Hopkins, 1915: 16; Basham, 1954: 35).

25 | Rig Veda | Translation in H. H. Wilson, 1866–88 |
|---|---|
| I, 61, 12 | 1: 165 |
| II, 7, 5 | 2: 225 |
| VI, 16, 47 | 3: 414 |
| VI, 17, 11 | 3: 416 |
| VI, 28, 3–4 | 3: 439–40 |
| X, 27, 2 | 6: 67 |
| X, 28, 3 | 6: 74 |
| X, 89, 14 | 6: 248 |
| X, 91, 14 | 6: 257 |

26 Atharva Veda, VI, 70, 1; trans. in Bloomfield, 1897: 144.

27 Śatapatha Brāhmaṇa, III, 1, 2, 21; trans. in Eggeling, 1885: 11.

28 Atharva Veda, XI, 7, 7; trans. in Bloomfield, 1897: 226.

29 Dutt, 1893, 1: 166; Crooke, 1896, 2: 226.

30 | Śatapatha Brāhmaṇa | Translation in Eggeling |
|---|---|
| IV, 5, 1, 5–6 | 1885: 387 |
| IV, 5, 1, 11–12 | 1885: 388–89 |
| VI, 2, 13–18 | 1894: 165–66 |

31 Bloomfield, 1897: 656 and

Atharva Veda	Translation in Bloomfield, 1897
V, 18, 1–3, 7, 11	169–70
V, 19, 4–5	171
XII, 4	174–79

32 Dutt, 1893, 1: 166.

33 Śatapatha Brāhmaṇa, III, 1, 2, 21; trans. in Eggeling, 1885: 11.

34 Gautama Dharma Sūtra, X, 17–18; trans. in Bühler, 1896: 229.

35 Baudhāyana Dharma Sūtra, II, 2, 4, 17–18; trans. in Bühler, 1882: 236.

36 Vasiṣṭha Dharma Sūtra, IV, 8; trans. in Bühler, 1882: 27. Sāṅkhāyana Gṛhya Sūtra, I, 12, 10 and II, 15, 1–3; trans. in Oldenberg, 1886: 34, 87.

37 Āpastamba, I, 5, 17, 28–31; trans. in Bühler, 1896: 64.

38 Vasiṣṭha Dharma Sūtra, XIV, 30; trans. in Bühler, 1882: 73.

39 Gautama Dharma Sūtra, XXII, 18; trans. in Bühler, 1896: 285. Vasiṣṭha Dharma Sūtra, XXI, 18–22; trans. in Bühler, 1882: 113.

40 Institutes of Viṣṇu, V, 48; XLV, 19; trans. in Jolly, 1900: 29, 148.

41 Institutes of Viṣṇu, LI, 64; trans. in Jolly, 1900: 170.

42 Kauṭilya's Arthaśāstra, II, 26 and 29; trans. in Shamasastry, 1951: 135–36, 143–44.

43 Mahāvagga, VI, 23, 9–15; trans. in Davids and Oldenberg, 1882: 84–86.

44 Davids, 1903: 294–95; Ambedkar, 1948: 98–99.

45 Buddha was pushed in the direction of a more general prohibition of flesh food by certain of his followers, but this apparently did not involve beef to any greater extent than other flesh foods. Resisting pressures for a more general prohibition, Buddha expounded his famous principle permitting three pure kinds of flesh, a principle which has been tersely described as "unseen, unheard, and unsuspected." Fish and meat were permitted if the monk did not see the animal killed or hear the slaughter or suspect that it was done on his account (Mahāvagga, VI, 31, 14; trans. in Davids and Oldenberg, 1882: 117. And Kullavagga, VII, 3, 14–15; trans. in Davids and Oldenberg, 1885: 251–53).

In keeping with this principle, the Pātimokkha, one of the oldest Buddhist textbooks, declared that no monk should, when he is not sick, request for his own use and eat fish and flesh (Pātimokkha, Pākittiyā Dhammā, 39; trans. in Davids and Oldenberg, 1881: 40).

The followers of Buddha divided into two groups with respect to the use of flesh food: those who believed in the "gradual" acceptance of Buddha's teachings and who adhered to the "threefold pure" system described above, and those who believed in the "instantaneous" acceptance of the higher truths expounded late in Buddha's ministry, and who demanded a more thorough self-denial; some of the latter were so strict that they abstained not only from all types of flesh food but from milk and milk products as well (Watters, 1904–5, 1: 54–57).

46 Sometimes feasts were held which rivaled those of the ancient Germans in the number of animals slaughtered and quantity of alcohol consumed (Sanjana, 1946: 106). At the home of one Rantideva a thousand cattle are said to have been slaughtered daily.

Incidentally, some Indian doctors in the first century recommended eating beef for its medicinal value (*ibid.*, 106–7).

47 Laws of Manu, XI, 60, 109–17; trans. in Bühler, 1886: 442, 453–54.
48 Watters, 1904–5, 1: 178; Beal, 1958, 2: 143.
49 Basham, 1954: 120.
50 Though in India common cattle outnumber water buffalo by a ratio of 3.5 to 1, in most of mainland Southeast Asia the proportion of water buffalo is far higher, and in Burma they outnumber common cattle. Since people in Southeast Asia generally have similar attitudes toward both animals, and since many writers on the region use the word "beef" to refer to the flesh of both animals, the two types of flesh will not be distinguished in this section.
51 Fielding Hall, 1917: 230.
52 Landon, [1939]: 92.
53 Gourou, 1936: 428–29.
54 Crawfurd, 1830, 2: 268–69.
55 White, 1823: 253.

56 Orléans, 1894: 123.
57 Reinach, 1901, 1: 403–4.
58 There are references to beef use in modern Burma (Andrus, 1947: 54), Thailand (V. Thompson, 1941: 332–33), and Indochina (White, 1823: 253; E. Brown, 1861: 252; Reinach, 1901, 1: 180; League of Nations, 1937: 78; Andrus, 1943: 31; Janse, 1944: 6; Gourou, 1945: 236).
59 V. Thompson, 1941: 332–33.
60 de Young, 1955: 91–92.
61 Fielding Hall, 1917: 229.
62 Mi Mi Khaing, 1946: 86.
63 C. J. Richards, 1945: 42.
64 Landon, [1939]: 92.
65 Grist, 1936: 309, 311; Rosemary Firth, 1943: 71–72.
66 Williams-Hunt, 1952: 94.
67 Maxwell, 1881: 22.
68 Loeb, 1935: 166.
69 Featherman, 1885–91, 2: 402.
70 Roth, 1896, 1: 388.

Hose and McDougall say that the Sea Dyak will eat the flesh of cattle, but few of them like it because it is not a common meat for them (1912, 2: 90).
71 Kroeber, 1943: 84.
72 Common cattle are kept principally by farmers in Tibet. Nomads ordinarily keep only one bull for crossbreeding with their yak cows (Combe, 1926: 126). The crossbred animals, or *dzo*, are more docile than yaks, and the females give more milk than do yak cows (Bell, 1928: 53–54).
73 Combe, 1926: 127–28.

Unfortunately it is not clear whether by "cow" Combe refers in a general sense to all bovine animals or the females of all bovine species, to common cattle as a group or to their females.
74 Friters, 1949: 14.
75 Przhevalskii, 1876: 56.
76 Bell, 1928: 53–54.
77 H. Ramsay, 1890: 306.
78 Friters, 1949: 14.
79 Though bones of cattle have been found in Shantung and at Anyang in excavations of one north Chinese Neolithic culture, that of the black pottery people, it is not certain whether the cattle were domesticated or wild. It appears, however, that domestic cattle were kept in

eastern Chinghai, quite close to the Tibetan plateau, by contemporaries of the north China Neolithic people. Since it is generally believed that domestic cattle were introduced to China from some region to the west, the Neolithic people of eastern Chinghai probably represent one step in the diffusion of cattle into China. In any event, domestic cattle were numerous in north China in Shang times and were common sacrificial victims. The water buffalo seems to have come there from the south (Gibson, 1935: 344; Creel, 1937: 182–83, 188–89, 192–93, 244, 251; Creel, 1937a: 78–79).

80 The water buffalo is the most common bovine species in the south today, and common cattle in the north. Both are found not only among the Chinese population on the mainland and on Formosa (Yamasaki, 1900: 233; Grajdanzev, 1942: 68–69) but among various aboriginal groups, such as the Miao of the south (Moninger, 1921: 46; D. C. Graham, 1937: 20; Mickey, 1947: 23). A farmer generally had only one or two oxen or water buffaloes for plowing and for other heavy farm labor, and did not keep herds of animals for beef or dairy products.

81 Ekvall, 1939: 23.

82 M.C. Yang, 1945: 48–49.

83 *Ibid.,* 47–48.

84 Gamble, 1954: 281.

85 Griffis, 1882: 267, 269–70; Hulbert, 1906: 270–71.

86 Griffis, 269–70.

87 Osgood, 1951: 77.

88 Shirokogoroff, 1924: 130–31.

89 Lattimore, 1933: 31.

90 Galitzin, 1856: 148; Bush, 1871: 180; Lansdell, 1882: 301.

91 Batchelor, 1901: 108.

92 Keir, 1914: 817.

93 The ancient Zoroastrians of Iran, for example, had a ceremony in which the urine of the sacred bull was consecrated and employed in purificatory rites (A. V. W. Jackson, 1928: 197–98). The bull was also an important figure among the deities, or a companion of the deities, in Mesopotamia and adjacent areas. The Sumerians regarded it both as a kindly protector of the home and as a malevo-

lent storm demon; the one conception perhaps derived from the character of the domestic animal, the other from that of the wild bull (Hastings, 1908–22, 2: 888). The Hittites of Asia Minor worshiped the bull god as the guardian of the agricultural land. This concept and those of the Sumerians apparently were taken over, intermingled, and modified by other groups of the area. Thus the beliefs of the Sumerians were adopted by the Semitic Babylonians, who designated their divine bulls by words of Sumerian origin. Perhaps because bulls were associated with the supernatural, perhaps because they symbolized strength, colossal stone or metal statues of them were frequently built at the entrances of temples, houses, and gardens as protection from evil spirits. These and other bull figures were often given wings and, in Assyrian times, a human face (see Fig. 7). There are assertions in Mesopotamian history and legend that when the figures were destroyed or had departed the temple they guarded fell to the enemy.

Bull worship occurred among the Jews, whether introduced from Syria or from Egypt. Aaron, during the absence of Moses, set up a golden bull as an object of worship (Exod. 32:1–7) and a visible manifestation of the god who had brought them from Egypt. In later times Jeroboam erected images of bulls in the sanctuaries of the northern kingdom, Israel. These bulls were then worshiped—which was regarded as a great sin and an affront to Jahweh (I Kings 12:28–33; II Kings 10:29; Hosea 8:5–6, 10:5). The use of oxen or bull figures to support the famous brazen sea that was constructed in Solomon's temple (I Kings 7:25; II Chron. 4:4; Jer. 52:20) suggests a survival, at least in form, of the ancient belief in the sacredness of bulls. There are hints of a similarly supported sea in a Babylonian temple (Hastings, 1908–22, 2: 888), from which the Jews may have derived their inspiration.

The rise of anthropomorphic gods in western Asia meant that animals alone were no longer the objects of worship, though they continued to appear as companions of the human deities. The bull, for example, was designated the son of the storm god in western Asia, and the storm god was frequently pictured standing on the back of a bull. In the north of Syria, a center of worship of the storm god Hadad, the bull was sacred to the god. When this god was introduced to Rome, where he was known as Jupiter Dolichenus, he was depicted as standing on a bull, with a thunderbolt in one hand and a battle ax in the other (*ibid.*).

In ancient Egypt, from which Israel to some extent derived its religious inspiration, cattle were among the most important deities. There was the bull god Mnevis of Heliopolis, who was associated with the sun; the bull god Apis of Memphis, associated either with the sun or with the moon; and the cow goddess Hathor of Momemphis (see Fig. 4), who was called the Egyptian Venus and is believed to have been associated with the moon. The Egyptian bovine gods are thought to have been embodied in live animals, which were cared for and honored, and when they died were ceremonially buried amid great mourning. In some places in Egypt people kept animals which they regarded as sacred but not as incarnations of a god (Plutarch, *Isis and Osiris*, 33; Strabo, *Geography*, XVII.1.22, 31; Wilkinson, 1878, 3: 86-94, 115-18, 305-8; W. R. Smith, 1914: 302).

In ancient Greece the ox was an attendant or servant of Demeter (Varro, *On Farming*, II.5.4; Columella, *On Agriculture*, VI. Pref. 7); and at the ancient seat of Demeter worship at Eleusis near Athens sacred cattle were maintained (Varro, 1912: 183, n. 1). In addition, both bulls and cows were sacrificed in Greece, bulls usually to gods and cows to goddesses (Pausanias, *Description of Greece*, II.35.4; II.11.7; IV.32.3; V.16.2; VII. 22.7; VIII.19.1; IX.3.4; X.9.2). In Rome, too, bulls and oxen were sacrificed to the gods, bulls being the choicest of the victims (Pliny, *Natural History*, VIII.70; Varro, *On Farming*, II.5.10-11, and 1912: 189, n. 3).

94 Wilkinson, 1878, 2: 22; 3: 305-6; W. R. Smith, 1914: 302.

95 Porphyry, "On Abstinence from Animal Food," II.11.

96 Herodotus, *History*, II.18; IV.186.

97 Porphyry, "On Abstinence from Animal Food," II.11.

98 Varro, *On Farming*, II.5.4; Columella, *On Agriculture*, VI. Pref. 7.

99 Pliny, *Natural History*, VIII.70.180.

1 Varro, *On Farming*, II.5.11.

2 The Koran specifically permits beef to the faithful (5: 1; 6: 143-45).

3 R. C. Thompson, 1908: 210.

4 Drower, 1937: 37-38, 47-48.

It has been claimed that among the Druses of Lebanon there are survivals of the worship of the sacred calf. This is doubtful; if true, it is inconspicuous and limited to small numbers of people (Guys, 1863: 146-59). There is nothing to suggest the existence of an avoidance of beef among the Druses.

5 Great Britain Colonial Office, 1953: 32.

6 Johnston, 1910, 2: 623.

7 Huntingford, 1953a: 20-21, 80, 107.

8 Evans-Pritchard, 1940: 16.

9 Ratzel, 1896-98, 2: 414.

10 Huntingford, 1953: 27-28.

11 Schapera, 1953: 23.

12 Middleton, 1953: 19-20.

13 Herskovits, 1952: 174.

14 Schneider, 1957: 286-87.

15 Great Britain Colonial Office, 1953: 9.

16 Prins, 1952: 15, 56-57.

17 Gulliver and Gulliver, 1953: 98.

18 Huntingford, 1953: 27.

19 Westermarck, 1924, 2: 494.

20 Gulliver and Gulliver, 59.

21 Huntingford, 1953a: 20.

22 Tew, 1950: 103.

23 The Marille (Nalder, 1937: 150) and Bari of the Sudan (Huntingford, 1953: 27-28), the Pakot of Kenya (Schneider, 1957: 293), and certain peoples of southwest Ethiopia (Cerulli, 1956: 54) are examples of this tie between man and bull.

24 Some peoples, such as the Nuer of the Sudan (Huffman, 1931: 11-12), regard long, wide-spreading horns as most desirable, a preference which may have led to the preservation of such exceptionally long-horned breeds as the Galla or Sanga cattle (Fig. 5). Other groups, in a curious parallel with ancient Egyptian custom, train the horns of their cattle

into unusual shapes. The Nandi and the Suk of Kenya prefer one horn trained forward and the other backward; indeed, it is a social necessity for a Nandi man to possess such an animal at some time during his life (Huntingford, 1953a: 20–21, 80).

25 The pattern of consuming beef only when an animal dies naturally or on ceremonial occasions has been reported for the Nuba (Nadel, 1947: 517), Mondari (Huntingford, 1953: 59, 61), Nuer (Evans-Pritchard, 1940: 26), and Dinka (W. R. Smith, 1914: 297; Westermarck, 1924, 2: 330), the Swazi (Kuper, 1952: 28), Southern Sotho (Sheddick, 1953: 21), Ndebele (Hughes and van Velsen, 1954: 58), and Thonga (Junod, 1913, 2: 50), the Venda (Stayt, 1931: 39), Mbundu (McCulloch, 1952: 13; Hambly, 1934: 153), Herero (Hambly, 1937, 1: 356), Lugbara (Baxter and Butt, 1953: 120), and Ila (Smith and Dale, 1920, 1: 130), and on Madagascar for the Tanala (Linton, 1933: 49).

26 Linton, 1933: 49.

27 Refusal to slaughter has been noted for the Nilotic peoples (Ratzel, 1896–98, 2: 418), the Masai and Kamba (*ibid.*, 523), Ila (Smith and Dale, 1920, 1: 130), Hima (Wahuma) (Herskovits, 1926: 265), Venda (Hambly, 1937, 2: 594, 595), Giryama (Herskovits, 1926: 258), and Ganda (*ibid.*, 261).

28 Among the groups reported as eating beef are the Bari (Huntingford, 1953: 27–28), Mondari (*ibid.*, 59, 61), Nuer (Evans-Pritchard, 1940: 26), Nuba (Nadel, 1947: 67, 517), and Dinka (W. R. Smith, 1914: 297) of the Sudan; the Hima (Hutton Webster, 1942: 118), Lugbara (Baxter and Butt, 1953: 120), Jie (Schneider, 1957: 296), Pakot (*ibid.*, 289), Masai (Huntingford, 1953a: 107), Kikuyu (Routledge, 1910: 50; Middleton, 1953: 19), Turkana (Gulliver and Gulliver, 1953: 59), and Chagga (Gutmann, 1926: 39–40) of Kenya, Uganda, and Tanganyika; and the Ila (Smith and Dale, 1920, 1: 130), Venda (Stayt, 1931: 39–41; Hambly, 1937, 2: 594–95), Swazi (Kuper, 1952: 28), Lozi (Herskovits, 1952: 294), Ndebele (Hughes and van Velsen, 1954:

58), Sotho (Ashton, 1939: 160–61; Sheddick, 1953: 21–22), Zulu (Ratzel, 1896–98, 2: 415), Thonga (Junod, 1913, 2: 49–50), Mbundu (McCulloch, 1952: 13; Hambly, 1934: 153–54), Kuanyama Ambo (Hambly, 1937, 2: 594), and Herero (*ibid.*, 1: 356) of the southern parts of Africa.

29 Ratzel, 1896–98, 2: 415.

30 Gutmann, 1926: 378–79.

31 Huntingford, 1953a: 107, 109.

32 Hambly, 1934: 154.

33 Herskovits, 1952: 295.

34 Schneider, 1957: 293.

35 Cattle markets had become an important part of rural life in the British African territories about the mid-century, especially in East, Central, and South Africa; and tens of thousands of animals were sold annually in such markets in each country (Great Britain Colonial Office, 1953: 9–10). In the Nandi Reserve of Kenya there are now regular sales of breeding stock (*ibid.*). The Pojulu of the Sudan do not object to selling their animals, even though they have few of them (Huntingford, 1953: 68). The Teso of Uganda have established a large trade in cattle in recent years with the towns and heavily populated areas; in 1949, for example, they sold more than 2,400 cattle (Gulliver and Gulliver, 1953: 16). The Teita of Kenya, although they rarely sell animals, occasionally slaughter some in the local markets (Prins, 1952: 109). The Southern Sotho sell animals to livestock merchants and traveling meat venders when they need the money (Sheddick, 1953: 21); it was estimated that 76,000 cattle were eaten in Basutoland in 1937 (Ashton, 1939: 160–61). The Luena of Angola regularly butcher their animals and sell them for meat (McCulloch, 1951: 61). The Ndebele of Southern Rhodesia now fairly widely follow the practice of selling cattle, though conservative persons still object; many Ndebele cattle owners, indeed, regularly sell part or all of the natural increase of their herds (Hughes and van Velsen, 1954: 58). For the Tswana of southern Africa the sale of cattle and other types of livestock is the main local source of cash income (Schapera, 1953: 23).

36 Schneider, 1957: 289, 295.
37 Hambly, 1937, 1: 349.
38 Routledge, 1910: 50.
39 Schneider, 287–88, 292–93.
40 Among the groups reported as bleeding their cattle are the Konso of southern Ethiopia (Cerulli, 1956: 55), the Nuer of the Sudan (Evans-Pritchard, 1940: 27–28), the Turkana of Kenya (Gulliver and Gulliver, 1953: 59), the Ganda of Uganda (Ratzel, 1896–98, 2: 420), the Kikuyu of Kenya (Routledge, 1910: 174–75), the Ila of Northern Rhodesia (Smith and Dale, 1920, 1: 144–45; Verrill, 1946: 223), and the Antandroy of Madagascar (Verrill, 223).
41 Kipling, 1891: 117.
42 Hutton, 1946: 199–200; S. K. Das, 1953: 239–40.
43 Das, 239.
44 Ambedkar, 1948: 116–21.

Chapter 5—CHICKEN AND EGGS

1 Laufer, 1927: 254.
2 In his article on domestication Berthold Laufer (254–55) uses the terms "cock," "fowl," and "chicken" without distinction. The context suggests he means that the bones of both hens and cocks were important in divination but that the cock occupied a somewhat more exalted position; that perhaps only cocks, not chickens in general, were sacred— although this is not clear. Laufer says specifically, however, that cocks were kept as timekeepers.
3 H. I. Marshall, 1922: 281–82, 285.
4 Ratzel, 1896–98, 3: 434.
5 Featherman, 1885–91, 4: 39.
6 Gurdon, 1907: 48; Becker, 1924: 130.
7 H. I. Marshall, 1922: 284–85.
8 Fryer, 1909–15, 20: 68; Slater, 1918: 215; Fürer-Haimendorf, 1943, 2: 98.
9 In Indonesia the Javanese, Sumatrans, and Makasserese are enthusiastic about it (personal communication, Mr. Dyatmoko, Jogjakarta); and the Malays had a passion for it, too, though it was prohibited by the British (Dennys, 1894: 78–79).
10 Crawfurd, 1830, 2: 269.
11 Scott, 1910: 84.
12 Laufer, 1927: 255.
13 *Ibid.*
14 *Ibid.*, 254.

15 Hutton, 1921: 83.
16 Scott, 1910: 136–37.
17 Laufer, 1927: 251.
18 The groups eating chicken include:
   in INDIA: the Angami Naga (Hutton, 1921: 239, 240, 245), Khasi (Featherman, 1885–91, 4: 39), Chenchu of Hyderabad (Fürer-Haimendorf, 1943, 1: 75), Lushai of Assam (Shakespear, 1912: 80, 133), and Ho of Chota Nagpur (Majumdar, 1937: 26, 32);
   in SOUTHEAST ASIA and the PACIFIC ISLANDS: the Burmese (Andrus, 1947: 54), Karen of Burma (H. I. Marshall, 1922: 258–59), Miao of south China (Moninger, 1921: 46; D. C. Graham, 1937: 20–21), Thai (de Young, 1955: 99), Laotians (Reinach, 1901, 1: 180), Annamese (Gourou, 1936: 425), Malays (Rosemary Firth, 1943: 72) and most aborigines of Malaya (Williams-Hunt, 1952: 94), many peoples of Borneo (Roth, 1896, 1: 379–81, 426), the Bugi of Celebes (Featherman, 1885–91, 2: 446), Javanese (personal communication, Mr. Dyatmoko, Jogjakarta), Niasese (Loeb, 1935: 133), Batak of Sumatra (Loeb, 24–25), the people of Luzon, Cebu, and Mindanao in the Philippines (Rivera and McMillan, 1952: 212–13), those of Ifalik in the Caroline Islands (Spiro, [1949]: 7-8; E. G. Burrows, [1949]: 18), in Majuro village in the Marshall Islands (Spoehr, 1949: 150), and in Polynesia in such places as Pukapuka (Beaglehole and Beaglehole, 1938: 106), Futuna (E. G. Burrows, 1936: 133), Tubuai in the Austral Islands (Aitken, 1930: 38), Samoa (Pritchard, 1866: 126), Western Samoa (P. H. Buck, 1930: 119; Grattan, 1948: 87), and the Hawaiian Islands, where domestic fowls were eaten as early as the 18th century (J. Cook, 1784, 3: 141), and still are.
   Though chickens in some cases are killed specifically for food, more commonly they are slaughtered on ceremonial occasions. Among the aborigines in India the Khasi (Becker, 1924: 130-31), Lushai (Shakespear, 1912: 80, 133), and Angami Naga (Hutton, 1921: 246, 339) sacrifice them; the Reddi of Hyderabad consider chicken sacrifice necessary in almost all ceremonies and

religious rites (Fürer-Haimendorf, 1943,
2: 98); and the Ho of Chota Nagpur
sacrifice fowl to the spirits governing
the earth (Majumdar, 1937: 26, 32).
Similarly, the Karen of Burma slaughter
chickens to propitiate evil spirits (Ferrars, 1901: 150); the Annamese sacrifice them to spirits (Gourou, 1936:
425); the Niasese use them principally
for sacrifice (Loeb, 1935: 133); the
Sadang of Celebes use them as offerings
at feasts (Kennedy, 1953: 130); the
Bontoc Igorot of Luzon raise them only
for ceremonial consumption (Jenks,
1905: 110); the Ifugao kill fowl only
for sacrifice (Mead, 1955: 199); the
Tinguian of Luzon seldom kill them except for ceremonies (Cole, 1922: 412).

The use of eggs has also been reported widely in Southeast Asia and the
Pacific: in Burma (Ferrars and Ferrars,
1901: 91; Andrus, 1947: 54), though
some writers (Scott, 1910: 84; Boas,
1938: 303–4) say that eggs are seldom
used for food there; among the Miao
of south China (Moninger, 1921: 46;
D. C. Graham, 1937: 20–21); in Thailand (de Young, 1955: 99; V. Thompson, 1941: 333); in Malaya (Rosemary
Firth, 1943: 72); in Indochina (League
of Nations, 1937: 78; Gourou, 1945:
231); among the Laotians (Reinach,
1901, 1: 180); on Nias (Loeb, 1935:
133); among the Kenyah of Sarawak
(Hose and McDougall, 1912, 2: 65);
among the Land Dyak of Sarawak and
British North Borneo, though certain
groups of them do not permit young
men to eat eggs (Roth, 1896, 1: 379–
81, 388, 426); in the Philippines, where
they comprise an important part of the
food supply for the Tinguian of Luzon
(Cole, 1922: 412), and are a scarce
food for most other groups (Rivera and
McMillan, 1952: 212–13; Hart, 1954:
431); and on Ifalik, where chickens run
free, and since people do not know
where they have roosted, the eggs are
found and eaten only occasionally
(Spiro, [1949]: 7–8; E. G. Burrows,
[1949]: 18).
19 Sumner, 1906: 339; Seligman and Seligman, 1911: 178–80.
20 Skeat and Blagden, 1906, 1: 131, 134–
35.

21 Loeb, 1935: 24.
22 Gathering the eggs of the bush fowl
may be a survival of an ancient habit.
The Arunta aborigines of Australia, a
primitive hunting-gathering group, also
harvested the eggs of wild birds, especially the black swan and native goose;
in times of plenty they collected such
quantities of eggs that they carried on a
regular trade with less fortunate neighboring tribes (Basedow, 1925: 125).
23 Blackwood, 1935: 284.

On Tikopia in the Solomon Islands
domestic fowl are kept, but many people do not eat them (Rivers, 1914:
333); in Micronesia, too, some people
do not eat fowl (Sumner, 1906: 339).
Spiro reports chickens scarce on Ifalik
in the Caroline Islands and eaten in-
frequently; he says many people are not
especially fond of them ([1949]: 7–8);
E. G. Burrows holds chickens to be the
most numerous domestic animal on
Ifalik, and says their flesh is regarded
as a delicacy ([1949]: 18). In Polynesia the Samoans do not regularly
gather the eggs of their chickens and
profess to dislike them, though they eat
them occasionally (personal communication, Ward Barrett). On Pukapuka,
in the past, people probably left eggs
in the nest to hatch; even today they
rarely eat eggs, though they may occasionally give them as presents to visi-
tors (Beaglehole and Beaglehole, 1938:
106). On Futuna (E. G. Burrows,
1936: 133) and Tubuai (Aitken, 1930:
38) eggs are little used.
24 In addition to the restrictions associated
with fear of inhibiting fertility or childbirth, or fear of encouraging sexual deviation, there are those which apply to
particular prestigeful persons. Though
chicken flesh is the most common meat
of the Angami Naga, they prohibit both
the flesh and eggs to religious officials
responsible for ceremonies, and to others of high social status (Hutton, 1921:
91, 232, 339); among the Kedah Se-
mang, medicine men rarely eat the flesh
of fowl (Skeat and Blagden, 1906, 2:
226); and the Sow and some other
tribes of Sarawak forbid fowl to men,
though they permit women and children to eat them (Roth, 1896, 1: 389).

25 Williams-Hunt, 1952: 94.
26 Dê, [1951]: 4.
27 Vanoverbergh, 1936–38: 94.
28 Hutton, 1921a: 65, 95, 242.
29 Dube, 1951: 49.
30 W. C. Smith, 1925: 33, 113.
31 Hutton Webster, 1942: 118.
32 Crawfurd, 1830, 1: 408.
33 Ratzel, 1896–98, 1: 432; Renner, 1944: 73.
34 Jenks, 1905: 143.
35 Verrill, 1946: 211.
36 Hiralal, 1925: 64.
37 Cornell University, 1956, 1: 190.
38 Gangulee, 1939: 199.
39 Lawrence, 1895: 254; Modi, 1913–16: 480–81; Biscoe, 1922: 265.
40 Blunt, 1931: 96; Gangulee, 199.
41 Dubois, 1906: 282.
42 Majumdar, 1937: 26, 32.
43 Le May, 1930: 147.
44 Nāgarakṛtāgama, Zang 89; trans. in Kern, 1918: 107.
45 Heber and Heber, 1926: 96.
   Though Moslems in India generally do eat fowl and eggs, in the upper Indus Valley a nominally Moslem group, the Shin of Dardistan, have a horror of fowl and will neither touch nor eat them (Drew, 1875: 428; Ratzel, 1896–98, 3: 523–24; *Imperial Gazetteer,* 1909: 108).
46 Waddell, 1895: 225; Ekvall, 1939: 60; Bell, 1928: 53–54.
47 Ekvall, 60; Bell, 1946: 181; Kawaguchi, 1909: 605.
48 Bell, 1928: 233–34.
49 Ekvall, 60.
50 Combe, 1926: 128; Bell, 1928: 233–34.
51 Bell, 1946: 181.
52 Westermarck, 1924, 2: 325.
53 Przhevalskii, 1876: 56.
54 Creel, 1937a: 76.
55 Two principal ways of preserving eggs were followed: one enabled them to be kept for a few months without cold storage, one to be kept indefinitely. In the first method, eggs are "placed in strong brine for several days and then coated with a mixture of earth, salt, and chaff. On opening, the yolk and white have the general appearance of fresh eggs, but the yolks are almost solid and have a 'stale' odor. They are used either raw or for cooking in the same way as fresh eggs" (Ward, 1923: 188). In the second method, fresh eggs are soaked for three months or longer in an infusion of lime, salt, lye, and tea leaves; then they are drained, coated with a mixture of clay and other things, and aged further. The longer the aging, the more desirable the final product. Though they are known to some as "hundred-year eggs," actually most eggs of this type sold in China are only one to two years old. Eggs older than this are regarded as great delicacies, and are saved for important occasions. The contents of the eggs alter chemically in aging, as well as changing color and hardening; but they are very different chemically from eggs that have simply spoiled. Aged eggs are eaten raw and taste strangely different from any food used in the West. Nevertheless, acquiring this taste is probably no more difficult for a Westerner than it is for an adult Chinese to become fond of strong cheese. The taste does not seem to have spread beyond the areas of Chinese culture. In Japan, for example, aged eggs are found only among Chinese settlers and in Chinese restaurants.
   The Chinese also learned how to utilize the calcium contained in eggshells by dissolving the shells in vinegar and drinking the resulting solution.
   The Romans had a method of preparing eggs by soaking them in vinegar until the shell was soft (Pliny, *Natural History,* X.80; XXIX.11); such eggs were valued for certain medicinal purposes. Romans and Greeks also preserved eggs in the flour of beans, chaff, or bran (Paulus Aegineta, *Seven Books,* I.83). They do not appear to have known the Chinese methods of preserving eggs.
56 Cammann, 1951: 35.
57 Yamasaki, 1900: 233; Stanford University, 1956: 259.
58 Wiedfeldt, 1914: 9, 18, 133.
59 Shirokogoroff, 1924: 133.
60 Griffis, 1882: 267; Saunderson, 1894: 307–8; Van Buskirk, 1923: 1; Osgood, 1951: 77–78.
61 Norbeck, 1954: 72; Beardsley, Hall, and Ward, 1959: 201.
62 Hutton Webster, 1942: 333.

63 Dhalla, 1922: 185.
64 Hehn, 1885: 241–42.
65 Dhalla, 185.
66 *Hamlet*, I.1. 149–55.
67 Gregor, 1881: 140–41.
68 Dhalla, 187.
69 There are reports of chickens and eggs being eaten in Iran (Field, 1939: 350; Great Britain [Admiralty], Naval Intelligence Division, 1945: 352; Haas, 1946: 196), in al-Munsif village in Lebanon (Gulick, 1955: 41–42), in Jordan (Phillips, 1954: 131), in Syria (Simmons et al., 1954: 141), in Morocco (Westermarck, 1926, 2: 311; Coon, 1931: 41, 61); and in Yemen, where eggs are a rarity as a food but are sold in the market place (Heyworth-Dunne, 1952: 62). The Mandaeans of Iraq and Iran eat chickens and eggs, but elements of impurity cling to them. Thus eggs are never used as part of a ritual meal; and novice priests avoid them during the sixty-day "period of purity" when they are being consecrated (Drower, 1937: 48, 155).
70 Graves, 1927: 172–73.
71 Philby, 1952: 642.
72 Bertram Thomas, 1932: 59.
73 Philby, 642, 656–57, 661.
74 Thomas, 59, 79.
75 L. C. Briggs, 1958: 41, 90, 134–36.
76 Porphyry, "On Abstinence from Animal Food," IV.16.
77 *The Gallic War*, V.12.
78 Argenti and Rose, 1949: 113.
79 Bryant, 1949: 344–45.
80 Cerulli, 1956: 13.
81 Roscoe, 1923: 198, 210.
82 Steedman, 1835, 1: 254.
83 Speke, 1908: 44.
84 Trant, 1954: 704.
85 Salt, 1814: 179; Paulitschke, 1893: 157, 229; Lagercrantz, 1950: 41–42.
86 Sumner, 1906: 339.
87 Lagercrantz, 1950: 44.
88 Huntingford, 1955: 109.
89 Cerulli, 1956: 100, 113.
90 Schapera and Goodwin, 1950: 133–34.
91 Huffman, 1931: 14.
92 For ETHIOPIA, which may be the avenue by which chickens were introduced to Negro Africa, reports of such general avoidances occur for various Cushitic peoples but not for Semites. In the 19th century the Janjero, Danakil, Somali, and Galla all refused the flesh of chickens (Salt, 1814: 179; Paulitschke, 1893: 157, 229; Huntingford, 1955: 138). Where the Galla had chickens, they did not eat eggs but collected and gave them away (Paulitschke, 1893: 157). The Walamo, who still consider fowl sacred and eat them only at sacrifices, used to put to death anyone who violated the restrictions on eating them (Cerulli, 1956: 100, 113).
Restrictions on eating either chickens or eggs, or both, persist in Ethiopia even today, though they have broken down considerably. Many Galla, for example, still do not eat chicken flesh and eggs. Some Moslem Galla, such as those of Harrar, do eat them occasionally (Huntingford, 1955: 28; personal communication, Clarke Brooke); but more often, around Harrar, they sell their eggs to members of other ethnic groups (Clarke Brooke). There has also been a weakening of Somali feeling. Though noble Somali still will not eat poultry or eggs, they are probably less strict in this than formerly (I. M. Lewis, 1955: 74); Somali have been known to refuse even to use a pan in which a European traveler had cooked fowl (Hutton Webster, 1942: 334). In southern Ethiopia fowl are not kept in Eastern Sidamo (Smeds, 1955: 32); the Mekan and Bodi do keep them, but only ritual experts eat them (Cerulli, 1956: 50, 100); the Janjero will not eat eggs (Huntingford, 1955: 138). Elsewhere, however, most Ethiopians show no reluctance to keep or eat chickens and their eggs; in fact these are important and well-liked elements in the diet of the Amhara and other Semitic-speaking peoples.
For the SUDAN there are many reports of the avoidance of chickens or eggs. As in Ethiopia, the reports apply not to the Semitic-speaking peoples but to southern tribes, among whom the avoidance varies considerably in form. The Nuer tend to regard chickens as unclean scavengers, and are not fond of eating birds of any sort (Butt, 1952: 33); the men, moreover, avoid eating eggs, lest they be considered ef-

feminate (Huffman, 1931: 14). The Toposa do not eat eggs, and the Lokoiya rarely do (Nalder, 1937: 78, 117). The Kuku keep chickens but do not eat them (Huntingford, 1953: 44–45). Both sexes among the Makaraka eat chickens and eggs, as they apparently do among the Baka (Nalder, 1937: 186, 224). The Azande have been mentioned as using chickens as food (Casati, 1891: 211; Junker, 1892: 284), but they have few chickens today because of disease; they save the eggs for hatching, and eat chickens only after they have been used for divination (Baxter and Butt, 1953: 44).

EAST AFRICA: There are many reports of general or near general avoidance of fowl or eggs for East Africa. A generation ago the Kikuyu did not eat birds of any sort; and they did not keep fowl because, they said, the cocks' crowing would betray the location of their dwellings to raiding parties (Routledge, 1910: 49–50). Today among the Kikuyu proper, the Tharaka, and the northern tribes of Kikuyu-speaking people, no one eats eggs (Routledge, 1910: 50; Hutton Webster, 1942: 334; Middleton, 1953: 19). Among the Tharaka only uncircumcised children eat fowl. Their neighbors the Chuka do not eat fowl (Middleton, 1953: 19). The Masai do not eat either fowl or eggs (Huntingford, 1953a: 190), nor do the members of some Chagga clans (Raum, 1940: 188). The Hima refuse eggs (Westermarck, 1924, 2: 325). Nyoro farmers eat chickens and eggs, though the pastoralists do not eat them; the latter keep only a cock to wake them in the morning and a few other chickens for purposes of divination (Roscoe, 1923: 198, 210). The Nyamwezi of Tanganyika avoid eating eggs and poultry (Hutton Webster, 1942: 334).

In SOUTHERN AFRICA feeling against chickens and eggs is not as common as in East Africa. Among the Yao of Nyasaland, for example, chickens are a regular part of the diet (Stannus, 1922: 348). The Bemba of Northern Rhodesia have numerous chickens but value them so highly that they never kill them just for food. Chickens are presented to

honor a chief or important visitor, or used for important ceremonies. Each new brood of chicks is regarded as good fortune; hence eggs are used with reluctance (A. I. Richards, 1939: 63). The Ila-speaking peoples of Northern Rhodesia frequently use chickens for food (Smith and Dale, 1920, 1: 145). The Ndebele of Southern Rhodesia, though they often kill chickens for their flesh, which is used as a relish, do not eat eggs (Hughes and van Velsen, 1954: 59). The Sotho keep chickens for both flesh and eggs (Ashton, 1939: 161). Among the Bantu-speaking tribes of South Africa chickens are common scavengers and also serve for sacrifice, for exchange, or simply for food (Schapera and Goodwin, 1950: 140–41). Formerly, however, the Ngoni did not eat fowl (Earthy, 1933: 38); and in earlier times, the Zulu, too, did not regard fowl as fit for eating (Bryant, 1949: 290). Though the Manganja of Nyasaland and Mozambique do not eat eggs (Ratzel, 1896–98, 2: 508), the Tanala of Madagascar have numerous chickens, which comprise their principal fresh meat as well as being used for minor sacrifices and as payment for midwives, circumcisers, and native doctors; the eggs, moreover, are regarded as a delicacy (Linton, 1933: 51–52). In Angola the Mbundu keep chickens and esteem them for sacrificial purposes but do not usually eat their flesh (Hambly, 1934: 156). The Kuanyama Ambo of Southwest Africa "seldom eat chickens' eggs and never use them ceremonially," but they do kill and eat chickens (Loeb, n.d.: 255, 477).

In WEST and CENTRAL AFRICA, although there is some general avoidance of chickens and eggs, there also are many people who eat and relish both. For the Nupe of Nigeria chickens are the most important sacrificial animal and the most desirable food known; they are found in every house and in the markets of all the larger villages (Nadel, 1951: 204). In the Congo, on the other hand, people rarely eat eggs (Johnston, 1895: 294). The Negroes of the Loango coast north of the Congo River do not eat fowl for fear of losing their hair (Westermarck, 1924, 2: 332); and the Kalai (Kalay) of Gabon, though they have fowl, never eat them (Bowdich, 1819: 427). The tribes of Liberia eat chickens but do not appear to like the eggs (Johnston, 1906, 2: 998).

93 There is impressive documentation for the statement that women, especially of childbearing age, are singled out for avoidance customs.

In the SUDAN among the Pojulu, only men eat eggs (Huntingford, 1953: 68). Among the Kakwa both sexes eat chickens and eggs; but women of child-bearing age avoid eating chickens, and in one section all the women refuse eggs (Nalder, 1937: 213; Huntingford, 1953: 33, 53). Among the Nyangbara both sexes eat eggs, though women do not eat chicken (Nalder, 1937: 195; Huntingford, 1953: 72). Bari women do not eat chickens or eggs, though the men do (Nalder, 1937: 138). Lotuko women of childbearing age do not eat eggs, but all others do (ibid., 112). Kaliko women may not eat eggs (ibid., 184).

In EAST AFRICA the Lugbara of Uganda forbid eggs to women, lest they not bear children (Hutton Webster, 1942: 118); and they forbid chicken flesh to women, as well (Baxter and Butt, 1953: 121). The Teso of Uganda keep chickens in every homestead and sacrifice them in various ceremonies; yet they mainly forbid chicken flesh to women, and always forbid eggs to them —though the latter restriction may be relaxed for old women. Teso men enjoy chicken flesh but seldom eat eggs (Lawrance, 1957: 124, 147). Among the Ganda of Uganda only women are prohibited from eating eggs (Graubard, 1943: 85). Among the Lango of Uganda women are forbidden eggs (Driberg, 1923: 105). In Kenya, among the Bantu of North Kavirondo, men, and young girls under ten are permitted to eat chickens and eggs; women are not, and indeed consider it a disgusting and shameful thing for a woman to do. Even where Christian missions have been established the women still refuse to eat eggs, though a few Christian women have been persuaded with difficulty to abandon the avoidance of chicken flesh (Wagner, 1949–56, 1: 202–3; 2: 66, 74).

In SOUTHERN AFRICA, too, there are many cases of women being singled out in the avoidances. In Mozambique young Lenge women will not eat eggs, for fear of suffering if they have children (Earthy, 1933: 38). The Bantu-speaking tribes of South Africa believe eating eggs will make women lascivious (Schapera and Goodwin, 1950: 133). Among the Zulu, only the very young and the aged eat eggs (Hutton Webster, 1942: 334). In Angola the Mbundu formerly did not permit their women to eat eggs (Hambly, 1934: 285).

CONGO: In the Lower as well as the Upper Congo eggs are commonly "tabooed," says Comhaire-Sylvain, to expectant and suckling mothers and to children (1950: 61). Women of the Lele tribe in the Kasai region are forbidden to eat eggs and chicken, though the men may (M. Douglas, 1955: 5). Among the Yaka both chickens and eggs are forbidden to women (Johnston, 1910, 2: 614; Hutton Webster, 1942: 118).

WEST AFRICA: The Kpe (Bakwiri) of the Cameroons also forbid both to women (Hutton Webster, 1942: 334). The Kundu of the Cameroons forbid women the flesh of chickens, and forbid their eggs to men as well as women (ibid.). Some sections of the Tiv of Nigeria forbid eggs to women to assure successful childbirth, though women of other sections do eat them (East, 1939: 311–12). In northern Nigeria the Hausa forbid eggs to pregnant women (Meek, 1925, 1: 136); and the Kagoro do not allow women of childbearing age to eat chickens, though old women may (ibid.). In the Northern Territories of Ghana, chickens are kept in almost every compound and are the commonest sacrificial animals, but among most tribes adult women do not eat their flesh, nor do "first-born children in 'immigrant' clans" (Manoukian, 1952a: 22). The Tallensi of Ghana keep fowl for sacrificial purposes; at sacrifices the men eat the flesh; women and first-born children in some clans, on the other hand, refuse chicken and women will not even cook it for their men (Fortes and Fortes, 1936: 250, 272). The Ashanti of Ghana are said to forbid eggs, and people do not eat them (Westermarck, 1924, 2: 325–26; Hutton Webster, 1942: 334); R. S. Rattray mentions, however, that while Ashanti girls should not eat eggs before puberty, in their puberty rites they are given eggs to eat (1927: 73).

Additional African tribes who apply the egg prohibition to women are the Kwotto, Fulani in Keffi, Kunabembe, Lissel, Bomam, Besom, Bidjuk, Bjakum, Kabere, Ndzimu, Lakka, Pojulu (Fajelu), Karamojon, Soga, Rega, Bango-Bango, Ndali, Mambwe, Pondo, and Maka (Lagercrantz, 1950: 40–41).

Other peoples of Africa who have prohibitions against eggs, either general or applied to certain persons, include the Kissi, Gbande, Toma, Comendi, Khasonke, Ewe, Igara, Ibibio, Kundu, Batom, Mabum, Banjangi, Kossi, Fan (Pangwe), Vili (Fiote), Wadaians (Wadai), Reik Dinka, Agar Dinka, Anuak, Kuku, Ruanda, Haya (Ziba), Ha, Kafa (Kafitsho), Nandi, Mwimbe, Chuka, Embu, Emberre, Pare, Shashi, Sukuma, Vende, Rangi, Hehe, Bena, Bemba (Wemba), Nyamwanga (Winamwanga), Sena, and Lovedu (Lagercrantz, 1950: 39–40).

94 Hutton Webster, 1942: 118.
95 Stannus, 1922: 348; Tew, 1950: 8.
96 Nalder, 1937: 177; Baxter and Butt, 1953: 109.
97 Trant, 1954: 704.
98 Cerulli, 1956: 94.
99 Among the Bongo of the Sudan, for instance, only women eat fowl (Baxter and Butt, 1953: 131); among the Cape Nguni, men do not usually eat poultry, which they consider women's food (Schapera and Goodwin, 1950: 133–34); and among the Chopi of Mozambique, boys avoid eating eggs lest they fail their initiation rites (Earthy, 1933: 38).
1 Gangulee, 1939: 199.
2 Cornell University, 1956, 1: 190.
3 Lagercrantz, 1950: 42–44.
4 M. Leach, 1949–50, 1: 335.
5 Ibid., 1: 341.
6 Westermarck, 1926, 1: 581; 2: 311.

7 Massé, 1938: 48, 153.
8 Hutson, 1921: 2; Adolph, 1956: 69.
9 Lagercrantz, 1950: 44.
10 Drower, 1956: 8, 37–38.
11 The Mandaeans of Iraq and Iran think a death will occur in the household if an egg is given away after dark (Drower, 1937: 48).
12 Drower, 1956: 8, 38.
13 Blackman, 1927: 108.
14 Pliny, Natural History, X.77.
15 Lagercrantz, 1950: 42.
16 Nadel, 1951: 204.
17 Some African groups will eat eggs only if they are hard-boiled or fried (Lagercrantz, 1950: 41). The Bantu of North Kavirondo eat only hard-boiled eggs, and consider both soft-boiled and fried eggs disgusting (Wagner, 1949–56, 2: 66). The Luba of the Congo will eat boiled or fried eggs, but only after the hen has sat on them and they have been proved sterile (Lagercrantz, 1950: 41). The Lendu of the Congo reserve fresh eggs for old people, though ordinary people will eat bad eggs (Baxter and Butt, 1953: 126). The Tallensi of northern Ghana never eat fresh eggs, which they consider potential chickens, but their children like rotten eggs (Fortes and Fortes, 1936: 251). The Ila-speaking peoples of Northern Rhodesia seldom eat eggs, but when they do they apparently prefer the fetus to be well developed (Smith and Dale, 1920, 1: 145; Lagercrantz, 1950: 41). The Bontoc Igorot of the Philippines feed hard-boiled fresh eggs to their infants, but themselves eat stale eggs, and prefer eggs with "something in them" (Jenks, 1905: 143).
18 It is useful, in this connection, to note whether the groups having one of the avoidances more commonly avoid eggs or chickens. Summing up the references in preceding pages, we find that many groups eat chicken while restricting the use of eggs, whereas only a few use eggs freely while restricting the eating of fowl. There are examples of the former in both Africa and Asia. The Yao of Nyasaland eat fowl, but only children and old people eat eggs. The Ndebele of Southern Rhodesia eat chicken frequently but never eggs. The

Nupe of Nigeria prefer chicken to all other food, but do not market eggs and in certain sections do not eat them. The Moru of the Sudan keep chickens and eat them, but only very old men and women eat eggs (Nalder, 1937: 177). Among the Teso of Uganda men eat chicken but rarely eggs; women, though they are sometimes forbidden chicken flesh, are always forbidden eggs unless they are past childbearing. Among the Bantu of North Kavirondo in Kenya, who traditionally prohibit women, especially those of childbearing age, from eating either chicken or eggs, a few Christian women have been persuaded to eat chicken flesh—but they still refuse eggs. In Asia the Malayan aborigines keep chickens and eat them, but most groups do not eat eggs, and people may be gravely offended if asked for them. The Khasi of Assam consider chicken flesh a favorite food, but never touch fowl's eggs. And adult Bontoc Igorot in the Philippines, who eat fowl on ceremonial occasions, eat stale eggs, but will not eat fresh ones (Jenks, 1905: 110, 143).

Only two groups that we have examined use eggs while restricting the eating of chickens; both are in the Sudan. Among the Kakwa, except for one section, men and women eat eggs, but young women will eat chicken only after they have had a number of children. Nyangbara men and women eat eggs, but the women do not eat chicken.

Chapter 6—HORSEFLESH

1 Ratzel, 1896–98, 3: 329.
2 Jochelson, 1906: 262–63.
3 Sarytschew, 1806: 9; Dobell, 1830, 1: 307; Erman, 1850: 299, 309; Lansdell, 1882: 301.
4 Lansdell, 301.
5 *Ibid.*
6 Dobell, 1830, 1: 307.
7 Minns, 1913: 49, 85, 86.
8 Clavijo, 1859: 134, 139, 142.
9 Rae, 1881: 124.
10 Kler, 1947: 24.
11 Przhevalskii, 1876: 56; Howey, 1923: 201; Friters, 1949: 17.
12 Hehn, 1885: 36.
There are reports of horseflesh being eaten among the "Altaian Turks" (Altai

Tatars) (Great Britain Admiralty, n.d.: 143), the "Karachai Turks" (Karachai Tatars) (*ibid.,* 199), the Bashkir (Langkavel, 1888: 51), the pagan tribes of Chuvash of the Volga region in southeast Russia (Featherman, 1885–91, 4: 515–16; MacCulloch, 1916–32, 4: 46), the Cheremis of Perm (Molotov) (MacCulloch, 4: 55, 57), the Crimean and Nogay Tatars (Featherman, 4: 212, 222), the Kazakh (Kirghiz-Kazakh) (*ibid.,* 4: 255–56), the Minusinsk Tatars (*ibid.,* 4: 228), and the Lapps (*ibid.,* 4: 447).
13 M. S. Stevenson, 1930: 6; G. W. Briggs, 1920: 45.
14 Crooke, 1896, 2: 207.
15 Mahāvagga, VI, 23, 11; trans. in Davids and Oldenberg, 1882: 85.
16 Hermanns, 1949: 163.
17 Combe, 1926: 127–28, 163.
18 It is generally believed that the horse was introduced to ancient China from the west, but the date is unknown. The Shang people of north China kept domesticated horses, and probably also hunted wild horses; they used horses to pull chariots and for sacrificial purposes. Thus they may also have eaten horseflesh (Sowerby, 1935: 234, 237; Gibson, 1935: 344; Creel, 1937: 182–83, 191, 193; Creel, 1937a: 76, 149–54, 200).
19 L. H. Buxton, 1929: 81; Yetts, 1934.
20 Eberhard, 1942: 16.
21 Burton, 1948: 201; Hahn, 1896: 195.
22 Batchelor, 1901: 198.
23 Burkill, 1935, 1: 1197.
24 Horse sacrifice has been recorded on Sumatra (Hutton, 1946: 202). Horseflesh is scarce among the Javanese but is esteemed as food (Featherman, 1885–91, 2: 368). In the Philippines the Bukidnon of Mindanao eat the flesh of decrepit horses (Cole, 1956: 56); the Bisayans of Barrio Caticugan on Negros eat horseflesh, but will kill horses only when they are very old, injured, or sickly (Hart, 1954: 427); the Igorot of Luzon keep horses and use them for food (Ratzel, 1896–98, 1: 431; Jenks, 1905: 107–8); and the Ifugao of Luzon eat horseflesh (Barton, 1922: 416).
25 Philby, 1928: 45.
26 T. P. Hughes, 1885: 130.
27 Herklots, 1921: 315.

28 The tenth-century Persian doctor Avicenna included horseflesh in his classification of foodstuffs and mentioned that it was very nutritious (Gruner, 1930: 219). In modern Iran horsemeat is recorded as a remedy for colic (Massé, 1938: 341). Curiously, Arabs not far from the birthplace of Islam have been reported as eating horseflesh (Hahn, 1896: 195).
29 Jochelson, 1928: 112.
30 Huntingford, 1955: 109; Cerulli, 1956: 19.
31 Nadel, 1947: 189.
32 Langkavel, 1881: 659.
33 Meek, 1925, 1: 136; Gunn, 1956: 28.
34 Bascom, 1951: 42.
35 Gunn, 1956: 71, and 1953: 80.
36 Temple, 1922: 46.
37 Gunn, 1956: 28.
38 Ardener, 1956: 47–48.
39 Ashton, 1939: 161.
40 Hahn, 1896: 195.
41 W. R. Smith, 1908: 367.
42 London Times, Jan. 25, 1868: 6.
43 Hehn, 1885: 37; Howey, 1923: 72.
44 Hahn, 1896: 195.
45 Hehn, 1885: 37.
46 Howey, 1923: 190.
47 De Paor and De Paor, 1958: 89.
48 Graves, 1957: 74.
49 Burton, 1948: 201.
50 Graves, 74.
51 Fernie, 1899: 250–51; Drummond and Wilbraham, 1940: 364.
52 Fernie reports that the people of Cleckheaton, West Yorkshire, formerly ate horseflesh, which was called "kicker," and that in Leeds they were disapprovingly referred to as "kicker eaters" (1899: 250). He does not mention whether this preceded or followed the introduction of chevaline in London.
53 London Times, Feb. 11, 1868: 7.
54 Drummond and Wilbraham, 364–65.
55 For example, the Harvard Faculty Club served horsemeat during World War II (Bates, 1957–58: 452).
56 Gerard, 1952: 254.
57 Reich, 1935: 211.
58 Personal communication, Hugh Iltis.
59 Personal communication, Alicja Iwanska.
60 Pegasus was a symbol sacred to the Carthaginians in classical times (W. R. Smith, 1914: 293–94); and in much of the ancient world the horse was associated with the gods. The association with the Sun God, to whom horses were commonly sacrificed, may have come from Iran; the Medes, Bactrians, Persians, and Massagetae (Herodotus, History, I.215; VII.60, 113; Strabo, Geography, XI.6; Hehn, 1885: 45–48) all regarded horses as the swiftest of animals and held them sacred—especially white ones. In Judah, too, the horse was sacred to the Sun God. Horses were sacrificed to him in Rhodes (W. R. Smith, 1914: 293–94); among the Spartans (Hehn, 1885: 54); and apparently among the Armenians (Xenophon, Anabasis, IV.5.35). The medieval Slavs worshiped the horse and dedicated a white horse to the God of Light and a black one to the Evil One, and the Germans had a cult of the horse similar to that of Iran (Tacitus, Germania, 10).

In ancient India the horse was prized and worshiped by the Aryans and sacrificed on certain religious occasions (Dutt, 1893, 1: 41–42; Crooke, 1896, 2: 204). Similar practices are still found in modern India, particularly in the northwest, which was most influenced by the Aryan invasion and was presumably the spot where horses and horse worship were first introduced from inner Asia. The aboriginal Bhil of that region are said to venerate the horse more than any other animal (Hutton, 1946: 19), and some "Rajput Bhil" worship a stone horse (Crooke, 2: 208). The Gond aborigines of Kodapen in south India honor a horse god at the beginning of the rainy season by worshiping a stone, by offering a pottery image of a horse, and by sacrificing a heifer (ibid.). The non-Hindu Garo of the Assam Hills sacrifice horses as part of a fertility rite (Hutton, 1946: 202). Though the custom of horse sacrifice is not followed by orthodox Hindus, various Hindu castes still persist in the view that the horse is pure and has the power to cleanse and to bestow luck. When a cooking pot has become impure, a usual way to cleanse it is to have a horse smell it. In northern India it is considered auspicious to have a horse and rider enter a field of sugar cane; and in the Deccan people believe that evil spirits will not approach a horse (Crooke, 2: 207).

Chapter 7—CAMEL FLESH

1 Fryer, 1915, 3: 141; Massé, 1938: 143.
2 Donaldson, 1938: 85.
3 In spite of the close association of camel sacrifice and Islam, we must look beyond Islam for the origin of the practice, for it was already common in pre-Islamic Arabia (Hastings, 1908–22, 3: 173; Henninger, 1948: 10).
4 Westermarck, 1926, 2: 290, 291.
5 Massé, 1938: 143.
6 Ibn el-Beïthar, 1877: 292, 368–70.
7 E. C. Sykes, 1910: 245.
8 Twitchell, 1953: 20.
9 Musil, 1928: 97; Raswan, 1947: 77.
10 Robinson, 1936: 55; Platt and Hefny, 1958: 189.
11 Hrdlička, 1912: 12.
12 L. C. Briggs, 1958: 32.
13 Central Asian Moslems eat camel flesh (Lattimore, 1929: 161); the Kazakh (Kirghiz-Kazakh) consider it a valuable food (Featherman, 1885–91, 4: 257); the Turkomans of Turkestan regard it as a dainty (Jochelson, 1928: 94–95). In the Sudan, the Kababish slaughter camels for food on important ceremonial occasions such as weddings (Seligman and Seligman, 1918: 151; Hambly, 1937, 1: 383), and the people of Kordofan eat camel flesh on ceremonial occasions (Hambly, 1935: 471). In Nigeria camels are slaughtered for both sacrifice and food (Robinson, 1936: 56), but the flesh is forbidden to Hausa women when they are pregnant, because it is believed to injure the unborn child or to make the woman barren (Meek, 1925, 1: 136). The camel has long been known in northeast Africa and has gradually spread southward until today it is found in the arid parts of Kenya. As early as 1330 Ibn Batuta described the Somali town of Berbera as filthy with the blood of camels that people slaughtered for food (Robinson, 1936: 56); and among the Somali of today the flesh is a highly prized staple (I. M. Lewis, 1955: 68, 74).
14 It has been reported that camels are now bred for food by the tribes on the shores of Lake Rudolf (Robinson, 1936: 65); that though the camel is a fairly recent introduction among the Turkana, it is used in bride price payments and other compensation, and its flesh is eaten (Gulliver and Gulliver, 1953: 60); and that the Pakot of Kenya sometimes substitute a camel for a steer in a ritual feast, in spite of camels not being so highly esteemed or having the same ritual status (Schneider, 1957: 291). The rejection of camel flesh by the pagan Katab of northern Nigeria (Gunn, 1956: 71) may be from unfamiliarity or in negative reaction to Islamic ways—but the latter is a rather rare phenomenon among the pagan groups of this area.
15 Leviticus, 11: 4.
16 Dussaud, 1900: 94.
17 W. R. Smith, 1908: 367.
18 Nweeya, 1910: 241.
19 Drower, 1937: 47–48.
20 Dussaud, 94.
21 Robinson, 1936: 55.
22 L. C. Briggs, 1958: 132–33.
23 Parkyns, 1868: 291–92; Reale Società Geografica Italiana, 1936: 256.
24 Trimingham, 1952: 162–63.
25 Thompson, 1908: 210.
26 Graves, 1927: 280.
27 G. W. Briggs, 1920: 45.
28 Przhevalskii, 1876: 56, 129; Lattimore, 1929: 160, 162.
29 Lattimore, 162.

Chapter 8—DOGFLESH

1 *Wisconsin State Journal,* Aug. 11, 1959: 3.
2 Personal communication, Judge Charles W. Iben.
3 Dog eating was also widely practiced by Indians in the New World; reports occur in Maine, for the Iroquois of New York, along the Upper Missouri River, for groups in the West and South of the United States, in Mexico, Nicaragua, the Antilles, and Peru (Humboldt, 1811, 3: 47; Humboldt, 1850: 85–86; Langkavel, 1881: 658; G. M. Allen, 1919–20: 454, 461, 468–69, 483, 489–90; Lowie, 1940: 39; Driver and Massey, 1957: 181–82).
4 Lindeman, 1906: 16–32; Fortes and Fortes, 1936: 249.

5 Schweinfurth, 1873, 1: 393-94.
6 Johnston, 1910, 2: 614-15.

In addition to the groups mentioned in the text, dog eating has been reported for the peoples of many parts of interior Liberia (Johnston, 1906, 2: 1000); in Nigeria among the Bedde, Chamba, Ngamo (Gamawa), and Bassa (Temple, 1922: 46, 61, 81, 110), the Pyem of Gindiri District of the Central Plateau (Gunn, 1953: 102), the Afusare of Bauchi (*ibid.*, 66), the Warjawa (Gunn, 1956: 28), and the Yoruba (Bascom, 1951: 42). To the east of Nigeria along the Sudan belt the Baghirmi like and use dogflesh (Nachtigal, 1874: 324, 329). Dog eating has also been mentioned in general terms for the Cameroons (Langkavel, 1881: 659), as well as for the Fia and Yambasa of that country, though some people in the Cameroons today are reluctant to kill dogs (Dugast, 1954: 158). There are many references to the eating of dogflesh in the Congo Basin and Angola: among the Banziri (Sumner, 1906: 339), Azande (Casati, 1891: 213-14; Junker, 1891: 305; Ratzel, 1896-98, 3: 81), Mangbetu (Peschel, 1906: 163), Ngala (Baumann, 1887: 173; Johnston, 1910: 614-15), Bunda (Kroll, 1928: 193), Yanzi (Baumann, 1887: 170), Luchazi (McCulloch, 1951: 62); among the Kwangari (Ovakwangari), who "seem" to eat it (Kroll, 1928: 193); the Ambo, who eat it sacrificially and as food (Dornan, 1933: 632; Loeb, n.d.: 256-57, 476); and the Mbundu, who consider it desirable food (Hambly, 1934: 155).

7 Exceptions are the Sango of Tanganyika (Kroll, 1928: 193), who apparently slaughter dogs for their flesh, and the Negroid Berta of the Ethiopian borderlands, who will eat any kind of flesh, including dogs (Cerulli, 1956: 19).
8 Kroll, 1928: 193.
9 Ratzel, 1896-98, 2: 415.
10 Driberg, 1923: 96.
11 Evans-Pritchard, 1932: 44-46; Frazer, 1935, 4: 16-17.
12 Cerulli, 1956: 26, 33.
13 The importance of dogs for the Koma and the people of Fazogli recalls Pliny's statement that the Ptoemphani, a Su-

danese group, had a dog as king and deciphered his commands from his movements (*Natural History,* VI.35). The high position of the dog among the Koma today is paralleled among various other groups of the region. The Sakalava of Madagascar are said to esteem dogs highly, and almost to worship them (Dornan, 1933: 620). The Kuku of the Sudan believe that dogs taught them to grind cereals, to use herbs for seasoning, to use fire for cooking, and explained to them the process of childbirth; people honor them and treat them well, as benefactors to the tribe (Huntingford, 1953: 44). The people of Dahomey regard the dog as sacred to the god Legba, and are pleased to see a dog eat the food that has been offered to the deity (Herskovits, 1938: 229).

14 Bowdich (1819: 429) however wrote that the Paämway (Mpongwe?) of Gabon early in the nineteenth century raised a breed of large dogs for eating.
15 Castrating dogs has been reported for the Ekoi, Banjangi, Yaunde, Bunda, Chewa (Kroll, 1928: 192), and for the Kuanyama Ambo (Loeb, n.d.: 256-57).
16 Fattening dogs has been reported for the Azande (Casati, 1891: 213-14; R. G. Anderson, 1911: 274), the peoples of the western Upper Congo (Johnston, 1910, 2: 614-15), and the Luchazi of Northern Rhodesia and Angola (McCulloch, 1951: 62).
17 Kroll, 1928: 192-93.
18 These reports are for the Birom of the Central Plateau of Nigeria (Gunn, 1953: 80) and for the Ambo of Angola (Dornan, 1933: 632).
19 Junker, 1891: 305.
20 Johnston, 1895: 294.
21 Hambly, 1934: 155.
2 The Tallensi of Ghana sacrifice dogs on special occasions such as the New Year festival (Fortes and Fortes, 1936: 249). The Baghirmi people of Chad slaughter them on the conclusion of peace (Dornan, 1933: 631). The Yoruba of Nigeria sacrifice a dog twice a year to Ogun, patron of blacksmiths and god of war, and then hang the dog's head, symbol of the sacrifice, conspicuously in the blacksmith's shop (Ham-

bly, 1935: 408, 465). The Tiv of Nigeria sometimes sacrifice a dog, and then give the body to the Utanje, a bush tribe, to eat, for the Tiv themselves are not dog eaters (East, 1939: 274). After a youth has served his apprenticeship and is about to be inaugurated as a blacksmith among the Mbundu of Angola, a dog is slaughtered and its blood spread on the tools in order to consecrate them (Hambly, 1935: 407). The Ambo of southern Angola and Southwest Africa sacrifice a dog in ceremonies involving witchcraft, sickness, or misfortune of any sort; some of the flesh of the sacrificed animal is eaten by the patient, and the rest by his relatives (Dornan, 1933: 632). And the Shona of Southern Rhodesia sacrifice a specially fed black dog at the time of sowing to encourage rain to fall on the crops (*ibid.*, 631).

23 Dornan, 1933: 630.

24 Frazer, 1935, 10: 4.

25 Fortes and Fortes, 1936: 272.

26 Gunn, 1953: 66.

27 Among the Lange of the southwest Congo, for example, only the western groups will eat dogflesh; hence they are known as Baschilambua, or "dog people" (Kroll, 1928: 193). There are further references to group avoidance of dogflesh for the Birom of the Bachit area (Gunn, 1953: 80), the Bolewa (Temple, 1922: 68), the Katab (Gunn, 1956: 70–71), and the Tiv in Nigeria (East, 1939: 274); the Sokoro and Bua of the Sudan borderlands (Nachtigal, 1874: 324, 329); the Kpe of the Cameroons (Ardener, 1956: 47–48); the Bubi of Fernando Po (Kroll, 1928: 193); the Kongo and Songo (*ibid.*), and Bango (Bobango) and Soko (Comhaire-Sylvain, 1950: 61) of the Congo and Angola; and apparently the Twa (Batwa) Pygmies of the northwestern Luba country (Johnston, 1910, 2: 507).

28 The South African Bantu-speaking tribes, for example, never eat or sacrifice dogs (Schapera and Goodwin, 1950: 141; Dornan, 1933: 632). The Tanala of Madagascar consider the idea of eating dogs disgusting (Linton, 1933: 48). The Nandi of Kenya sacrifice dogs on special occasions, but throw them into the bush rather than eat them (Dornan, 1933: 631). In Uganda the Karamojon, Jie, and Dodos prohibit dogs as food (Gulliver and Gulliver, 1953: 35); and the Lendu, who live nearby in the Congo, never eat dogflesh (Baxter and Butt, 1953: 126). In Ethiopia dogflesh is strongly rejected by Semites, Cushites, and most Negroes; in the Sudan, neither Nuba (Nadel, 1947: 189), Bongo (Peschel, 1906: 159), nor Dinka eat it.

29 Comhaire-Sylvain, 1950: 61.

30 Gunn, 1956: 28.

31 Kroll, 1928: 193.

32 Bryant, 1949: 290.

33 Schweinfurth, 1873, 1: 158–59.

34 Creel, 1937: 182–83, 210; 1937a: 76–77.

35 Vesey-Fitzgerald, 1957: 39.

36 Verrill, 1946: 208.

37 *China Post,* Jan. 27, 1960.

38 Personal communication, John Street.

39 Personal communication, Prof. Lin Lin.

40 Kinmond, 1957: 163–65.

41 Griffis, 1882: 267–69; Saunderson, 1894: 308; Hulbert, 1906: 21, 26; Keir, 1914: 817; Kang, 1931: 107–9; Osgood, 1951: 77–78.

42 Personal communication, John D. Donoghue.

43 Langkavel, 1881: 659; Jochelson, 1905–8: 519–20; Shinichirō, 1960: 13, 14.

44 Bogoras, 1904–9: 101.

45 Seeland, 1882: 110.

46 Hawes, 1903: 259.

47 Jochelson (1904–8: 519–20) says the Koryak throw the carcasses away; Bogoras (1904–9: 101) implies that they eat dogflesh, though he may be referring only to times of famine.

48 A traveler reported seeing two Lisu tribesmen driving a dozen dogs from China to northeast Burma to sell for their flesh (Kingdon-Ward, 1949: 218). That this is not an isolated case is suggested by the wooden yokes some of the dogs wore, apparently to facilitate controlling them. In Burma and Assam dog eating has been reported for various aboriginal groups, including the Chin (C. J. Richards, 1945: 52), Garo (Featherman, 1885–91, 4: 82; Gurdon, 1904: 58; Gurdon, 1907: 51), Kuki (Gurdon, 1907: 51), Lushai (Shake-

spear, 1912: 32, 36), Abor (Elwin, 1959: 285), and the Lhota (*ibid.*), An-gami, and Sema Naga.

49 Hutton, 1921: 81, 100.

50 Hutton, 1921a: 69, 71, 104, 123.

51 These include the Pani-Kocchi (Featherman, 1885–91, 4: 21), Bodo (Kachari) and Dhimal (*ibid.*, 4: 26), Khasi (Gurdon, 1904: 58; Gurdon, 1907: 51), Synteng (Gurdon, 1904: 58), and Lynngam (Gurdon, 1907: 195).

52 Elwin, 1959: 182.

53 Westermarck, 1924, 2: 332.

54 Ferrars and Ferrars, 1901: 89; C. J. Richards, 1945: 52.

55 Mahāvagga, VI, 23, 12–13; trans. in Oldenberg, 1886: 85.

56 Scott, 1910: 83; Fielding Hall, 1917: 244; C. J. Richards, 1945: 41–42.

57 *New York Times*, Sept. 16, 1959: 5.

58 Scott, 1910: 83, 542–43.

59 *Wall Street Journal*, July 23, 1959: 9.

60 Baudesson, [1919]: 105–6.

61 Langkavel, 1898: 673–74; Koppers, 1930; Kretschmar, 1938, 1: 170–92, 212.

62 Hutton, 1946: 225.

63 *Ibid.*, 225–26.

64 Frazer, 1935, 11: 222–23.

65 Crooke, 1896, 2: 222.

66 League of Nations, 1937: 78.

67 Gourou, 1936: 426–27.

68 Nāgarakṛtāgama, Zang 89; trans. in Kern, 1918: 107.

69 On Sumatra, for example, most Batak aboriginals still fatten dogs and eat them (Langkavel, 1881: 659; Featherman, 1885–91, 2: 321; Hahn, 1896: 71; Loeb, 1935: 24–25; personal communication, Mr. Dyatmoko, Jogjakarta). On Java, Chinese settlers eat dogflesh to some extent, as do non-Moslem immigrants from Celebes (Mr. Dyatmoko), and an exceptional Hollander (Hahn, 1896: 71). On Celebes such non-Moslem groups as the Sadang (Kennedy, 1953: 43, 130) and the Minahasa (Mr. Dyatmoko) still eat dogmeat, as do a few other Indonesian peoples.

On Buru and Aru islands in the Moluccas men eat dogflesh to aid them in becoming brave and quick in war (Frazer, 1935, 8: 145). On Borneo some Dyak eat it (Langkavel, 1881: 659; Ratzel, 1896–98, 1: 431; Roth, 1896, 1:

390, 425). The Kenyah, on the other hand, believe killing a dog would cause a man to go insane (Hose and McDougall, 1912, 2: 70–71). The Klemantan of Borneo are afraid to kill dogs, though one group of them will sometimes slaughter a dog ceremonially, or simply cut off its tail; in the latter event, a man who is taking an oath licks blood from the stump of the tail, an act which makes a solemn and binding oath and is known as "the eating of the dog" (*ibid.*, 2: 80).

70 Verrill, 1946: 209.

71 Malcolm, 1951: 57.

72 Jenks, 1905: 142–43, 110–11.

73 Vanoverbergh, 1936–38: 206; L. L. Wilson, 1947: 11.

74 Barton, 1922: 416.

75 Jenks, 142.

76 In Melanesia and Micronesia dog eating has been reported for (1) the Roro-speaking tribes of New Guinea (Seligman, 1910: 230, 257); (2) the southern Massim of New Guinea, except for members of the Elewa clan, for whom the dog is a totemic animal and who feed dogs the same food they themselves eat (*ibid.*, 450, 454, 455); (3) Rossel Island, southeast of New Guinea, where dogs are eaten at feasts (Armstrong, 1928: 19); (4) the Biara of New Britain, who regard dogflesh as a delicacy, though it is a luxury which they rarely obtain (Featherman, 1885–91, 2: 47); (5) the people of Kambara in the Fiji Islands, where dogs were eaten formerly (L. Thompson, 1940: 141); and (6) the people of Ifalik in the Caroline Islands, who eat dogs occasionally (Burrows, [1949]: 18). It is said, moreover, that though the Papuans of the Trans-Fly region of New Guinea regard the eating of dogs with abhorrence, certain groups of them—the Kaunje and Gambadi—formerly ate dogflesh (Williams, 1936: 420). The people of Sa'a village on Marmasike Island and those of Ulawa Island in the southeast Solomons have been reported as sacrificing dogs (Ivens, 1927: 241, 405); it is not stated whether they eat the flesh.

77 Renner, 1944: 74; Smyth, 1878: 148–49.

78 The Tasmanians, it is true, had no dogs

before the Europeans introduced them, but the Australian aborigines captured and tamed the wild dingo (Smyth, 1878: 147; Basedow, 1925: 118).

79 Roth, 1890: 123; Smyth, 1878: 147–48.

However strange it may seem to us, the practice of suckling dogs has been widely reported: among the Malayan aborigines (Williams-Hunt, 1952: 94), the people of Engano Island near Sumatra (Loeb, 1935: 211), in Upper Burma, New Guinea, the Society Islands, Tahiti, Hawaii, as well as among the Paumari in Peru, and in the Gran Chaco in South America (Langkavel, 1898: 654).

80 Dogs were not present on Easter Island, Manihiki, Rakahanga, Mangareva, Rapa, or in the Tuamotu and Marquesas islands (P. H. Buck, 1932: 83; 1938a: 155, 175, 189, 212, 310, 312).

81 Dog eating occurred, among other places, in Tahiti, Hawaii (Cook, 1784, 3: 141), Futuna (E. G. Burrows, 1936: 133), Samoa (Pritchard, 1866: 126; P. H. Buck, 1930: 127), and New Zealand. That it was regarded as respectable is shown by the assertion that on Futuna dogmeat was served to guests, and that on New Zealand (Tregear, 1904: 105, 167, 172) the Maori priest generally ate it.

82 J. Cook, 1955: 102–3, 121–22, 262, 506; Corney, 1915: 287-88.

83 P. H. Buck, 1950: 110–11.

84 Pritchard, 1866: 126; P. H. Buck, 1930: 127.

85 Sorokin, 1942: 77; Fedenko, 1951: 41.

86 The needy weavers in Gerhart Hauptmann's play, *Die Weber*, whose setting was the Sudetenland in the 1840's, ate dogflesh, but not without qualms (Hauptmann, 1951: 28–29).

87 G. M. Allen, 1919–20: 461, 490.

88 In the Graeco-Roman world, the dog occupied an ambiguous position. Dogs were not permitted to enter the Athenian Acropolis or the island of Delos (Plutarch, *The Roman Questions*, 111), and were never sacrificed to the Olympian gods. The priest of Jupiter in Rome avoided dogs and neither mentioned them nor touched them. Plutarch explains that the priest was the embodiment and sacred image of the god, a refuge for petitioners and suppliants, and that if dogs were present they might frighten people away (*ibid.*). Once each year the Romans crucified dogs in punishment for some wrong dogs had done the city (Pliny, *Natural History*, XXIX.14). One might conclude that this animal was not highly regarded by the Greeks and Romans. Yet it was looked on as the faithful friend of man; and Pliny (VIII.61) wrote of dogs in terms that would warm the heart of the modern dog lover. The Greek goddess Hecate was pictured in the company of mad dogs and liked to be addressed by the name "dog" (Dornan, 1933: 630). That the Greeks sacrificed dogs to certain deities, such as Hecate, indicates that it was thought to be an animal acceptable to them. The Spartans considered it appropriate to sacrifice the bravest of animals to the war god Enyalius, the bravest of the gods (Plutarch, *The Roman Questions*, 52, 68, 111). The Boeotians and Argives of Greece sacrificed dogs (*ibid.*, 52, 111; Athenaeus, *The Deipnosophists*, III.56). In Asia Minor, at the Ionian city of Colophon, people sacrificed a black female puppy to a wayside goddess (Pausanias, *Description of Greece*, III.xiv.9); and in Rome a bitch was sacrificed to the goddess called Geneta Mana (Plutarch, *The Roman Questions*, 52).

89 Hippocrates, "Regimen," II.46.

90 Sextus Empiricus, *Outlines of Pyrrhonism*, III.225.

91 *Natural History*, XXIX.14.

92 Personal communication, James J. Parsons.

Apart from the classical references to dog eating in the Mediterranean, there is the assertion of Thomas Muffett (*Healths Improvement*, London, 1655, p. 78) that puppies were eaten in Corsica in his time, and that of John Josselyn (*New-Englands Realities Discovered: In Birds, Beasts, Fishes, Serpents, and Plants of That Country*, London: G. Widdowes, 1672, p. 19) that the flesh of young spaniel puppies was extolled in seventeenth-century England and France! It may be that the practice of dog eating was briefly introduced to France and England from Spain along with spaniels.

93 Justin, *History*, XIX.1.

94 Hooton, 1925: 56.
95 Bertholon, 1897: 563; Canard, 1952: 298.
96 Bertholon, 561; Canard, 298–99; L. C. Briggs, 1958: 40.
97 Westermarck, 1926, 2: 306–7; O. Bates, 1914: 177.
98 Hrdlička, 1912: 12.
   The only reference I have found to the consumption of dogflesh in modern times in the Middle East outside of North Africa is for Bahrein (de Planhol, 1959: 59).
99 L. C. Briggs, 1958: 40.
 1 Bertholon, 1897: 561; O. Bates, 1914: 177.
 2 Westermarck, 1926, 2: 306–7.
 3 Canard, 1952: 299.
 4 Frazer, 1935, 7: 22.
 5 Westermarck, 1924, 2: 501.
 6 The beliefs of the Zoroastrians led to some curious customs among them and others influenced by them. They used dogs in ceremonies to cleanse the living body and to purify a corpse (A. V. Jackson, 1928: 101). The Parsi of India have a dog nearby when a man is dying, muzzle near the dying man's mouth so that it may receive his last breath and carry it to the waiting angel. The Parsi do not look with horror at the practice of dogs eating corpses; the Tibetans in recent times even bred and trained dogs especially to devour corpses, and regarded this as the most honorable disposition of the body, reserved for monks and important people (Crooke, 1896, 2: 219). In many other parts of the Old World (Langkavel, 1898: 661–63) feeding human corpses to dogs was not unusual, but it was generally restricted to the poor and the disgraced. Reports of dogs devouring live people appear in various classical accounts, including a report by Onesicritus (c. 325 B.C.) for the Bactrians, who threw persons disabled by disease and old age to the dogs to be eaten (Strabo, *Geography*, XI. 11.3). Though the custom was not widespread, apparently there was considerable strength of feeling associated with it, for Stasanor, one of Alexander's prefects, nearly lost his power by attempting to destroy it (Porphyry, "On Abstinence from Animal Food," IV.21).

 7 Dussaud, 1900: 94.
 8 W. R. Smith, 1914: 291; Dornan, 1933: 630.
 9 Strabo, *Geography*, XVII.1.40.
10 Plutarch, *Isis and Osiris*, 72.
   It is clear from paintings that in Egypt the dog was a respected companion of people of all classes and a favorite household animal. According to Plutarch, in early times it had a place of honor in Egypt over all other animals (*Isis and Osiris*, 44). Herodotus says that on the death of a dog in Egypt every member of the family shaved his head and body in sorrow; a female dog was buried in a consecrated chest (*History*, II.66–67). Dogs were embalmed and interred with great honor in special tombs (Wilkinson, 1878, 3: 274). It is not certain how the dog became a sacred animal in Egypt; was the idea diffused from Persia or elsewhere; did it come from the identification with the canine deity Anubis, who was called "dog" and was symbolized by a recumbent jackal; or did it happen in some other way? In later times the dog lost its position of primacy among the animals; according to one tradition, this took place when, after the Persian conqueror Cambyses had slain the sacred bull of Apis in Egypt (c. 525 B.C.), the dog was the only animal to eat its body (Plutarch, *Isis and Osiris*, 44), degrading itself by such repulsive behavior.
11 As these notes show, the position of the dog in the ancient Middle East and Mediterranean varied considerably from group to group, and even within a group was sometimes not clearly defined. The ancient Babylonians pictured their god Marduk as accompanied by four dogs, who were named Iltebu, "the pursuer"; Ukkumu, "the seizer"; Iksuda, "the capturer"; and Akkulu, "the devourer." The names give reason to suspect that the dogs may originally have been "devastating winds who followed in the track of a death-dealing god" (Sayce, 1888: 288). The Babylonians regarded the dog as an animal of omen, and observed and interpreted its movements carefully. It was believed to possess elements of sacredness, and was regarded sometimes as good, sometimes as evil.

Though the presence of dogs in the roads was believed essential to the welfare of a place, care was taken lest they defile a person or house (Jastrow, 1898: 398–99, 661–62). The Assyrians had a huntsman-god who was accompanied by a dog; so was Heracles, at Tyre in Phoenicia (W. R. Smith, 1914: 291–92). The Lycians and Carians of southwest Asia Minor claimed that they were descended "from the dog Apollo" (Dornan, 1933: 630).

Dogs were used by the ancient Jews for hunting and to protect their flocks, but they also congregated in pariah packs and prowled about the streets, living as scavengers. Perhaps because of the food they ate and their dirty habits, they were regarded as unclean. To call a man a dog was an insult (I Sam. 17:43; II Kings 8:13). The term "dog" was also sometimes applied in a figurative sense to refer to those who did not appreciate what is sacred (Matt. 7:6), to those who introduced untrue doctrines cynically (Phil. 3:2), and to a sinner who repeated his sins (II Peter 2:22; Prov. 26:11). In later times the Jews called the heathen "dogs" because they were ceremonially unclean; even Jesus used this expression on occasion (Matt. 15:26; Mark 7:27). There are allusions to the sacrifice of dogs in Isaiah (66:3), which indicates that the practice was known to them, perhaps from the mixed Samaritan population, who may not have regarded the dog in the same light as the Jews did.

12 T. P. Hughes, 1885: 91.

Attitudes toward dogs in the Islamic world are ambivalent. In Palestine early in the century stricter Moslems, especially members of the Shafe'i sect, regarded dogs as so dirty that if a wet dog shook itself forty steps from the place where they were at prayer they stopped the proceedings, performed certain ablutions, and started their prayers over again (Hanauer, 1935: 194). At Andjra in Morocco people believe that if a dog should eat from a vessel or lick it, it would break unless washed seven times in hot water; the Ait Waryager require that the washing be with water which has been made pure by

putting seven stones in it. Moroccans also believe that a man who kills a dog becomes polluted, that the meat of any animal he slaughters is unfit to eat, and that he should not be permitted to perform certain religious sacrifices (Westermarck, 1926, 2: 303–4). Because of these attitudes, most dogs are neglected, noisy pariahs in Arab towns (Doughty, 1888, 1: 337–38; Cheesman, 1926: 108) and are kept from entering the mosques.

On the other hand, Moslem peoples have a certain respect and affection for dogs, especially for their pets. The killing of a dog arouses considerable feeling; in the Islamic world generally it is considered a good act for a man to feed a dog and give it drink (W. R. Smith, 1914: 292). "It is better to feed a dog than to feed a man" they say in Palestine, meaning that the dog is grateful and will not forget the kindness; the man may (Hanauer, 1935: 195–96). Greyhounds are believed in Morocco to be possessed of a good spirit; in Tangier and among the Ait Waryager, people believe that the house in which a greyhound lives is not molested by spirits. In Andjra a good hunting dog is respected and prayed for; when it dies its body, unlike those of ordinary dogs, is buried or hidden (Westermarck, 1926, 2: 103, 308).

There are indications of varying attitudes toward dogs in these regions in pre-Islamic times. Pliny wrote that no dogs were admitted into the interior of "the island of Sygaros" off the southern coast of Arabia (*Natural History,* VI. 32), and that they wandered about on the seashore until they died. But in ancient Palestine one who killed a neighbor's dog was liable to pay blood compensation just as for killing a man (Hanauer, 1935: 195).

The dog was a holy animal in ancient Iran. With the acceptance of Islam, however, it lost its position of prestige and became unclean (Dhalla, 1922: 367). Even Zoroastrians have adopted this Moslem notion and forgotten their former high regard for the dog (P. M. Sykes, 1906: 758). In Iran today, though people are fond of the dogs they keep as pets, and though huntsmen are proud of their greyhounds and pointers, most dogs are pariahs, wandering half starved through the streets (E. C. Sykes, 1910: 247–48). Some people believe that whereas man is the noblest creature the dog is the lowest. On the other hand, it is said that a grateful dog is better than a thankless man and that if a man had one of the seven qualities a dog has he would go to heaven. It is also believed that any person who sheds the blood of a dog will die (Massé, 1938: 196).

13 Langkavel, 1898: 652–53.

Chapter 9—CONCLUSION

1 M. Bates, 1957–58: 452.
2 *Antony and Cleopatra,* I.4.66–68.
3 Angyal, 1941: 401–3, 408–9.
4 Hall and Hall, 1939: 541, 547.

5 Porphyry, "On Abstinence from Animal Food," II.61.
6 Thomson, 1885: 430–31.
7 Spencer and Gillen, 1904: 611–14.
8 Townsend, 1928: 65.
9 Hearne, 1795: 204–6.
10 Adair, 1775: 133.
11 Hutton, 1946: 225.
12 Spencer and Gillen, 1904: 164, 166, 283, 291.
13 Frazer, 1935, 8: 29–30.
14 DuBois, 1944: 165, 292.
15 Allport, 1958: 127.
16 Masuoka, 1945: 759.
17 Stefansson, 1920: 543.
18 DuBois, 1941: 276.
19 Trant, 1954: 704.
20 Stefansson, 1920: 540–43.
21 Jochelson, 1926: 417.
22 Masuoka, 1945: 763.
23 Tussing, 1939: 198–99; Wallen, 1943: 288–98.

REFERENCES

Adair, James. 1775. *A History of the American Indians*. London: Edward and Charles Dilly. 464 pp.

Adolph, William H. 1956. "What Early Man Discovered about Food," *Harper's Magazine*, May, pp. 67–70.

Ahmad, Jamal-ud-din, and Muhammad Abdul Aziz. 1934. *Afghanistan: A Brief Survey*. Kabul: Dar-ut-talif. 160 pp.

Aitken, Robert T. 1930. *Ethnology of Tubuai*. Bernice P. Bishop Museum, Bul. 70. Honolulu. 169 pp.

Albright, William Foxwell. 1942. *Archaeology and the Religion of Israel*. Baltimore: Johns Hopkins Press. 238 pp.

Ali, Maulvi Muhammad. 1935. *The Holy Qur-án*. With English trans. and commentary. 3d ed. Lahore: Ahmadiyya Anjuman-I-Isháat-I-Islam. 1275 pp.

Allen, Glover M. 1919–20. "Dogs of the American Aborigines," *Bulletin of the Museum of Comparative Zoology at Harvard*, 63: 431–517.

Allen, William E. D. 1932. *A History of the Georgian People*. London: Kegan Paul, Trench, Trubner. 429 pp.

Allport, Gordon W. 1958. *The Nature of Prejudice*. Abridged ed. Anchor Books. Garden City, N.Y.: Doubleday. 496 pp.

Ambedkar, B. R. 1948. *The Untouchables*. New Delhi: Amrit Book Company. 158 pp.

Amschler, J. Wolfg. 1939. "Tierreste der Ausgrabungen von dem 'Grossen Königschügel' Shah Tepé, in Nord-Iran," *Reports from the Scientific Expedition to the North-western Provinces of China under the Leadership of Dr. Sven Hedin*, 7 (No. 4): 35–129. Stockholm: Bokförlags Aktiebolaget Thule.

Anderson, Albert W. 1934. "Report on 46 Cases of Trichiniasis," *Nebraska State Medical Journal*, 19: 379–82.

Anderson, R. G. 1911. "Some Tribal Customs in Their Relation to Medicine and Morals of the Nyam-nyam and Gour People Inhabiting the Eastern Bahr-El-Ghazal," *Fourth Report of Wellcome Tropical Research Laboratories at the Gordon Memorial College, Khartoum,* Vol. B, 239–77. London: Baillière, Tindall, and Cox.

Andrews, Roy C. 1919. "Exploring Unknown Corners of the 'Hermit Kingdom'," *National Geographic Magazine,* 36: 25–48.

Andrus, J. Russell. 1943. *Preliminary Survey of the Economy of French Indochina.* Washington: Bureau of Foreign and Domestic Commerce, Far Eastern Unit. 116 pp.

————. 1947. *Burmese Economic Life.* Stanford: Stanford Univ. Press. 362 pp.

Angyal, A. 1941. "Disgust and Related Aversions," *Journal of Abnormal and Social Psychology,* 36: 393–412.

Anonymous. 1950. "Report on Agriculture, Fishing and Forestry." U.S. Economic Survey Mission to the Philippines. Sept. 26 pp. (mimeographed).

Anstey, Vera. 1952. *The Economic Development of India.* London: Longmans, Green. 677 pp.

Ardener, Edwin. 1956. *Coastal Bantu of the Cameroons.* Ethnographic Survey of Africa. Western Africa, Pt. 11. London: International African Institute. 116 pp.

Argenti, Philip P., and H. J. Rose. 1949. *The Folk-Lore of Chios.* Cambridge: Cambridge Univ. Press. 2 vols.

Arkell, A. J. 1949. *Early Khartoum.* London: Oxford Univ. Press. 145 pp.

Armstrong, W. E. 1928. *Rossel Island.* Cambridge: Cambridge Univ. Press. 274 pp.

Ashton, E[dmund] H[ugh]. 1939. "A Sociological Sketch of Sotho Diet," *Transactions of the Royal Society of South Africa,* 27: 147–214.

Ashton, [Edmund] Hugh. 1952. *The Basuto.* London: Oxford Univ. Press. 355 pp.

Athenaeus. 1854. *The Deipnosophists.* Trans. by C. D. Yonge. London: Henry G. Bohn. 3 vols.

Baikie, James. 1923. *The Life of the Ancient East.* New York: Macmillan. 463 pp.

Baker, John R. 1929. *Man and Animals in the New Hebrides.* London: George Routledge and Sons. 200 pp.

Baker, Sir Samuel W. 1867. *The Nile Tributaries of Abyssinia.* Philadelphia: J. B. Lippincott. 596 pp.

Ball, Charles James. 1893–94. "Israel and Babylon," *Proceedings of the Society of Biblical Archeology,* 16: 188–200.

Barbosa, Duarte. 1866. *A Description of the Coasts of East Africa and Malabar in the Beginning of the Sixteenth Century.* Hakluyt Society Works, Vol. 35. Trans. by H. E. J. Stanley. London: Hakluyt Society. 336 pp.

Barton, Roy Franklin. 1922. "Ifugao Economics," University of California Publications in American Archaelogy and Ethnology, 15 (No. 5): 385–446.

Barton, R[oy] F[ranklin]. 1935. "Ispol'zovanie mifov kak magii u gornykh plemen filippin" (The Use of Myths as Magic among the Mountain Tribes of the Philippines), *Sovetskaia Etnografiia*, No. 3, pp. 77–95. Trans. for the Human Relations Area Files.

Bascom, William R. 1951. "Yoruba Food," *Africa*, 21: 41–53.

Basedow, Herbert. 1925. *The Australian Aboriginal.* Adelaide: F. W. Preece and Sons. 422 pp.

Basham, Arthur L. 1954. *The Wonder That Was India.* London: Sidgwick and Jackson. 568 pp.

Batchelor, John. 1901. *The Ainu and Their Folk-Lore.* London: Religious Tract Society. 604 pp.

Bate, Dorothea M. A. 1938. "Animal Remains," pp. 209–14 in P. L. O. Guy, *Megiddo Tombs.* Oriental Institute Publications, Vol. 33. Chicago: Univ. of Chicago Press.

———. 1953. "The Vertebrate Fauna," pp. 11–19 in A. J. Arkell, *Shaheinab.* London: Oxford Univ. Press.

Bates, Marston. 1957–58. "Man, Food and Sex," *American Scholar,* 27: 449–58.

Bates, Oric. 1914. *The Eastern Libyans.* London: Macmillan. 298 pp.

———. 1917. "Ancient Egyptian Fishing," Harvard African Studies, 1: 199–271.

Baudesson, Henry. [1919.] *Indo-China and Its Primitive People.* London: Hutchinson. 328 pp.

Baumann, Oscar. 1887. "Beiträge zur Ethnographie des Congo," *Mittheilungen der Anthropologischen Gesellschaft in Wien,* 17: 160–81.

Baxter, P. T. W., and Audrey Butt. 1953. *The Azande, and Related Peoples of the Anglo-Egyptian Sudan and Belgian Congo.* Ethnographic Survey of Africa. East Central Africa, Pt. 9. London: International African Institute. 152 pp.

Beaglehole, Ernest and Pearl. 1938. *Ethnology of Pukapuka.* Bernice P. Bishop Museum, Bul. 150. Honolulu. 419 pp.

Beal, Samuel. 1958. *Chinese Accounts of India.* New ed. Calcutta: Susil Gupta (India). 4 vols.

Beardsley, Richard K., J. W. Hall, and R. E. Ward. 1959. *Village Japan.* Chicago: Univ. of Chicago Press. 498 pp.

Becker, C. 1924. "Familienbesitz und Mutterrecht," *Zeitschrift für Buddhismus und verwandte Gebiete,* 6: 127–38, 300–310. Trans. for the Human Relations Area Files by E. Knight.

Beech, Mervin Worcester Howard. 1911. *The Suk, Their Language and Folklore.* Oxford: Clarendon Press. 151 pp.

Belding, David Lawrence. 1958. *Basic Clinical Parasitology.* New York: Appleton-Century-Crofts. 469 pp.

Belgrave, James H. D. 1953. *Welcome to Bahrain.* Stourbridge, England: Published privately. 154 pp.

Bell, Sir Charles. 1928. *The People of Tibet.* Oxford: Clarendon Press. 319 pp.

———. 1931. *The Religion of Tibet.* Oxford: Clarendon Press. 235 pp.

————. 1946. *Portrait of the Dalai Lama*. London: Collins. 414 pp.

Benet, Sula. 1951. *Song, Dance and Customs of Peasant Poland*. New York: Roy Publishers. 247 pp.

Bennett, John W. 1943. "Food and Social Status in a Rural Society," *American Sociological Review*, 8: 561–69.

Bennett, John W., H. L. Smith, and H. Passin. 1942. "Food and Culture in Southern Illinois—A Preliminary Report," *ibid.*, 7: 645–60.

Bergman, Sten. 1938. *In Korean Wilds and Villages*. London: John Gifford. 232 pp.

Bernatzik, Hugo A. 1954. *Die neue grosse Völkerkunde*. Frankfurt: Herkul G.M.B.H. 3 vols.

Bertholon, L. 1897. "Ethnologie de l'île de Gerba," Pt. 2 of "Exploration anthropologique de l'île de Gerba," *L'Anthropologie*, 8: 539–83.

Best, Elsdon. 1924. *The Maori*. Vol. 2. Wellington, New Zealand: Board of Maori Ethnological Research. 637 pp.

Bigandet, Paul A. 1911–12. *The Life or Legend of Gaudama the Buddha of the Burmese*. 4th ed. London: Kegan Paul, Trench, Trübner. 2 vols.

Biscoe, C. E. Tyndale. 1922. *Kashmir in Sunlight and Shade*. London: Seeley, Service. 315 pp.

Blackman, Winifred S. 1927. *The Fellahin of Upper Egypt*. London: George G. Harrap. 331 pp.

Blackwood, Beatrice. 1935. *Both Sides of Buka Passage*. Oxford: Clarendon Press. 624 pp.

Bliss, Frederick Jones. 1912. *The Religions of Modern Syria and Palestine*. New York: Charles Scribner's Sons. 354 pp.

Bloomfield, Maurice, trans. 1897. *Hymns of the Atharva-Veda*. Vol. 42 of The Sacred Books of the East, ed. by F. Max Müller. Oxford: Clarendon Press. 716 pp.

Blunt, E. A. H. 1931. *The Caste System of Northern India*. London: Oxford Univ. Press. 374 pp.

Blunt, Sir Edward, ed. 1938. *Social Service in India: An Introduction to Some Social and Economic Problems of the Indian People*. London: H. M. Stationery Office. 446 pp.

Boas, Franz. 1938. *General Anthropology*. Boston: D. C. Heath. 718 pp.

Boettger, Caesar Rudolf. 1958. *Die Haustiere Afrikas*. Jena: Gustav Fischer. 314 pp.

Bogoras, Waldemar (Bogaraz-Tan, Vladimir Germanovich). 1904–9. *The Chukchee*. Pt. 1 (1904): *Material Culture;* Pt. 2 (1907): *Religion;* Pt. 3 (1909): *Social Organization*. American Museum of Natural History, Memoirs, Vol. 11. Leiden: E. J. Brill, and New York: G. E. Stechert. 733 pp.

Bourne, F. S. A. 1889. "Report by Mr. F. S. A. Bourne of a Journey in South-Western China," Parliamentary Papers, No. 6, *Archaeological Review*, 3: 53–67, 118–33.

Bowdich, Thomas Edward. 1819. *Mission from Cape Coast Castle to Ashantee*. London: John Murray. 512 pp.

Braidwood, Robert J. 1952. *The Near East and the Foundations for Civilization.* Eugene: Oregon State System of Higher Education. 45 pp.

Brant, Charles. 1954. *Tadagale: A Burmese Village in 1950.* Cornell University, Southeast Asia Program, Date Paper No. 13. Ithaca. 41 pp.

Breeks, James Wilkinson. 1873. *An Account of the Primitive Tribes and Monuments of the Nilagiris.* London: India Museum. 137 pp.

Briggs, George W. 1920. *The Chamars.* Calcutta: Association Press. 270 pp.

Briggs, Lloyd Cabot. 1958. *The Living Races of the Sahara Desert.* Harvard University, Peabody Museum of American Archaeology and Ethnology, Papers, Vol. 28, No. 2. Cambridge. 217 pp.

Brodrick, Alan Houghton. 1942. *Little China: The Annamese Lands.* London: Oxford Univ. Press. 332 pp.

Broomhall, Marshall. 1910. *Islam in China.* London: Morgan and Scott, and China Inland Mission. 334 pp.

Brown, Edward. 1861. *A Seaman's Narrative of His Adventures during a Captivity among Chinese Pirates, on the Coast of Cochin-China, and Afterwards during a Journey on Foot across That Country, in the Years 1857–8.* London: Charles Westerton. 292 pp.

Brown, T. Burton, 1951. *Excavations in Azarbaijan, 1948.* London: John Murray. 279 pp.

Browne, Edward Granville. 1927. *A Year amongst the Persians.* Cambridge: Cambridge Univ. Press. 650 pp.

Bruce, James. 1790. *Travels to Discover the Source of the Nile, in the Years 1768, 1769, 1770, 1771, 1772, and 1773.* London: G. G. J. and J. Robinson. 5 vols.

Bryant, Alfred T. 1949. *The Zulu People.* Pietermaritzburg: Shuter and Shooter. 769 pp.

Buck, John Lossing. 1930. *Chinese Farm Economy: A Study of 2866 Farms in Seventeen Localities and Seven Provinces in China.* Chicago: Univ. of Chicago Press. 476 pp.

Buck, Peter H. 1930. *Samoan Material Culture.* Bernice P. Bishop Museum, Bul. 75. Honolulu. 724 pp.

———. 1932. *Ethnology of Manihiki and Rakahanga.* Bernice P. Bishop Museum, Bul. 99. Honolulu. 238 pp.

———. 1938. *Ethnology of Mangareva.* Bernice P. Bishop Museum, Bul. 157. Honolulu. 519 pp.

———. 1938[a]. *Vikings of the Sunrise.* New York: Frederick A. Stokes. 335 pp.

———. 1944. *Arts and Crafts of the Cook Islands.* Bernice P. Bishop Museum, Bul. 179. Honolulu. 533 pp.

———. 1950. *Material Culture of Kapingamarangi.* Bernice P. Bishop Museum, Bul. 200. Honolulu. 291 pp.

———. 1950[a]. *The Coming of the Maori.* Wellington: Maori Purposes Fund Board. 551 pp.

Budge, Sir E. A. Wallis. 1928. *A History of Ethiopia.* London: Methuen. 2 vols.

Bühler, Georg, trans. 1882. *The Sacred Laws of the Âryas, as Taught in the Schools of Âpastamba, Gautama, Vâsishtha, and Baudhâyana,* Pt. 2. Vol. 14 of The

Sacred Books of the East, ed. by F. Max Müller. Oxford: Clarendon Press. 360 pp.

———. 1886. *The Laws of Manu.* Vol. 25 of The Sacred Books of the East, ed. by F. Max Müller. Oxford: Clarendon Press. 620 pp.

———. 1896. *The Sacred Laws of the Âryas, as Taught in the Schools of Âpastamba, Gautama, Vâsishtha, and Baudhâyana,* Pt. 1. Vol. 2 of The Sacred Books of the East, ed. by F. Max Müller. 2d ed. Oxford: Clarendon Press. 314 pp.

Burkill, I. H. 1935. *A Dictionary of the Economic Products of the Malay Peninsula.* London: Crown Agents for the Colonies. 2 vols.

Burkitt, F. C. 1925. *The Religion of the Manichees.* Cambridge: Cambridge Univ. Press. 130 pp.

Burrows, Edwin Grant. 1936. *Ethnology of Futuna.* Bernice P. Bishop Museum, Bul. 138. Honolulu. 239 pp.

———. [1949.] "The People of Ifalik: A Little-Disturbed Atoll Culture." Unpublished manuscript submitted as a final report, Coordinated Investigation of Micronesian Anthropology. Washington: Pacific Science Board, National Research Council. 246 pp.

Burrows, Guy. 1898. *The Land of the Pigmies.* London: C. Arthur Pearson. 299 pp.

———. 1899. "On the Natives of the Upper Welle District of the Belgian Congo," *Journal of the Anthropological Institute of Great Britain and Ireland,* O.S. 28 (N.S. 1): 35–48.

Burton, Richard F. 1856. *Personal Narrative of a Pilgrimage to El-Medinah and Meccah.* New York: G. P. Putnam. 492 pp.

Burton, Robert. 1948. *The Anatomy of Melancholy.* New York: Tudor Publishing Company. 1036 pp.

Bush, Richard J. 1871. *Reindeer, Dogs, and Snow-Shoes: A Journal of Siberian Travel and Explorations.* New York: Harper and Brothers. 529 pp.

Butt, Audrey. 1952. *The Nilotes of the Anglo-Egyptian Sudan and Uganda.* Ethnographic Survey of Africa. East Central Africa, Pt. 4. London: International African Institute. 198 pp.

Butzer, Karl W. 1960. "Archeology and Geology in Ancient Egypt," *Science,* Dec. 2, pp. 1617–24.

Buxton, David. 1950. *Travels in Ethiopia.* New York: Medill McBride. 200 pp.

Buxton, L. H. Dudley. 1929. *China, the Land and the People: A Human Geography.* Oxford: Clarendon Press. 333 pp.

Caesar, Julius. 1952. *The Gallic War.* With an English trans. by H. J. Edwards. Cambridge: Harvard Univ. Press. 620 pp.

Cammann, Schuyler. 1951. *The Land of the Camel: Tents and Temples of Inner Mongolia.* New York: Ronald Press. 200 pp.

Campbell, Dugald. 1922. *In the Heart of Bantuland.* Philadelphia: J. B. Lippincott. 313 pp.

Canard, Marius. 1952. "L'autobiographie d'un chambellan du Mahdî'Obeidallâh le Fâṭimide," *Hespéris,* 39: 279–329.

Casati, Gaetano. 1891. *Ten Years in Equatoria and the Return with Emin Pasha,* Vol. 1. London and New York: Frederick Warne. 376 pp.

Cato, Marcus Portius. 1934. *On Agriculture.* Loeb Classical Library. London: William Heinemann. 157 pp.

Čech, Jan, and J. E. Mellon. 1944. *Czechoslovakia: Land of Dream and Enterprise.* London: Lawrence Press. 184 pp.

Cerulli, Ernesta. 1956. *Peoples of South-West Ethiopia and Its Borderland.* Ethnographic Survey of Africa. North-Eastern Africa, Pt. 3. London: International African Institute. 148 pp.

Cervinka, M. Vladimir. 1950. *Afghanistan.* Office Suisse d'Expansion Commerciale. Rapport spécial No. 58, Série A. Lausanne. 83 pp. Trans. for the Human Relations Area Files by A. Kalmykov.

Chandler, Asa Crawford. 1955. *Introduction to Parasitology.* 9th ed. New York: John Wiley and Sons. 799 pp.

Chang, Yin-t'ang. 1933. *The Economic Development and Prospects of Inner Mongolia (Chahar, Suiyuan and Ningsia).* Shanghai: Commercial Press. 243 pp.

Chaudhuri, Sashi Bhusan. 1957. *Civil Rebellion in the Indian Mutinies (1857–1859).* Calcutta: World Press Private. 367 pp.

Cheesman, R. E. 1926. *In Unknown Arabia.* London: Macmillan. 447 pp.

———. 1936. *Lake Tana and the Blue Nile.* London: Macmillan. 400 pp.

Chen, Ta. 1940. *Emigrant Communities in South China.* New York: Institute of Pacific Relations. 287 pp.

Chewings, Charles. 1936. *Back in the Stone Age: The Natives of Central Australia.* Sydney: Angus and Robertson. 161 pp.

Cheyne, T. K., and J. Sutherland Black. 1899–1903. *Encyclopaedia Biblica.* New York: Macmillan. 4 vols.

Childe, V. Gordon. 1926. *The Aryans.* New York: Alfred A. Knopf. 221 pp.

———. 1952. *New Light on the Most Ancient East.* London: Routledge and Kegan Paul. 255 pp.

———. 1957. *The Dawn of European Civilization.* London: Routledge and Kegan Paul. 368 pp.

Childs, Gladwyn Murray. 1949. *Umbundu Kinship and Character.* London and New York: International African Institute. 245 pp.

Chotek, Karel. 1936. "Výživa: Zaměstnání" (Nutrition; Occupations), *Československá Veastiveda,* Series 2, Národopis (Ethnography), pp. 249–58. Prague: Sfinx (Bohumil Janda). Trans. for the Human Relations Area Files by G. Kreshka.

Christian, John Leroy. 1942. *Modern Burma: A Survey of Political and Economic Developments.* Berkeley and Los Angeles: Univ. of California Press. 381 pp.

Church, R. J. Harrison. 1957. *West Africa.* London: Longmans, Green. 547 pp.

Chwolsohn, D. 1856. *Die Ssabier und der Ssabismus.* St. Petersburg: Buchdruckerei der Kaiserlichen Akademie der Wissenschaften. 2 vols.

Clarac-Schwarzenbach, Annemarie. 1940. "Afghanistan in Transition," *Geographical Magazine,* 2: 326–41.

Clark, Grahame. 1947. "Sheep and Swine in the Husbandry of Prehistoric Europe," *Antiquity,* 21: 122–36.

Clark, Harlan B. 1947. "Yemen—Southern Arabia's Mountain Wonderland," *National Geographic Magazine*, 92: 631–72.

Clavijo, Ruy Gonzalez de. 1859. *Narrative of the Embassy of Ruy Gonzalez de Clavijo to the Court of Timour, at Samarcand, A.D. 1403–6.* Hakluyt Society Works, Vol. 26. Trans. by C. R. Markham. London: Hakluyt Society. 200 pp.

Cole, Fay-Cooper. 1913. "The Wild Tribes of Davao District, Mindanao." Field Museum of Natural History, Anthropological Series, 12 (No. 2): 49–203. Chicago.

———. 1922. "The Tinguian. Social, Religious, and Economic Life of a Philippine Tribe." Field Museum of Natural History, Anthropological Series, 14 (No. 2): 227–493. Chicago.

———. 1945. *The Peoples of Malaysia.* New York: D. Van Nostrand. 354 pp.

———. 1956. "The Bukidnon of Mindanao." Chicago Natural History Museum, Fieldiana: Anthropology, 46: 1–140.

Columbia University. 1955–56. *The Caucasus.* Subcontractor's Monograph HRAF–35, Columbia–1. New Haven: Human Relations Area Files. 1008 pp.

Columella, Lucius Junius Moderatus. 1941–55. *On Agriculture.* Trans. by H. B. Ash, E. S. Forster, and E. H. Heffner. Cambridge: Harvard Univ. Press. 3 vols.

Combe, G. A. 1926. *A Tibetan on Tibet.* London: T. Fisher Unwin. 212 pp.

Comhaire-Sylvain, Suzanne. 1950. *Food and Leisure among the African Youth of Leopoldville (Belgian Congo).* Communications from the School of African Studies, University of Capetown, N.S., No. 25. Capetown: Univ. of Capetown. 124 pp.

Connolly, R. M. 1897. "Social Life in Fanti-Land," *Journal of the Anthropological Institute of Great Britain and Ireland*, 26: 128–53.

Conrad, Agnes. 1937. "The Attitude toward Food," *American Journal of Orthopsychiatry*, 7: 360–67.

Cook, Elsie K. 1951. *Ceylon.* Madras: Macmillan. 360 pp.

Cook, James. 1784. *A Voyage to the Pacific Ocean.* London: G. Nicol and T. Cadell. 3 vols.

———. 1955. *The Journals of Captain James Cook on His Voyages of Discovery*, Vol. 1, "The Voyage of the Endeavour, 1768–1771." Hakluyt Society Extra Series, No. 34. Cambridge: Cambridge Univ. Press. 684 pp.

Coon, Carleton Stevens. 1931. *Tribes of the Rif*, Harvard African Studies, Vol. 9. 417 pp.

———. 1951. *Caravan.* New York: Henry Holt. 376 pp.

———. [1951a.] *Cave Explorations in Iran 1949.* Philadelphia: University Museum, University of Pennsylvania. 125 pp.

———. 1954. *The Story of Man.* New York: Alfred A. Knopf. 437 pp.

Corfield, F. D. 1938. "The Koma," *Sudan Notes and Records*, 21: 123–65.

Cornell University. 1956. *India: A Sociological Background.* Subcontractor's Monograph HRAF–44, Cornell–8. New Haven: Human Relations Area Files. 2 vols.

Corney, Bolton Glanvill, trans. 1915. *The Quest and Occupation of Tahiti by*

Emissaries of Spain during the Years 1772–1776, Vol. 2. Hakluyt Society Works, Series 2, No. 36. London: Hakluyt Society. 521 pp.

Craster, J. E. E. 1913. *Pemba, the Spice Island of Zanzibar.* London: T. Fisher Unwin. 358 pp.

Crawfurd, John. 1830. *Journal of an Embassy from the Governor-General of India to the Courts of Siam and Cochin China.* London: Henry Colburn and Richard Bentley. 2 vols.

Creel, Herrlee Glessner. 1937. *Studies in Early Chinese Culture.* Baltimore: Waverly Press. 266 pp.

————. [1937a.] *The Birth of China.* New York: Frederick Ungar. 402 pp.

Cressey, George Babcock. 1934. *China's Geographic Foundations: A Survey of the Land and Its People.* New York: McGraw-Hill. 436 pp.

Crooke, William. 1896. *The Popular Religion and Folklore of Northern India.* Westminster: Archibald Constable. 2 vols.

Crowfoot, J. W. 1925. "Further Notes on Pottery," *Sudan Notes and Records,* 8: 125–36.

Cruickshank, Brodie. 1853. *Eighteen Years on the Gold Coast of Africa.* London: Hurst and Blackett. 2 vols.

Crumbine, Samuel J., and James A. Tobey. 1929. *The Most Nearly Perfect Food.* Baltimore: Williams and Wilkins. 292 pp.

Cunningham, Alexander. 1854. *Ladák, Physical, Statistical and Historical; with Notices of the Surrounding Countries.* London: W. H. Allen. 485 pp.

Cussler, Margaret, and Mary L. de Give. 1952. *'Twixt the Cup and the Lip.* New York: Twayne Publishers. 262 pp.

Czekanowski, Jan. 1924. "Forschungen im Nil-Kongo Zwischengebiet," *Wissenschaftliche Ergebnisse der Deutschen Zentral Afrika Expedition,* 1907–1908, *unter Führung Adolf Friedrichs, Herzogs zu Mecklenburg,* 6 (Pt. 2): 21–110. Leipzig: Klinkhardt and Biermann. Trans. for the Human Relations Area Files.

Daguio, Amador Taguinod. 1952. "Hudhud Hi Aliguyon: A Translation of an Ifugao Harvest Song with Introduction and Notes." Unpublished Master's thesis, Stanford University. 121 pp.

Das, S. K. 1953. "A Study of Folk Cattle Rites," *Man in India,* 33: 232–41.

Das, Sarat Chandra. 1902. *Journey to Lhasa and Central Tibet.* London: John Murray. 285 pp.

Davids, Thomas W. Rhys. 1903. *Buddhist India.* New York: G. P. Putnam's Sons. 332 pp.

Davids, Thomas W. Rhys, and Hermann Oldenberg, trans. 1881–85. *Vinaya Texts,* Pts. 1, 2, and 3. Vols. 13 (1881), 17 (1882), and 20 (1885) respectively of The Sacred Books of the East, ed. by F. Max Müller. Oxford: Clarendon Press. 360, 444, and 444 pp.

Davis, John D. 1944. *The Westminster Dictionary of the Bible.* Rev. and rewritten by H. S. Gehman. Philadelphia: Westminster Press. 658 pp.

Dê, Tran Dinh. [1951.] "Notes on Birth and Reproduction in Vietnam." Unpublished manuscript by M. Coughlin. 9 pp.

Deacon, Arthur Bernard. 1934. *Malekula*. London: George Routledge. 789 pp.

Deffontaines, Pierre. 1932. *La vie forestière en Slovaquie*. Paris: Honoré Champion. 94 pp. Trans. for the Human Relations Area Files by L. Greene.

Del Re, Arundel. n.d. *Creation Myths of the Formosan Natives*. Tokyo: Hokuseido Press. 75 pp.

Dennys, N. B. 1894. *A Descriptive Dictionary of British Malaya*. London: "London and China Telegraph" Office. 423 pp.

De Paor, Máire, and Liam De Paor. 1958. *Early Christian Ireland*. New York: Frederick A. Praeger. 263 pp.

de Planhol, Xavier. 1959. *The World of Islam*. A trans. of *Le monde islamique: Essai de géographie religieuse*. Ithaca: Cornell Univ. Press. 142 pp.

de Young, John E. 1955. *Village Life in Modern Thailand*. Berkeley and Los Angeles: Univ. of California Press. 225 pp.

Dhalla, Maneckji Nusservanji. 1922. *Zoroastrian Civilization*. New York: Oxford Univ. Press. 395 pp.

Dickson, H. R. P. 1951. *The Arab of the Desert*. London: George Allen & Unwin. 664 pp.

Diodorus Siculus. 1933–57. *The Library of History*. English trans. by C. H. Oldfather. London: W. Heinemann. 10 vols.

Dobell, Peter. 1830. *Travels in Kamchatka and Siberia; with a Narrative of a Residence in China*. London: Henry Colburn and Richard Bentley. 2 vols.

Dodge, Stanley D. 1928. "The Samoyed Culture," *Papers of the Michigan Academy of Science, Arts, and Letters*, 8: 1–9.

Doke, Clement M. 1931. *The Lambas of Northern Rhodesia*. London: George G. Harrap. 408 pp.

Dollot, René. 1937. *L'Afghanistan: Histoire-Description-Moeurs et Coutumes-Folklore-Fouilles*. Paris: Payot. 318 pp. Trans. for the Human Relations Area Files by D. D. Kostich.

Donaldson, Bess Allen. 1938. *The Wild Rue: A Study of Muhammadan Magic and Folk-Lore in Iran*. London: Luzac. 208 pp.

Donner, Kai. 1926. *Bei den Samojeden in Sibirien*. Stuttgart: Strecker and Schröder. 202 pp. Trans. for the Human Relations Area Files.

Donoghue, John D. 1957. "An Eta Community in Japan: The Social Persistence of Outcaste Groups," *American Anthropologist*, 59: 1000–1017.

Dore, R. P. 1958. *City Life in Japan: A Study of a Tokyo Ward*. Berkeley and Los Angeles: Univ. of California Press. 472 pp.

Dornan, S. S. 1933. "Dog Sacrifice among the Bantu," *South African Journal of Science*, 30: 628–32.

Doughty, Charles Montagu. 1888. *Travels in Arabia Deserta*. Cambridge: Cambridge Univ. Press. 2 vols.

Douglas, Mary. 1955. "The Lele of Kasai," pp. 1–26 in Daryll Forde, *African Worlds*. London: International African Institute. 243 pp.

Douglas, William O. 1953. *Beyond the High Himalayas*. Garden City, N.Y.: Doubleday. 352 pp.

Drew, Frederic. 1875. *The Jummoo and Kashmir Territories: A Geographical Account.* London: Edward Stanford. 568 pp.

Driberg, Jack Herbert. 1923. *The Lango.* London: T. Fisher Unwin. 468 pp.

Driver, Harold E., and William C. Massey. 1957. "Comparative Studies of North American Indians," *Transactions of the American Philosophical Society,* N.S., 47 (Pt. 2): 165–456.

Drower, Ethel S. 1937. *The Mandaeans of Iraq and Iran. Their Cults, Customs, Magic, Legends, and Folklore.* Oxford: Clarendon Press. 436 pp.

———. 1956. *Water into Wine. A Study of Ritual Idiom in the Middle East.* London: John Murray. 273 pp.

Drummond, J. C., and Anne Wilbraham. 1940. *The Englishman's Food.* London: Jonathan Cape. 574 pp.

Dube, S. C. 1951. *The Kamar.* Lucknow: Universal Publishers. 216 pp.

———. 1955. *Indian Village.* Ithaca, N.Y.: Cornell Univ. Press. 248 pp.

DuBois, Cora. 1941. "Attitudes toward Food and Hunger in Alor," pp. 272–81 in Leslie Spier, A. I. Hallowell, and S. S. Newman, *Language, Culture, and Personality.* Menasha, Wis.: Sapir Memorial Publication Fund. 298 pp.

———. 1944. *The People of Alor.* Minneapolis: Univ. of Minnesota Press. 654 pp.

Dubois, J. A. 1906. *Hindu Manners, Customs and Ceremonies.* Oxford: Clarendon Press. 741 pp.

Dugast, I. 1954. "Banen, Bafia, and Balom," pp. 134–69 in *Peoples of the Central Cameroons.* Ethnographic Survey of Africa. Western Africa, Pt. 9. London: International African Institute.

Dumarest, André. 1935. *La formation de classes sociales en pays Annamite.* Lyon: P. Ferréol. 267 pp. Trans. for the Human Relations Area Files by T. R. Whitaker.

Durand, Algernon. 1900. *The Making of a Frontier.* London: John Murray. 298 pp.

Dussaud, René. 1900. *Histoire et religion des Nosairîs.* Bibliothèque de l'École des Hautes Études, Sciences Philologiques et Historiques, No. 129. Paris: Librairie Émile Bouillon. 211 pp.

Dutt, Romesh C. 1893. *A History of Civilisation in Ancient India.* London: Kegan Paul, Trench, Trübner. 2 vols.

Dyson, Robert H. 1953. "Archeology and the Domestication of Animals in the Old World," *American Anthropologist,* 55: 661–73.

Earthy, Emily Dora. 1933. *Valenge Women.* London: International Institute of African Languages and Cultures. 251 pp.

East, Rupert, ed. 1939. *Akiga's Story: The Tiv Tribe as Seen by One of Its Members.* London: International Institute of African Languages and Cultures. 436 pp.

Eberhard, Wolfram. 1942. *Lokalkulturen im alten China.* Leiden: E. J. Brill. 447 pp.

————. 1952. *Chinese Festivals.* New York: Henry Schuman. 152 pp.

Eggan, Fred, and Michel Pijcán. 1943. "Some Problems in the Study of Food and Nutrition," *América Indígena,* 3: 9–22.

Eggeling, Julius, trans. 1885–94. *The Satapatha-Brâhmana according to the Text of the Mâdhyandina School,* Pts. 2 and 3. Vols. 26 (1885) and 41 (1894) of The Sacred Books of the East, ed. by F. Max Müller. Oxford: Clarendon Press. 480 and 424 pp.

Ekvall, Robert B. 1939. *Cultural Relations on the Kansu-Tibetan Border.* University of Chicago Publications in Anthropology, Occasional Papers, No. 1. Chicago: Univ. of Chicago Press. 87 pp.

Elwin, Verrier. 1942. *The Agaria.* Calcutta: Oxford Univ. Press. 292 pp.

————. 1959. *India's North-East Frontier in the Nineteenth Century.* London: Oxford Univ. Press. 473 pp.

Embree, John F. 1939. *Suye Mura, A Japanese Village.* Chicago: Univ. of Chicago Press. 354 pp.

Endle, Sidney. 1911. *The Kacharis.* London: Macmillan. 121 pp.

Engert, Cornelius van H. 1924. *A Report on Afghanistan.* U. S. Department of State, Division of Publications, Series C, No. 53. Washington, D.C. 225 pp.

Epictetus. 1926–28. *Discourses.* The Discourses as reported by Arrian, the Manual, and Fragments. Trans. by W. A. Oldfather. Loeb Classical Library. London: William Heinemann. 2 vols.

Eppstein, John, ed. 1945. *Hungary.* British Survey Handbooks, Vol. 4. Cambridge: Cambridge Univ. Press. 88 pp.

Epstein, Eliahu. 1938. "Kuwait," *Journal of the Royal Central Asian Society,* 25: 595–603.

Erman, Adolph. 1850. *Travels in Siberia: Including Excursions Northwards, down the Obi, to the Polar Circle, and Southwards, to the Chinese Frontier,* Vol. 2. Philadelphia: Lea and Blanchard. 400 pp.

————. 1894. *Life in Ancient Egypt.* London: Macmillan. 570 pp.

Espinosa, Friar Alonso de. 1907. *The Guanches of Tenerife, The Holy Image of Our Lady of Candelaria,* and *The Spanish Conquest and Settlement.* Hakluyt Society Works, Series 2, No. 21. Trans. and ed. by Sir C. Markham. London: Hakluyt Society. 221 pp.

Evans-Pritchard, Edward E. 1932. "Ethnological Observations in Dar Fung," *Sudan Notes and Records,* 15: 1–61.

————. 1940. *The Nuer.* Oxford: Clarendon Press. 271 pp.

Farnell, Lewis R. 1911. *Greece and Babylon.* Edinburgh: T. and T. Clark. 311 pp.

Faroughy, Abbas. 1951. *The Bahrein Islands (750–1951).* New York: Verry, Fisher. 128 pp.

Faust, Ernest Carroll. 1955. *Animal Agents and Vectors of Human Disease.* Philadelphia: Lea and Febiger. 660 pp.

Featherman, A. 1885–91. *Social History of the Races of Mankind.* London: Trübner. 4 vols.

Fedenko, Panas. 1951. *Ukraine, the Struggle for Freedom.* Augsburg, Germany: Free Ukraine. 80 pp.

Fei, Hsiao-Tung. 1946. *Peasant Life in China.* New York: Oxford Univ. Press. 300 pp.

Fernie, William T. 1899. *Animal Simples Approved for Modern Uses of Cure.* Bristol: John Wright. 565 pp.

Ferrars, Max, and Bertha Ferrars. 1901. *Burma.* London: Sampson Low, Marston. 237 pp.

Field, Henry. 1939. *Contributions to the Anthropology of Iran.* Field Museum of Natural History, Anthropological Series, Vol. 29. Chicago. 706 pp.

Fielding Hall, Harold. 1917. *The Soul of a People.* London: Macmillan. 314 pp.

Firth, Raymond. 1930. "Report on Research in Tikopia," *Oceania,* 1 (No. 1): 105–17.

Firth, Rosemary. 1943. *Housekeeping among Malay Peasants.* London School of Economics and Political Science. Monographs on Social Anthropology, No. 7. 198 pp.

Fisher, William B. 1950. *The Middle East: A Physical, Social, and Regional Geography.* London: Methuen. 514 pp.

Fleure, H. J., and E. Estyn Evans, eds. 1939. *Romania II.* South Carpathian Studies. London: Le Play Society. 60 pp.

Forbes, Robert James. 1955. *Studies in Ancient Technology,* Vol. 2. Leiden: E. J. Brill. 215 pp.

Forde, C. Daryll. 1949. *Habitat, Economy and Society.* London: Methuen. 500 pp.

————. 1951. *The Yoruba-Speaking Peoples of South-Western Nigeria.* Ethnographic Survey of Africa. Western Africa, Pt. 4. London: International African Institute. 102 pp.

————. 1955. "The Nupe," pp. 17–52 in *Peoples of the Niger-Benue Confluence.* Ethnographic Survey of Africa. Western Africa, Pt. 10. London: International African Institute.

Forde, Daryll, and G. I. Jones. 1950. *The Ibo and Ibibio-Speaking Peoples of South-Eastern Nigeria.* Ethnographic Survey of Africa. Western Africa, Pt. 3. London: International African Institute. 94 pp.

Fortes, M., and S. L. Fortes. 1936. "Food in the Domestic Economy of the Tallensi," *Africa,* 9: 237–76.

Foucart, P. 1873. *Des associations religieuses chez les Grecs.* Paris: Chez Klincksieck. 243 pp.

Fox, Ernest F. 1943. *Travels in Afghanistan.* New York: Macmillan. 280 pp.

Frazer, James George. 1887. *Totemism.* Edinburgh: Adam and Charles Black. 96 pp.

————. 1935. *The Golden Bough.* New York: Macmillan. 12 vols.

————. 1939. *The Native Races of Asia and Europe.* Anthologia Anthropologica. London: Percy Lund Humphries. 399 pp.

Friters, Gerard M. 1949. *Outer Mongolia and Its International Position.* Baltimore: Johns Hopkins Press. 358 pp.

Fryer, John. 1909–15. *A New Account of East India and Persia.* Hakluyt Society Works, Series 2, Nos. 19 (1909), 20 (1912), and 39 (1915). Ed. by W. Crooke. London: Hakluyt Society. 3 vols.

Fürer-Haimendorf, Christoph von. 1943. *The Aboriginal Tribes of Hyderabad.* London: Macmillan. 2 vols.

Gaillard, Claude. 1934. "Contribution à l'étude de la faune préhistorique de l'Égypte," *Archives du Muséum d'Histoire Naturelle de Lyon,* 4 (Mémoire 3): 1–126.

Galitzin, Ern. 1856. "Manners and Customs of the Yacoutes," *Journal of the Ethnological Society of London,* 4: 144–48.

Gamble, Sidney. 1954. *Ting Hsien, a North China Rural Community.* New York: Institute of Pacific Relations. 472 pp.

Gandhi, M. K. 1949. *Diet and Diet Reform.* Ahmedabad: Navajivan Publishing House. 176 pp.

Gangulee, Nagendranath. 1939. *Health and Nutrition in India.* London: Faber and Faber. 337 pp.

Gautier, Émile F. 1935. *Sahara, the Great Desert.* New York: Columbia Univ. Press. 264 pp.

Gazetteer of the Kangra District. 1883–84. "Kulu, Lahaul and Spiti," pp. 77–149 of Vol. 2. Calcutta: Punjab Government.

Gejvall, Nils Gustaf. 1937–38. "The Fauna of the Different Settlements of Troy. Preliminary Report," *Årsberättelse,* Kungl. Humanistiska Vetenskapssamfundet I Lund. Pp. 51–57.

Gerard, Ralph W. 1952. *Food for Life.* Chicago: Univ. of Chicago Press. 306 pp.

Ghurye, G. S. 1950. *Caste and Class in India.* Bombay: G. R. Bhatkal for the Popular Book Department. 246 pp.

Gibson, H. E. 1935. "Animals in the Writings of Shang," *China Journal,* 23: 342–51.

Goetze, Albrecht. 1938. *The Hittite Ritual of Tunnawi.* American Oriental Series, Vol. 14. New Haven: American Oriental Society. 129 pp.

Golish, Vitold de. 1954. *Primitive India.* London: George G. Harrap. 52 pp.

Gondal, Ram Pratap. 1948. "Changes in Customs and Practices among some Lower Agricultural Castes of the Kotah State," *Eastern Anthropologist,* 1 (No. 4, June): 21–28.

Goudal, Jean. 1938. *Labour Conditions in Indo-China.* International Labour Office. Studies and Reports, Series B, No. 26. Geneva. 331 pp.

Gould, Sylvester E. 1945. *Trichinosis.* Springfield, Ill.: Charles C Thomas. 356 pp.

Gourou, Pierre. 1936. *Les paysans du Delta Tonkinois. Étude de géographie humaine.* Publications de l'École Française d'Extrême-Orient. Vol 27. Paris: Éditions d'Art et d'Histoire. 666 pp.

——. 1945. *Land Utilization in French Indochina.* Washington: Institute of Pacific Relations. 588 pp.

Graffen, Enrico, and Edoardo Columbo. 1906. "Les Niam-Niam," *Revue Internationale de Sociologie,* 14: 769–99. Trans. for the Human Relations Area Files.

Graham, David Crockett. 1937. "The Customs of the Ch'uan Miao," *Journal of the West China Border Research Society,* 9: 13–70.

Graham, W. A. 1924. *Siam.* London: Alexander Moring. 2 vols.

Grajdanzev, Andrew J. 1942. *Formosa Today: An Analysis of the Economic Development and Strategic Importance of Japan's Tropical Colony.* New York: Institute of Pacific Relations. 193 pp.

Grattan, F. J. H. 1948. *An Introduction to Samoan Custom.* Apia, Western Samoa: Samoa Printing and Publishing Company. 189 pp.

Graubard, Mark. 1942. "Food Habits of Primitive Man," *Scientific Monthly,* 55: 342–49, 453–60.

———. 1943. *Man's Food, Its Rhyme or Reason.* New York: Macmillan. 213 pp.

Graves, Robert. 1927. *Lawrence and the Arabs.* London: Jonathan Cape. 454 pp.

———. 1957. "Mushrooms, Food of the Gods," *Atlantic Monthly,* 200 (No. 2, Aug.): 73–77.

Great Britain Admiralty. 1920. *A Handbook of Siberia and Arctic Russia,* Vol. 1. Oxford: H. M. Stationery Office. 384 pp.

Great Britain [Admiralty], Naval Intelligence Division. 1945. *Persia.* Geographical Handbook Series, B.R. 525. London: H. M. Stationery Office. 638 pp.

Great Britain Admiralty. n.d. *A Manual on the Turanians and Pan-Turanianism.* London: H. M. Stationery Office. 256 pp.

Great Britain Colonial Office. 1953. *The Improvement of Cattle in British Colonial Territories in Africa.* Colonial Advisory Council of Agriculture, Animal Health, and Forestry, Pub. No. 3. London: H. M. Stationery Office. 144 pp.

Gregor, Walter. 1881. *Notes on the Folk-Lore of the North-East of Scotland.* London: The Folk-Lore Society. 238 pp.

Griffis, William Elliot. 1882. *Corea: The Hermit Nation.* New York: Charles Scribner's Sons. 462 pp.

Grist, D. H. 1936. *An Outline of Malayan Agriculture.* Malayan Planting Manual No. 2. Kuala Lumpur: Straits Settlement Department of Agriculture. 378 pp.

Groot, Gerard J. 1951. *The Prehistory of Japan.* New York: Columbia Univ. Press. 128 pp.

Gruner, O. Cameron. 1930. *A Treatise on the Canon of Medicine of Avicenna.* London: Luzac. 612 pp.

Guérin and Bernard. 1868. "Les aborigènes de l'île de Formose," *Bulletin de la Société de Géographie (Paris),* Série 5, 15: 542–68. Trans. for the Cross-Cultural Survey by C. Sherman.

Gulick, John. 1955. *Social Structure and Culture Change in a Lebanese Village.* Viking Fund Publications in Anthropology, No. 21. New York: Wenner-Gren Foundation for Anthropological Research. 188 pp.

Gulliver, Pamela, and P. H. Gulliver. 1953. *The Central Nilo-Hamites.* Ethnographic Survey of Africa. East Central Africa, Pt. 7. London: International African Institute. 106 pp.

———. 1956. *Pagan Peoples of the Central Area of Northern Nigeria.* Ethnographic Survey of Africa. Western Africa, Pt. 12. London: International African Institute. 146 pp.

Gunn, Harold D. 1953. *Peoples of the Plateau Area of Northern Nigeria.* Ethnographic Survey of Africa. Western Africa, Pt. 7. London: International African Institute. 111 pp.

Gurdon, P. R. T. 1904. "Note on the Khasis, Syntengs, and Allied Tribes Inhabiting the Khasi and Jaintia Hills District in Assam," *Journal of the Asiatic Society of Bengal,* 73 (Pt. 3, No. 4): 57–74.

———. 1907. *The Khasis.* London: David Nutt. 277 pp.

Gutmann, Bruno. 1926. *Das Recht der Dschagga.* Arbeiten zur Entwicklungspsychologie, No. 7. Munich: C. H. Beck. Trans. for the Human Relations Area Files by A. M. Nagler.

Guys, M. Henri. 1863. *La nation Druse.* Paris: Challamel Ainé. 231 pp.

Haas, William S. 1946. *Iran.* New York: Columbia Univ. Press. 257 pp.

Hadas, Moses, ed. and trans. 1953. *The Third and Fourth Books of Maccabees.* New York: Harper. 248 pp.

Hahn, Eduard. 1896. *Die Haustiere und ihre Beziehungen zur Wirtschaft des Menschen.* Leipzig: Verlag von Duncker und Humblot. 581 pp.

Hall, Irene S., and Calvin S. Hall. 1939. "A Study of Disliked and Unfamiliar Foods," *Journal of the American Dietetic Association,* 15: 540–48.

Hall, Maurice C. 1938. "Studies on Trichinosis. VI. Epidemiological Aspects of Trichinosis in the United States as Indicated by an Examination of 1,000 Diaphragms for Trichinae," *Public Health Reports,* 53: 1086–1105.

Hambly, Wilfrid D. 1934. *The Ovimbundu of Angola.* Field Museum of Natural History, Anthropological Series, 21 (No. 2): 89–362. Chicago.

———. 1935. *Culture Areas of Nigeria.* Field Museum of Natural History, Anthropological Series, 21 (No. 3): 365–502. Chicago.

———. 1937. *Source Book for African Anthropology.* Field Museum of Natural History, Anthropological Series, Vol. 26. Chicago. 2 vols.

Hanauer, J. E. 1935. *Folk-Lore of the Holy Land.* London: Sheldon Press. 280 pp.

Handcock, Percy S. P. 1912. *Mesopotamian Archaeology.* New York: G. P. Putnam's Sons. 423 pp.

Hardy, Robert Spence. 1850. *Eastern Monachism.* London: Partridge and Oakey. 443 pp.

Harmer, Walter J. n.d. "Mother Magic. An Inquiry into the Origin of Domestic Plants and Animals." Unpublished manuscript. 444 pp.

Harnack, Adolf, and Frederic C. Conybeare, "Manichaeism," *Encyclopaedia Britannica,* 11th ed., 17: 572–78.

Harrison, Paul W. 1924. *The Arab at Home.* New York: Thomas Y. Crowell. 345 pp.

Harrisson, Tom. 1937. *Savage Civilisation.* London: Victor Gollancz. 461 pp.

Hart, Donn Vorhis. 1954. "Barrio Caticugan: A Visayan Filipino Community." Unpublished Ph.D. thesis, Syracuse University. 768 pp.

Harting, J. E. 1884. "Dogs: Ancient and Modern," *Zoologist,* Series 3, 8: 393–411.

Hartley, Robert M. 1842. *An Historical, Scientific and Practical Essay on Milk as an Article of Human Sustenance.* New York: Jonathan Leavitt. 358 pp.

Hartmann, R. 1883. *Abyssinien und die übrigen Gebiete der Ostküste Afrikas.* Leipzig: G. Freytag. 304 pp.

Hasluck, Margaret. 1954. *The Unwritten Law in Albania.* Cambridge: Cambridge Univ. Press. 285 pp.

Hastings, James, ed. 1908–22. *Encyclopaedia of Religion and Ethics.* Edinburgh: T. and T. Clark. 12 vols.

Hauptmann, Gerhart Johann Robert. 1951. *The Weavers. Hannele. The Beaver Coat.* Trans. by H. Frenz and M. Waggoner. New York: Rinehart. 218 pp.

Hawes, Charles H. 1903. *In the Uttermost East.* London and New York: Harper and Brothers. 478 pp.

Hearne, Samuel. 1795. *A Journey from Prince of Wales's Fort in Hudson's Bay to the Northern Ocean.* London: A. Strahan and T. Cadell. 458 pp.

Heber, A. Reeve, and Kathleen M. Heber. 1926. *In Himalayan Tibet.* Philadelphia: J. B. Lippincott. 283 pp.

Hehn, Victor. 1885. *The Wanderings of Plants and Animals from their First Home.* Ed. by J. S. Stallybrass. London: Swan Sonnenschein. 523 pp.

Heineman, Paul G. 1921. *Milk.* Philadelphia: W. B. Saunders. 684 pp.

Henninger, Joseph. 1948. "Le sacrifice chez les Arabes," *Ethnos,* 13: 1–16.

Herklots, Gerhard Andreas. 1921. *Islam in India.* London: Oxford Univ. Press. 374 pp.

Hermanns, Matthias. 1949. *Die Nomaden von Tibet.* Vienna: Herold. 325 pp.

Herodotus. 1858. *The Ancient History.* Trans. by W. Beloe. New York: Derby and Jackson. 489 pp.

Herskovits, Melville J. 1926. "The Cattle Complex in East Africa," *American Anthropologist,* N.S., 28: 230–72, 361–88, 494–528, 633–64.

———. 1938. *Dahomey. An Ancient West African Kingdom.* New York: J. J. Augustin. 2 vols.

———. 1952. *Economic Anthropology.* New York: Alfred A. Knopf. 547 pp.

Heydrich, M. 1931. "Koreanische Landwirtschaft: Beiträge zur Völkerkunde von Korea," *Abhandlungen und Berichte der Museen für Tierkunde und Völkerkunde zu Dresden,* 19: 1–44.

Heyworth-Dunne, Gamal-Eddine (James). 1952. *Al-Yemen: A General Social, Political and Economic Survey.* Muslim World Series, No. 5. Cairo: Renaissance Bookshop. 118 pp.

Hikage, Shigeru. 1938. "Eisei" (Health and Living Conditions). Pt. 3, pp. 96–106 of *Moco daikan* (A General Survey of Mongolia), compiled by Zenrin Kyokai chosa-bu. Tokyo: Kaizosha. Trans. for the Human Relations Area Files.

Hill, J. F. R., and J. P. Moffett. 1955. *Tanganyika: A Review of Its Resources and Their Development.* Dar es Salaam: Government of Tanganyika. 924 pp.

Hilton, Richard. 1957. *The Indian Mutiny.* London: Hollis and Carter. 232 pp.

Hilzheimer, Max. 1941. *Animal Remains from Tell Asmar.* Oriental Institute of the University of Chicago, Studies in Ancient Oriental Civilization, No. 20. Chicago: Univ. of Chicago Press. 52 pp.

Hippocrates. 1931. "Regimen," pp. 225–447 in Vol. 4, W. H. S. Jones, *Hippocrates.* London: William Heinemann.

Hiralal, Rai Bahadur. 1925. "Some Notes about Marriage, Food, Drink, and

Occupations of Castes Affecting Social Status in the Central Provinces," *Man in India*, 5: 56–68.

Hofmann, Amerigo. 1912. "Aus Formosa," *Mitteilungen der K. K. Geographischen Gesellschaft in Wien*, 55: 600–638. Trans. for the Human Relations Area Files.

Hooper, David. 1937. "Useful Plants and Drugs of Iran and Iraq." Field Museum of Natural History, Botanical Series, 9 (No. 3) : 69–241. Chicago.

Hooton, Earnest A. 1925. *The Ancient Inhabitants of the Canary Islands*, Harvard African Studies, Vol. 7. 401 pp.

Hopkins, E. Washburn. 1915. *Epic Mythology*. Grundriss der Indo-Arischen Philologie und Altertumskunde. Band 3, Heft 1B. Strassburg: Karl J. Trübner. 277 pp.

Hose, Charles, and William McDougall. 1912. *The Pagan Tribes of Borneo*. London: Macmillan. 2 vols.

Howey, M. Oldfield. 1923. *The Horse in Magic and Myth*. London: W. Rider and Son. 238 pp.

Hrdlička, Aleš. 1912. *The Natives of the Kharga Oasis, Egypt*. Smithsonian Miscellaneous Collections, Vol. 59, No. 1. Washington: Smithsonian Institution. 188 pp.

Huffman, Ray. 1931. *Nuer Customs and Folk-Lore*. London: Oxford Univ. Press. 108 pp.

Hughes, A. J. B., and J. van Velsen. 1954. "The Ndebele," pp. 41–126 in *The Shona and Ndebele of Southern Rhodesia*. Ethnographic Survey of Africa. Southern Africa, Pt. 4. London: International African Institute.

Hughes, Thomas Patrick. 1885. *A Dictionary of Islam*. New York: Scribner, Welford. 750 pp.

Huke, Robert E. 1954. *Economic Geography of a North Burma Kachin Village*. Presented at meetings of the Far Eastern Association, New York. 23 pp.

Hulbert, Homer B. 1906. *The Passing of Korea*. New York: Doubleday, Page. 473 pp.

Humboldt, Alexander von. 1811. *Political Essay on the Kingdom of New Spain*. London: Longman, Hurst, Rees, Orme, and Brown. 4 vols.

———. 1850. *Views of Nature*. London: Henry G. Bohn. 452 pp.

Huntingford, G. W. B. 1953. *The Northern Nilo–Hamites*. Ethnographic Survey of Africa. East Central Africa, Pt. 6. London: International African Institute. 108 pp.

———. [1953a.] *The Southern Nilo–Hamites*. Ethnographic Survey of Africa. East Central Africa, Pt. 8. London: International African Institute. 152 pp.

———. 1955. *The Galla of Ethiopia; The Kingdoms of Kafa and Janjero*. Ethnographic Survey of Africa. North–Eastern Africa, Pt. 2. London: International African Institute. 156 pp.

Hurlbut, Floy. 1939. *The Fukienese: A Study in Human Geography*. Published by the author. 143 pp.

Hutchison, Sir Robert. 1940. *Food and the Principles of Dietetics*. Baltimore: Williams and Wilkins. 648 pp.

Hutson, James. 1921. *Chinese Life on the Tibetan Foothills.* Shanghai: Far Eastern Geographical Establishment. 210 pp.

Hutton, J. H. 1921. *The Angami Nagas.* London: Macmillan. 480 pp.

———. [1921a.] *The Sema Nagas.* London: Macmillan. 463 pp.

———. 1946. *Caste in India.* Cambridge: Cambridge Univ. Press. 279 pp.

———. 1951. *Caste in India: Its Nature, Function, and Origins.* 2d ed. Bombay: Oxford Univ. Press. 315 pp.

Ibn el-Beïthar. 1877. *Traité des simples,* Vol. 1. Notices et Extraits des Manuscrits de la Bibliothèque Nationale et Autres Bibliothèques, 23 (1): 1–476.

Ikbal, 'Ali Shāh Sirdar. 1930. *Eastward to Persia.* London: Wright and Brown. 292 pp.

Imperial Gazetteer of India. 1909. Provincial Series: Kashmir and Jammu. Calcutta: Superintendent of Government Printing. 140 pp.

Inayatullah, Shaikh. 1942. *Geographical Factors in Arabian Life and History.* Kashmiri Bazar, Lahore: Sh. Muhammad Ashraf. 160 pp.

Indiana University. 1955. *Esthonia.* Subcontractor's Monograph, HRAF–2, Indiana–8. New Haven: Human Relations Area Files. 392 pp.

———. [1955a.] *The Hungarians.* Subcontractor's Monograph, HRAF–5, Indiana–19. New Haven: Human Relations Area Files. 267 pp.

———. [1955b.] *The Livonians.* Subcontractor's Monograph, HRAF–9, Indiana–37. New Haven: Human Relations Area Files. 61 pp.

Ingrams, W. H. 1936. *A Report on the Social, Economic and Political Condition of the Hadhramaut.* Colonial Office Report No. 123. London: H. M. Stationery Office. 177 pp.

Islavin, Vladimir. 1847. *Samoiedy v domashnem i obshchestvennom bytu* (The Samoyed in Their Domestic and Social Life). St. Petersburg: Ministerstva Gosudarstvennykh Imshchestv. 142 pp. Trans. for the Cross-Cultural Survey and the Human Relations Area Files.

Ivens, W. G. 1927. *Melanesians of the South-East Solomon Islands.* London: Kegan Paul, Trench, Trübner. 529 pp.

Jackson, A. V. Williams. 1928. *Zoroastrian Studies.* Iranian Religion and Various Monographs. New York: Columbia Univ. Press. 325 pp.

Jackson, Frederick George. 1894. "Notes on the Samoyads of the Great Tundra, collected from the Journals of F. G. Jackson," *Journal of the Anthropological Institute of Great Britain and Ireland,* 24: 388–410.

———. 1899. *A Thousand Days in the Arctic.* New York: Harper and Brothers. 940 pp.

Janse, Olov R. T. 1944. *The Peoples of French Indochina.* Smithsonian Institution, War Background Studies, No. 19. Washington. 28 pp.

Jastrow, Morris. 1898. *The Religion of Babylonia and Assyria.* Boston: Ginn. 780 pp.

Jenks, Albert Ernest. 1905. *The Bontoc Igorot.* Department of the Interior, Ethnological Survey Publications, Vol. 1. Manila: Bureau of Public Printing. 266 pp.

Jensen, P. 1886. "Das Wildschwein in den assyrisch-babylonischen Inschriften," *Zeitschrift für Assyriologie,* 1: 306–12.

Jettmar, Karl. 1954. "Les plus anciennes civilisations d'éleveurs des steppes d'Asie Centrale," *Cahiers d'Histoire Mondiale,* 1: 760–83.

Jevons, Frank Byron. 1904. *An Introduction to the History of Religion.* London: Methuen. 443 pp.

Jochelson, Waldemar. 1905–8. *The Koryak.* American Museum of Natural History, Memoirs, Vol. 10. 842 pp. [Vol. 6 of the Jesup North Pacific Expedition Publications.]

———. 1906. "Kumiss Festivals of the Yakut and the Decoration of Kumiss Vessels," *Boas Anniversary Volume,* pp. 257–71. New York: G. E. Stechert.

———. 1926. *The Yukaghir and the Yukaghirized Tungus.* American Museum of Natural History, Memoirs, Vol. 13. 469 pp. [Vol. 9 of the Jesup North Pacific Expedition Publications.]

———. 1928. *Peoples of Asiatic Russia.* New York: American Museum of Natural History. 277 pp.

Joest, W. 1882. "Beiträge zur Kenntniss der Eingebornen der Inseln Formosa und Ceram," *Verhandlungen der Berliner Gesellschaft für Anthropologie, Ethnographie, und Urgeschichte,* 14: 53–63. Trans. for the Cross-Cultural Survey by M. Switzer.

Johnston, Harry Hamilton. 1895. *The River Congo.* London: Sampson Low, Marston. 300 pp.

———. 1906. *Liberia.* London: Hutchinson. 2 vols.

———. 1910. *George Grenfell and the Congo.* New York: D. Appleton. 2 vols.

Jolly, Julius, trans. 1900. *The Institutes of Vishnu.* Vol. 7 of The Sacred Books of the East, ed. by F. Max Müller. Oxford: Clarendon Press. 316 pp.

Julianus, Flavius Claudius. 1913. *The Orations of the Emperor Julian.* Vol. 1 of The Works of the Emperor Julian. Loeb Clasical Library. London: William Heinemann. 511 pp.

Junker, Wilhelm. 1891. *Travels in Africa during the Years 1879–1883.* London: Chapman and Hall. 447 pp.

———. 1892. *Travels in Africa during the Years 1882–1886.* London: Chapman and Hall. 573 pp.

Junod, Henri A. 1913. *The Life of a South African Tribe.* Neuchatel: Imprimerie Attinger Frères. 2 vols.

Justin (Justinus, Marcus Junianus). 1903. *Historiae Philippicae ex Trogo Pompeio.* Paris: Librairie Hachette. 330 pp.

Kang, Younghill. 1931. *The Grass Roof.* New York: Charles Scribner's Sons. 367 pp.

Karutz, Richard. 1925. *Atlas der Völkerkunde,* Vol. 1. Stuttgart: Frankhsche Verlagshandlung. Trans. for the Human Relations Area Files by B. Cooke and R. Neuse.

Kawaguchi, Ekai. 1909. *Three Years in Tibet.* Adyar, Madras: Theosophist Office. 719 pp.

Keesing, Felix M. 1949. "Some Notes on Bontoc Social Organization, Northern Philippines," *American Anthropologist,* 51: 578–601.

Keir, R. Malcolm. 1914. "Modern Korea," *Bulletin of the American Geographical Society,* 46: 756–69, 817–30.

Keller, C. 1901. *Madagascar, Mauritius, and the Other East–African Islands.* London: Swan Sonnenschein. 242 pp.

Kennan, George. 1870. *Tent Life in Siberia, and Adventures among the Koraks and Other Tribes in Kamchatka and Northern Asia.* New York: G. P. Putnam and Sons. 425 pp.

Kennedy, Raymond. 1953. *Field Notes on Indonesia: South Celebes, 1949–50.* Ed. by H. C. Conklin. New Haven: Human Relations Area Files. 269 pp.

Kenyon, Kathleen M. 1956. "Jericho and Its Setting in Near Eastern History," *Antiquity,* 30: 184–95.

Kern, H. 1918. *Verspreide Geschriften,* Vol. 8. The Hague: Martinus Nijhoff. 323 pp.

Kesteven, G. L. 1949. *Malayan Fisheries.* Singapore: Malaya Publishing House. 88 pp.

Kingdon-Ward, F. 1949. *Burma's Icy Mountains.* London: Jonathan Cape. 287 pp.

Kinmond, William. 1957. *No Dogs in China.* New York: Thomas Nelson and Sons. 211 pp.

Kipling, John Lockwood. 1891. *Beast and Man in India.* London and New York: Macmillan. 401 pp.

Kirk, George. 1952. *The Middle East in the War.* London: Oxford Univ. Press. 511 pp.

Kler, Joseph. 1938. "Birth, Infancy and Childhood among the Ordos Mongols," *Primitive Man,* 11: 58–66.

––––––. 1947. "The Horse in the Life of the Ordos Mongols," *ibid.,* 15–25.

Koppers, Wilhelm. 1930. "Der Hund in der Mythologie der zirkumpazifischen Völker," *Wiener Beiträge zur Kulturgeschichte und Linguistik,* 1: 359–99.

Krader, Lawrence. 1955. "Ecology of Central Asian Pastoralism," *Southwestern Journal of Anthropology,* 11: 301–26.

Krasheninnikov, Stepan. 1764. *The History of Kamtschatka, and the Kurilski Islands, with the Countries Adjacent.* Glocester: R. Raike's. 280 pp.

Kreinovich, E. A. 1934. "Morskoi promysel giliakov derevni Kul' " (The Fishing Industry of the Gilyaks in the Village Kul), *Sovetskaia Etnografia,* No. 5, pp. 78–96. Trans. for the Human Relations Area Files.

Kretschmar, Freda. 1938. *Hundestammvater und Kerberos.* Stuttgart: Strecker und Schröder. 2 vols.

Kroeber, Alfred Louis. 1919. *People of the Philippines.* New York: American Museum of Natural History. 224 pp.

––––––. 1943. *Peoples of the Philippines.* American Museum of Natural History, Handbook Series. 2d and rev. ed. New York. 244 pp.

Kroll, Hubert. 1928. "Die Haustiere der Bantu," *Zeitschrift für Ethnologie,* 60: 177–290.

Kuls, Wolfgang. 1956. "Bericht über Anthropogeographische Studien in Südä-thiopen," *Erdkunde,* 10: 216–27.
Kuper, Hilda. 1952. *The Swazi.* Ethnographic Survey of Africa. Southern Africa, Pt. 1. London: International African Institute. 89 pp.
———. 1954. "The Shona," pp. 9–40 in *The Shona and Ndebele of Southern Rhodesia.* Ethnographic Survey of Africa. Southern Africa, Pt. 4. London: International African Institute. 131 pp.

Lagae, C. R. 1926. *Les Azande ou Niam–Niam: L'organisation Zande, croyances religieuses et magiques, coutumes familiales.* Bibliothèque–Congo. Vol. 18. Brussels: Vromant. 224 pp. Trans. for the Human Relations Area Files.
Lagercrantz, Sture. 1950. *Contribution to the Ethnography of Africa.* Studia Ethnographica Upsaliensia. Vol. 1. Lund. 430 pp.
Lambrecht, Francis. 1932–41. *The Mayawyaw Ritual.* Publications of the Catholic Anthropological Conference, Vol. 4, Nos. 1–5. Washington, D.C. 754 pp.
Lambton, Ann K. S. 1953. *Landlord and Peasant in Persia.* London: Oxford Univ. Press. 459 pp.
Lamson, Herbert Day. 1934. *Social Pathology in China.* Shanghai: Commercial Press. 607 pp.
Landon, Kenneth P. [1939.] *Thailand in Transition: A Brief Survey of Cultural Trends in the Five Years since the Revolution of 1932.* Distributed in the United States by the Univ. of Chicago Press. 427 pp.
Lane, Rose Wilder. 1923. *Peaks of Shala.* New York: Harper and Brothers. 349 pp.
Lang, Olga. 1946. *Chinese Family and Society.* New Haven: Yale Univ. Press. 395 pp.
Langkavel, B. 1881. "Das Hunde-Essen bei den verschiedenen Völkern," *Das Ausland,* 54: 658–60.
———. 1888. "Pferde und Naturvölker," *Internationales Archiv für Ethnographie,* 1: 49–60.
———. 1898. "Dogs and Savages," *Annual Report of the Smithsonian Institution for the Year Ending June 30, 1898,* pp. 651–75.
Lansdell, Henry. 1882. *Through Siberia.* Boston: Houghton, Mifflin. 811 pp.
Larken, P. M. 1926, 1927. "An Account of the Zande," *Sudan Notes and Records,* 9: 1–55; 10: 85–134.
Latourette, Kenneth S. 1934. *The Chinese: Their History and Culture,* Vol. 2. New York: Macmillan. 389 pp.
Lattimore, Owen. 1929. *The Desert Road to Turkestan.* Boston: Little, Brown. 373 pp.
———. 1932. "Chinese Colonization in Inner Mongolia: Its History and Present Development," pp. 288–312 in *Pioneer Settlement: Cooperative Studies.* American Geographical Society, Special Publications, No. 14. New York.
———. 1933. "The Gold Tribe, 'Fishskin Tatars' of the Lower Sungari," *Memoirs of the American Anthropological Association,* No. 40, pp. 1–77.

————. 1941. *Mongol Journeys.* New York: Doubleday, Doran. 324 pp.

————. 1950. *Pivot of Asia: Sinkiang and the Inner Asian Frontiers of China and Russia.* Boston: Little, Brown. 288 pp.

Laufer, Berthold. 1927. "Methods in the Study of Domestications," *Scientific Monthly,* 25: 251–55.

Lawrance, J. C. D. 1957. *The Iteso.* London: Oxford Univ. Press. 280 pp.

Lawrence, Walter R. 1895. *The Valley of Kashmir.* London: Henry Frowde. 478 pp.

Layard, Henry Austen. 1849. *Ninevah and Its Remains.* London: John Murray. 2 vols.

Leach, E. R. 1940. *Social and Economic Organization of the Rowanduz Kurds.* London School of Economic and Political Science, Monographs on Social Anthropology, No. 3. 74 pp.

Leach, Maria, ed. 1949–50. *Standard Dictionary of Folklore.* New York: Funk and Wagnalls. 2 vols.

League of Nations. 1939. *Lithuania.* European Conference on Rural Life, 1939, Vol. 12. Geneva: League of Nations. 47 pp.

————. Health Organization, Intergovernmental Conference of Far-Eastern Countries on Rural Hygiene. 1937. *Preparatory Papers: Report of French Indochina.* League of Nations Publications, Series 3: Health. Geneva. 135 pp.

Lebkicher, Roy, G. Rantz, and M. Steineke. 1952. *The Arabia of Ibn Saud.* New York: Russell F. Moore. 179 pp.

Legendre, Aimé François. 1909. "Far West Chinois. Races aborigènes. Les Lolos. Étude ethnologique et anthropologique," *T'oung pao,* Série 2, 10: 340–80, 399–444, 603–665. Leiden: E. J. Brill.

Leitner, G. W. [1893.] *Dardistan in 1866, 1886, and 1893.* Working, England: Oriental University Institute. 251 pp.

Le May, Reginald. 1930. *Siamese Tales Old and New: The Four Riddles and Other Stories.* London: Noel Douglas. 192 pp.

Levi-Strauss, Claude. 1955. "I Starved with the World's Most Primitive Tribe," *Réalités,* Sept., pp. 56–76.

Lévy-Bruhl, Lucien. 1923. *Primitive Mentality.* New York: Macmillan. 458 pp.

Lewis, Albert Buell. 1932. *Ethnology of Melanesia.* Guide, Pt. 5. Chicago: Field Museum of Natural History. 209 pp.

Lewis, I. M. 1955. *Peoples of the Horn of Africa.* Ethnographic Survey of Africa. North–Eastern Africa, Pt. 1. London: International African Institute. 200 pp.

Lewis, Norman. 1951. *A Dragon Apparent: Travels in Indochina.* New York: Charles Scribner's Sons. 317 pp.

Li, Chi. 1957. *The Beginnings of Chinese Civilization.* Seattle: Univ. of Washington Press. 123 pp.

Lin Yueh-wha. 1944. "Social Life of the Aboriginal Groups in and around Yunnan," *Journal of the West China Border Research Society,* Series A, 15: 47–56.

Lindeman, M. 1906. "Les Upotos," *Bulletin de la Société Royale Belge de Géographie* (Brussels), 30: 16–32.

Linton, Ralph. 1926. *Ethnology of Polynesia and Micronesia.* Guide, Pt. 6. Chicago: Field Museum of Natural History. 191 pp.

———. 1933. *The Tanala: A Hill Tribe of Madagascar.* Field Museum of Natural History, Anthropological Series, Vol. 22. Chicago. 334 pp.

———. 1955. *The Tree of Culture.* New York: Alfred A. Knopf. 692 pp.

Liu En-lan. 1937. "Pootu, a Lost Island," *Economic Geography,* 13: 132–38.

Lobo, Jerome. 1734. *A Voyage to Abyssinia.* Trans. by M. LeGrand. London: A. Bettesworth and C. Hitch. 396 pp.

Loeb, Edwin M. 1935. "Sumatra. Its History and People," *Wiener Beiträge zur Kulturgeschichte und Linguistik,* 3: 1–303.

———. n.d. "In Feudal Africa. The Kwanyama Ambo Bantu of Southwest Africa." Unpublished manuscript. 481 pp.

Lorimer, Emily Overend. 1938. "The Burusho of Hunza," *Antiquity,* 12: 5–15.

———. 1939. *Language Hunting in the Karakoram.* London: George Allen and Unwin. 310 pp.

Lowie, Robert H. 1940. *An Introduction to Cultural Anthropology.* New York: Rinehart. 584 pp.

Lucian. 1913. *The Syrian Goddess.* Trans. by H. A. Strong. London: Constable. 111 pp.

Lužbetak, Louis J. 1951. *Marriage and the Family in Caucasia: A Contribution to the Study of North Caucasian Ethnology and Customary Law.* Vienna-Modling: St. Gabriel's Mission Press. 272 pp.

Ma, Ho–t'ien. 1949. *Chinese Agent in Mongolia.* Baltimore: Johns Hopkins Press. 215 pp.

Macalister, R. A. Stewart. 1913. *The Philistines: Their History and Civilization.* London: British Academy. 136 pp.

Maccabees. For Books I–IV of Maccabees see Moses Hadas, ed. and trans.; Sidney Tedesche, trans; Solomon Zeitlin, ed.

MacCulloch, John Arnott. 1916–32. *The Mythology of All Races.* Boston: Marshall Jones. 13 vols.

McCulloch, Merran. 1950. *Peoples of Sierra Leone Protectorate.* Ethnographic Survey of Africa. Western Africa, Pt. 2. London: International African Institute. 102 pp.

———. 1951. *The Southern Lunda and Related Peoples.* Ethnographic Survey of Africa. West Central Africa, Pt. 1. London: International African Institute. 110 pp.

———. 1952. *The Ovimbundu of Angola.* Ethnographic Survey of Africa. West Central Africa, Pt. 2. London: International African Institute. 50 pp.

———. 1954. "Tikar," pp. 11–52 in *Peoples of the Central Cameroons.* Ethnographic Survey of Africa. Western Africa, Pt. 9. London: International African Institute.

MacDonald, David. 1929. *The Land of the Lama.* London: Seeley, Service. 283 pp.

Macdonell, Arthur A. 1897. *Vedic Mythology.* Grundriss der Indo–Arischen

Philologie und Altertumskunde. Band 3, Heft 1A. Strassburg: Karl J. Trübner. 189 pp.

Mackay, Ernest J. H. 1943. *Chanhu–Daro Excavations 1935–36.* American Oriental Series, Vol. 20. New Haven: American Oriental Society. 338 pp.

Majumdar, D. N. 1937. *A Tribe in Transition.* Calcutta: Longmans, Green. 216 pp.

Malcolm, George A. 1951. *First Malayan Republic: The Story of the Philippines.* Boston: Christopher. 460 pp.

Malinowski, Bronislaw. 1935. *Coral Gardens and Their Magic.* New York: American Book Company. 2 vols.

Mallory, Walter H. 1926. *China, Land of Famine.* American Geographical Society, Special Publications, No. 6. New York. 199 pp.

Man, Edward Horace. 1932. *On the Aboriginal Inhabitants of the Andaman Islands.* London: Royal Anthropological Institute of Great Britain and Ireland. 224 pp.

Mann, Harold H. 1917. *Land and Labour in a Deccan Village.* Bombay: Oxford Univ. Press. 184 pp.

Manoukian, Madeline. 1950. *Akan and Ga-Adangme Peoples of the Gold Coast.* Ethnographic Survey of Africa. Western Africa, Pt. 1. London: International African Institute. 112 pp.

————. 1952. *Tribes of the Northern Territories of the Gold Coast.* Ethnographic Survey of Africa. Western Africa, Pt. 5. London: International African Institute. 102 pp.

————. [1952a.] *The Ewe–Speaking People of Togoland and the Gold Coast.* Ethnographic Survey of Africa. Western Africa, Pt. 6. London: International African Institute. 63 pp.

Marriott, McKim, ed. 1955. "Village India," *Memoirs of the American Anthropological Association,* No. 83, pp. 1–269.

Marshall, Harry Ignatius. 1922. *The Karen People of Burma: A Study in Anthropology and Ethnology.* Ohio State University Bul., Vol. 26, No. 13. Columbus: Ohio State University Press. 329 pp.

Marshall, John. 1931. *Mohenjo–Daro and the Indus Civilization.* London: Arthur Probsthain. 3 vols.

Marshall, William E. 1873. *A Phrenologist amongst the Todas.* London: Longmans, Green. 271 pp.

Martialis, Marcus Valerius. 1926. *The Epigrams.* Trans. by Henry G. Bohn. London: G. Bell. 660 pp.

Marty, Paul. 1930. "Les Nimadi, Maures sauvages et chasseurs," *Hespéris,* 11: 119–24.

Maspero, G. 1901. *The Dawn of Civilization.* New York: D. Appleton. 800 pp.

Massé, Henri. 1938. *Croyances et coutumes persanes suivies de contes et chansons populaires.* Paris: Librairie Orientale et Américaine. 533 pp. Trans. for the Human Relations Area Files.

Masuoka, Jitsuichi. 1945. "Changing Food Habits of the Japanese in Hawaii," *American Sociological Review,* 10: 759–65.

Mattingly, H. 1951. *Tacitus on Britain and Germany. A New Translation of the 'Agricola' and the 'Germania'*. Harmondsworth, England: Penguin Books. 175 pp.

Maxwell, W. E. 1881. "The Folklore of the Malays," *Journal of the Straits Branch of the Royal Asiatic Society,* 7: 11–29.

May, Jacques M. 1950. "Medical Geography: Its Methods and Objectives," *Geographical Review,* 40: 9–41.

Mead, Margaret. 1930. *Social Organization of Manua.* Bernice P. Bishop Museum, Bul. 76. Honolulu. 218 pp.

———, ed. 1955. *Cultural Patterns and Technical Change.* New York: New American Library. 352 pp.

Meek, C. K. 1925. *The Northern Tribes of Nigeria.* London: Oxford Univ. Press. 2 vols.

Menander. 1921. *The Principal Fragments.* With an English trans. by F. G. Allinson. London: William Heinemann. 540 pp.

Metcalf, John E. 1952. *The Agricultural Economy of Indonesia.* U.S. Department of Agriculture, Office of Foreign Affairs, Monograph No. 15. Washington: U.S. Government Printing Office. 100 pp.

Métraux, Alfred. 1940. *Ethnology of Easter Island.* Bernice P. Bishop Museum, Bul. 160. Honolulu. 432 pp.

Mi Mi Khaing. 1946. *Burmese Family.* Calcutta: Longmans, Green. 138 pp.

Mickey, Margaret Portia. 1947. *The Cowrie Shell Miao of Kweichow.* Harvard University, Peabody Museum of American Archaeology and Ethnology, Papers, Vol. 32, No. 1. Cambridge. 83 pp.

Middleton, John. 1953. *The Kikuyu and the Kamba of Kenya.* Ethnographic Survey of Africa. East Central Africa, Pt. 5. London: International African Institute. 105 pp.

Minns, Ellis H. 1913. *Scythians and Greeks.* Cambridge: Cambridge Univ. Press. 720 pp.

Mirchuk, I., ed. 1949. *Ukraine and Its People: A Handbook with Maps, Statistical Tables and Diagrams.* Munich: Ukrainian Free Univ. Press. 280 pp.

Modi, Jivanji Jamshedji. 1913–16. "The Pundits of Kashmir," *Journal of the Anthropological Society of Bombay,* 10: 461–85.

Moninger, M. M. 1921. "The Hainanese Miao," *Journal of the North China Branch of the Royal Asiatic Society,* 52: 40–50.

Montell, Gösta. 1937. "Distilling in Mongolia," *Ethnos,* 2: 321–32.

———. 1940. "The Torguts of Etsin-Gol," *Journal of the Royal Anthropological Institute of Great Britain and Ireland,* 70: 77–92.

Montet, Pierre. 1958. *Everyday Life in Egypt in the Days of Ramesses the Great.* London: Edward Arnold. 365 pp.

Moose, J. Robert. 1911. *Village Life in Korea.* Nashville: M. E. Church. 242 pp.

Morgan, Kenneth W. 1953. *The Religion of the Hindus.* New York: Ronald Press. 434 pp.

Morrison, Hyman. 1935. "Trichiniasis among Jews," *New England Journal of Medicine,* 213: 531–32.

Mukerjee, Radhakamal. 1938. *Food Planning for Four Hundred Millions*. London: Macmillan. 267 pp.

Mukhtyar, G. C. 1930. *Life and Labour in a South Gujarat Village*. Studies in Indian Economics, Vol. 3. Calcutta: Longmans, Green. 304 pp.

Musil, Alois. 1928. *The Manners and Customs of the Rwala Bedouins*. American Geographical Society, Oriental Explorations and Studies, No. 6. New York. 712 pp.

Nachtigal, G. 1874. "Nachrichten von Dr. G. Nachtigal in Inner-Afrika. Die tributären Heidenländer Baghirmi's," *Petermanns Mitteilungen*, 20: 323–31.

Nadel, Siegfried Ferdinand. 1947. *The Nuba*. London: Oxford Univ. Press. 527 pp.

———. 1951. *A Black Byzantium*. London: Oxford Univ. Press. 420 pp.

Nalder, Leonard Fielding, ed. 1937. *A Tribal Survey of Mongalla Province*. London: Oxford Univ. Press. 232 pp.

National Research Council. 1943. *The Problem of Changing Food Habits*. Report of the Committee on Food Habits, 1941–43. National Research Council, Bul. No. 108. October. 177 pp.

Newberry, P. E. 1928. "The Pig and the Cult-Animal of Set," *Journal of Egyptian Archaeology*, 14: 211–25.

Niedermayer, Oskar von. 1924. *Afghanistan*. Leipzig: Karl W. Hiersemann. 316 pp. Trans. for the Human Relations Area Files by W. Chafe.

Norbeck, Edward. 1954. *Takashima: A Japanese Fishing Community*. Salt Lake City: Univ. of Utah Press. 232 pp.

Norins, Martin R. 1944. *Gateway to Asia: Sinkiang, Frontier of the Chinese Far West*. New York: John Day. 200 pp.

Northampton, The Marquis of, W. Spiegelberg, and P. E. Newberry. 1908. *Report on Some Excavations in the Theban Necropolis during the Winter of 1898–9*. London: Archibald Constable. 40 pp.

Nweeya, Samuel K. 1910. *Persia the Land of the Magi*. Philadelphia: John C. Winston. 352 pp.

Oldenberg, Hermann, trans. 1886. *The Grihya-Sûtras*, Pt. 1. Vol. 29 of The Sacred Books of the East, ed. by F. Max Müller. Oxford: Clarendon Press. 440 pp.

O'Malley, L. S. S., ed. 1941. *Modern India and the West*. London: Oxford Univ. Press. 834 pp.

Onabamiro, Sanya Dojo. 1953. *Food and Health*. Penguin West African Series. London: Penguin Books. 124 pp.

Orléans, Prince Henri d'. 1894. *Around Tonkin and Siam*. London: Chapman and Hall. 426 pp.

Orlovskii, P. N. 1928. "God anadyrsko-Chukotskoga olenevoda" (A Year in the Life of an Anadyr-Chukchee Reindeer Raiser), *Severnaia Aziia*, No. 2, pp. 61–70. Trans. for the Human Relations Area Files by L. Bromwich.

Osgood, Cornelius. 1951. *The Koreans and Their Culture*. New York: Ronald Press. 387 pp.
Ovid (Publius Ovidius Naso). 1867. *The Metamorphoses of Ovid*. Trans. by H. T. Riley. Volume 2 of Works of Ovid. London: Bell and Daldy. 554 pp.

Parker, K. Langloh. 1905. *The Euahlayi Tribe*. London: Archibald Constable. 156 pp.
Parkyns, Mansfield. 1868. *Life in Abyssinia*. London: John Murray. 446 pp.
Paton, David. 1925. *Animals of Ancient Egypt*. Princeton: Princeton Univ. Press. 37 pp.
Patwardhan, V. N. 1952. *Nutrition in India*. Bombay: Indian Journal of Medical Sciences. 345 pp.
Paulitschke, Philipp. 1893. *Ethnographie Nordost-Afrikas. Die Materielle Cultur der Danâkil, Galla und Somal*. Berlin: Geographische Verlagshandlung Dietrich Reimer. 338 pp.
Paulus Aegineta. 1844–47. *The Seven Books of Paulus Aegineta*. Trans. by F. Adams. London: Sydenham Society. 3 vols.
Pausanias. 1898. *Description of Greece*. Trans. with a commentary by J. G. Frazer. London: Macmillan. 6 vols.
Pearce, F. B. 1920. *Zanzibar*. London: T. Fisher Unwin. 431 pp.
Pearce, Nathaniel. 1831. *The Life and Adventures of Nathaniel Pearce*, ed. by J. J. Halls. London: Henry Colburn and Richard Bentley. 2 vols.
Peschel, Oscar. 1906. *The Races of Man, and Their Geographical Distribution*. New York: D. Appleton. 528 pp.
Peters, John Punnett. 1897–98. *Nippur, or Explorations and Adventures on the Euphrates*. New York: Knickerbocker Press. 2 vols.
Philby, H. St. John B. 1928. *Arabia of the Wahhabis*. London: Constable. 422 pp.
———. 1952. *Arabian Highlands*. Ithaca: Cornell Univ. Press. 771 pp.
———. 1955. *Saudi Arabia*. London: Ernest Benn. 393 pp.
Phillips, Paul Grounds. 1954. *The Hashemite Kingdom of Jordan: Prolegomena to a Technical Assistance Program*. University of Chicago, Department of Geography, Research Paper No. 34. Chicago. 191 pp.
Phillott, D. C. 1907. "Bibliomancy, Divination, Superstitions, amongst the Persians," *Journal and Proceedings of the Asiatic Society of Bengal*, N.S., 2 (No. 8): 339–42.
Platt, Raye R., and Mohammed Bahy Hefny. 1958. *Egypt: A Compendium*. New York: American Geographical Society. 408 pp.
Pliny. 1942. *Natural History*. Cambridge: Harvard Univ. Press. 10 vols.
Plowden, Walter C. 1868. *Travels in Abyssinia and the Galla Country*. London: Longmans, Green. 485 pp.
Plutarch. [1905.] *Symposiacs*. Pp. 197–460 in Vol. 8 of The Writings of Plutarch, cor. and rev. by W. W. Goodwin. New York: Athenaeum Society. 518 pp.
———. 1936. *Isis and Osiris*. Pp. 1–191 in Vol. 5 of *Plutarch's Moralia*, trans. by F. C. Babbitt. Cambridge: Harvard Univ. Press. 515 pp.

————. 1936. *The Roman Questions*. Pp. 1–171 in Vol. 4 of *Plutarch's Moralia*, trans. by F. C. Babbitt. Cambridge: Harvard Univ. Press. 553 pp.

Pollard, Samuel. 1921. *In Unknown China*. Philadelphia: J. B. Lippincott. 324 pp.

Porphyry. 1823. *Select Works of Porphyry*. Trans. by T. Taylor. London: Thomas Rodd. 271 pp.

Powdermaker, Hortense. 1933. *Life in Lesu*. New York: W. W. Norton. 352 pp.

Price, Weston Andrew. 1939. *Nutrition and Physical Degeneration. A Comparison of Primitive and Modern Diets and Their Effects*. New York: Paul B. Hoeber. 431 pp.

Prins, A. H. J. 1952. *The Coastal Tribes of the North-Eastern Bantu*. Ethnographic Survey of Africa. East Central Africa, Pt. 3. London: International African Institute. 138 pp.

Pritchard, W. T. 1866. *Polynesian Reminiscences*. London: Chapman and Hall. 428 pp.

Przhevalskii, N. 1876. *Mongolia, the Tangut Country, and the Solitudes of Northern Tibet*, Vol. 1. Trans. by E. D. Morgan. London: Sampson Low, Marston, Searle, and Rivington. 287 pp.

Pumpelly, Raphael. 1908. *Explorations in Turkestan*. Washington: Carnegie Institution of Washington. 2 vols.

Radcliffe-Brown, A. R. 1933. *The Andaman Islanders*. Cambridge: Cambridge Univ. Press. 510 pp.

Rae, Edward. 1875. *The Land of the North Wind: or Travels among the Laplanders and the Samoyedes*. London: John Murray. 352 pp.

————. 1881. *The White Sea Peninsula: A Journey in Russian Lapland and Karelia*. London: John Murray. 347 pp.

Ramsay, Captain H. 1890. *Western Tibet: A Practical Dictionary of the Language and Customs of the Districts Included in the Ladak Wazarat*. Lahore: W. Ball, Government Printers. 190 pp.

Ramsay, W. M. 1890. *The Historical Geography of Asia Minor*. Royal Geographical Society, Supplementary Papers, Vol. 4. London: John Murray. 493 pp.

Raswan, Carl R. 1947. *Black Tents of Arabia*. New York: Creative Age Press. 206 pp.

Rattray, R. S. 1927. *Religion and Art in Ashanti*. Oxford: Clarendon Press. 414 pp.

Ratzel, Friedrich. 1896–98. *The History of Mankind*. London: Macmillan. 3 vols.

Raum, O. F. 1940. *Chaga Childhood: A Description of Indigenous Education in an East African Tribe*. London: Oxford Univ. Press. 422 pp.

Reale Società Geografica Italiana, Rome. 1936. *L'Africa Orientale*. Bologna: Zanichelli. 407 pp.

Reclus, Élisée. 1895. *The Earth and Its Inhabitants*, Vol. 1. New York: D. Appleton. 504 pp.

Reed, Charles A. 1959. "Animal Domestication in the Prehistoric Near East," *Science*, Dec. 11, pp. 1629–39.

Reich, Eduard. 1935. *Die tchechoslowakische Landwirtschaft.* Berlin: Verlags-buchhandlung Paul Parey. 312 pp. Trans. for the Human Relations Area Files by F. Schütze.

Reinach, Lucien de. 1901. *Le Laos.* Paris: A. Charles, Librairie-Editeur. 2 vols. Trans. for the Human Relations Area Files by C. A. Messner.

Remington, Roe E. 1936. "The Social Origins of Dietary Habits," *Scientific Monthly,* 43: 193–204.

Renner, H. D. 1944. *The Origin of Food Habits.* London: Faber and Faber. 261 pp.

Riasanovsky, Valentin Aleksandrovich. 1937. *Fundamental Principles of Mongolian Law.* London: Kegan Paul, Trench, Trübner. 338 pp.

Richard, P. C. 1867. "Notes pour servir à l'ethnographie de la Cochinchine," *Revue Maritime et Coloniale,* 21: 92–133. Trans. for the Human Relations Area Files by K. Botsford.

Richards, Audrey I. 1939. *Land, Labour and Diet in Northern Rhodesia.* London: International Institute of African Languages and Cultures. 423 pp.

⸺. 1948. *Hunger and Work in a Savage Tribe.* Glencoe, Ill.: Free Press. 238 pp.

Richards, C. J. 1945. *The Burman: An Appreciation.* Burma Pamphlets, No. 7. Calcutta: Longmans, Green. 55 pp.

Ritson, Joseph. 1802. *An Essay on Abstinence from Animal Food as a Moral Duty.* London: Richard Phillips. 236 pp.

Rivera, Generoso F., and Robert T. McMillan. 1952. *The Rural Philippines.* Manila: Office of Information, Mutual Security Agency. 217 pp.

Rivers, W. H. R. 1906. *The Todas.* London: Macmillan. 755 pp.

⸺. 1914. *The History of Melanesian Society,* Vol. 1. Cambridge: Cambridge Univ. Press. 400 pp.

Robinson, A. E. 1936. "The Camel in Antiquity," *Sudan Notes and Records,* 19: 47–70.

Rockhill, William Woodville. 1894. *Diary of a Journey through Mongolia and Tibet in 1891 and 1892.* Washington: Smithsonian Institution. 413 pp.

⸺. 1895. "Notes on the Ethnology of Tibet," *Report of the U.S. National Museum for 1893,* pp. 665–747. Washington: Smithsonian Institution.

Rombauer, Irma S. 1943. *The Joy of Cooking.* Indianapolis and New York: Bobbs-Merrill. 884 pp.

Roscoe, John. 1911. *The Baganda.* London: Macmillan. 547 pp.

⸺. 1915. *The Northern Bantu.* Cambridge: Cambridge Univ. Press. 305 pp.

⸺. 1923. *The Bakitara or Banyoro.* Cambridge: Cambridge Univ. Press. 370 pp.

Roth, Henry Ling. 1890. *The Aborigines of Tasmania.* London: Kegan Paul, Trench, Trübner. 224 pp.

⸺. 1896. *The Natives of Sarawak and British North Borneo.* London: Truslove and Hanson. 2 vols.

Routledge, W. Scoresby, and Katherine Routledge. 1910. *With a Prehistoric People.* London: Edward Arnold. 392 pp.

Ruey, Yih-fu, et al. 1955. "Ethnographical Investigation of Some Aspects of the Atayal, Chin-shui Ts'un, Miaoli Hsien," National Taiwan University, Department of Archaeology and Anthropology, Bul. No. 5, pp. 113–27. Trans. for the Human Relations Area Files by Chen Chi'lu.

Ruiz, Leopoldo T. 1945. "Farm Tenancy and Cooperatives in the Philippines," *Far Eastern Quarterly*, 4: 163–69.

Rushdy, Mahmud Effendi. 1911. "The Treading of Sown Seed by Swine," *Annales du Service des Antiquités de l'Égypte*, 11: 162–63.

Russell, Sir E. John. 1954. *World Population and World Food Supplies*. London: George Allen and Unwin. 513 pp.

Salt, Henry. 1814. *A Voyage to Abyssinia and Travels into the Interior of That Country*. London: F. C. and J. Rivington. 506 pp.

Sanders, Irwin T. 1949. *Balkan Village*. Lexington: University of Kentucky Press. 291 pp.

Sandford, K. S. 1934. *Paleolithic Man and the Nile Valley in Upper and Middle Egypt*. Oriental Institute of the University of Chicago. Prehistoric Survey of Egypt and Western Asia, Vol. 3. Chicago: Univ. of Chicago Press. 131 pp.

Sanjana, J. E. 1946. *Caste and Outcaste*. Bombay: Thacker. 249 pp.

Sarytschew (Sarychev), Gawrila. 1806. *Account of a Voyage of Discovery to the North–east of Siberia, the Frozen Ocean, and the North–east Sea*, Vol 1. London: Richard Phillips. 70 pp.

Sauer, Carl O. 1952. *Agricultural Origins and Dispersals*. Bowman Memorial Lectures, Series 2. New York: American Geographical Society. 110 pp.

Saunderson, H. S. 1895. "Notes on Corea and Its People," *Journal of the Anthropological Institute of Great Britain and Ireland*, 24: 299–316.

Sawitz, Willi. 1938. "The Prevalence of Trichinosis in the United States," *Public Health Reports*, 53: 365–83.

Sayce, A. H. 1888. *Lectures on the Origin and Growth of Religion as Illustrated by the Religion of the Ancient Babylonians*. Hibbert Lectures, 1887. London: Williams and Norgate. 558 pp.

Schapera, I. 1953. *The Tswana*. Ethnographic Survey of Africa. Southern Africa, Pt. 3. London: International African Institute. 80 pp.

Schapera, I., and A. J. H. Goodwin. 1950. "Work and Wealth," pp. 131–72 in I. Schapera, ed., *The Bantu–Speaking Tribes of South Africa*. London: Routledge and Kegan Paul.

Schneider, Harold K. 1957. "The Subsistence Role of Cattle among the Pakot and in East Africa," *American Anthropologist*, 59: 278–300.

Schrader, Otto. 1890. *Prehistoric Antiquities of the Aryan Peoples*. Trans. by F. B. Jevons. London: Charles Griffin. 486 pp.

Schulze, Louis. 1891. "The Aborigines of the Upper and Middle Finke River," *Transactions and Proceedings and Report of the Royal Society of South Australia*, 14: 210–46.

Schumacher, Robert. 1898. "Formosa und seine Gebirgsbewohner," *Petermanns Mitteilungen*, 44: 222–26. Trans. for the Cross–Cultural Survey by E. R. Field.

Schweinfurth, Georg. 1873. *The Heart of Africa*. London: Sampson Low. 2 vols.

Scott, Sir James George (Shway Yoe, pseud.). 1910. *The Burman: His Life and Notions*. London: Macmillan. 609 pp.

Seeland, Nicolas. 1882. "Die Ghiliaken: Eine ethnographische Skizze," *Russische Revue*, 21: 97–130, 222–54. Trans. for the Human Relations Area Files.

Seligman, Charles Gabriel. 1910. *The Melanesians of British New Guinea*. Cambridge: Cambridge Univ. Press. 766 pp.

Seligman, Charles Gabriel, and Brenda Z. Seligman. 1911. *The Veddas*. Cambridge: Cambridge Univ. Press. 463 pp.

——. 1918. "The Kababish, a Sudan Arab Tribe," Harvard African Studies, 2: 105–86.

——. 1932. *Pagan Tribes of the Nilotic Sudan*. London: George Routledge and Sons. 565 pp.

Sengupta, Padmini. 1950. *Everyday Life in Ancient India*. London: Oxford Univ. Press. 203 pp.

Sextus Empiricus. 1933. *Outlines of Pyrrhonism*. Vol. 1 of the works of Sextus Empiricus, trans. by R. G. Bury. London: William Heinemann. 513 pp.

Shah, Vimal, and Sarla Shah. 1949. *Bhuvel: Socio-economic Survey of a Village*. Bombay: Vora. 154 pp.

Shakespear, J. 1912. *The Lushei Kuki Clans*. London: Macmillan. 250 pp.

Shamasastry, R., trans. 1951. *Kauṭilya's Arthaśāstra*. 4th ed. Mysore: Sri Raghuveer Printing Press. 484 pp.

Sheddick, V. G. J. 1953. *The Southern Sotho*. Ethnographic Survey of Africa. Southern Africa, Pt. 2. London: International African Institute. 87 pp.

Shen, T. H. 1951. *Agricultural Resources of China*. Ithaca: Cornell Univ. Press. 407 pp.

Shên, Tsung-lien, and Shên-chi Liu. 1953. *Tibet and the Tibetans*. Stanford: Stanford Univ. Press. 199 pp.

Shinichirō, Takakura. 1960. "The Ainu of Northern Japan," *Transactions of the American Philosophical Society*, N.S., 50 (Pt. 4): 1–88. Trans. and ann. by J. A. Harrison.

Shirokogoroff, S. M. 1924. *Social Organization of the Manchus*. Royal Asiatic Society (North China Branch), Extra Vol. 3. Shanghai. 196 pp.

Shklovsky, I. W. 1916. *In Far North-East Siberia*. London: Macmillan. 264 pp.

Simmons, James Stevens, et al. 1954. *The Near and Middle East*. Vol. 3 in *Global Epidemiology: A Geography of Disease and Sanitation*. Philadelphia: J. B. Lippincott. 357 pp.

Simoons, Frederick. 1954. "The Non-Milking Area of Africa," *Anthropos*, 49: 58–66.

Simson, Alfred. 1886. *Travels in the Wilds of Ecuador, and the Exploration of the Putumayo River*. London: Sampson Low, Marston, Searle, and Rivington. 270 pp.

Singh, Mohinder. 1947. *The Depressed Classes: Their Economic and Social Condition*. Bombay: Hind Kitabs. 216 pp.

Skeat, Walter William, and Charles Otto Blagden. 1906. *Pagan Races of the Malay Peninsula*. London: Macmillan. 2 vols.

Skrine, C. P. 1926. *Chinese Central Asia.* London: Methuen. 306 pp.

Slaski, J. 1951. *Peoples of the Lower Luapula Valley.* Ethnographic Survey of Africa. East Central Africa, Pt. 2 of Pt. 2. pp. 77–100. London: International African Institute.

Slater, Gilbert, ed. 1918. *Some South Indian Villages.* University of Madras, Economic Studies, Vol. 1. London: Oxford Univ. Press. 265 pp.

Smeds, Helmer. 1955. "The Ensete Planting Culture of Eastern Sidamo, Ethiopia," *Acta Geographica,* 13 (No. 4): 1–39.

Smith, Edwin W., and Andrew Murray Dale. 1920. *The Ila-Speaking Peoples of Northern Rhodesia.* London: Macmillan. 2 vols.

Smith, W. Robertson. 1908. *The Old Testament in the Jewish Church.* London: Adam and Charles Black. 458 pp.

——. 1914. *Lectures on the Religion of the Semites.* London: Adam and Charles Black. 507 pp.

Smith, William, ed. 1893. *A Dictionary of the Bible.* London: John Murray. 3 vols.

Smith, William Carlson. 1925. *The Ao Naga Tribe of Assam.* London: Macmillan. 244 pp.

Smyth, R. Brough. 1878. *The Aborigines of Victoria,* Vol. 1. London: Trübner. 483 pp.

Sopher, David E. 1959. *Geography of Indian Coasts.* Dittoed Annual Summary Report, Office of Naval Research NR 388–041, Contract No. Nonr–2329(00). 37 pp.

Sorokin, Pitirim A. 1942. *Man and Society in Calamity.* New York: E. P. Dutton. 352 pp.

Sowerby, Arthur de Carle. 1935. "The Domestic Animals of Ancient China," *China Journal,* 23: 233–43.

Speke, John Hanning. 1908. *Journal of the Discovery of the Source of the Nile.* London: J. M. Dent. 480 pp.

Spencer, Baldwin, and F. J. Gillen. 1904. *The Northern Tribes of Central Australia.* London: Macmillan. 784 pp.

Spencer, Joseph E. 1954. *Land and People in the Philippines: Geographic Problems in Rural Economy.* Berkeley and Los Angeles: Univ. of California Press. 282 pp.

Spindler, Lloyd A. 1953. "Transmission of Trichinae to Swine through Feces," *Journal of Parasitology,* 39: 34.

Spiro, Melford E. [1949.] "Ifalik: A South Sea Culture." Unpublished manuscript submitted as a final report, Coordinated Investigation of Micronesian Anthropology. Washington: Pacific Science Board, National Research Council. 148 pp.

Spoehr, Alexander. 1949. *Majuro: A Village in the Marshall Islands.* Chicago Natural History Museum, Fieldiana: Anthropology, Vol. 39. 266 pp.

Srinivas, Mysore Narasimhachar. 1952. *Religion and Society among the Coorgs of South India.* Oxford: Clarendon Press. 267 pp.

Stadling, J. 1901. *Through Siberia.* Westminster: Archibald Constable. 315 pp.

Stanford University. 1956. *Taiwan (Formosa)*. Subcontractor's Monograph, HRAF–31, Stanford–5. New Haven: Human Relations Area Files. 680 pp.

Stanley, Henry Morton. 1885. *The Congo and the Founding of Its Free State*. New York: Harper & Brothers. 2 vols.

Stannus, Hugh S. 1922. "The Wayao of Nyasaland," Harvard African Studies, 3: 229–372.

Stayt, Hugh Arthur. 1931. *The Bavenda*. London: International Institute of African Languages and Cultures. 392 pp.

Steedman, Andrew. 1835. *Wanderings and Adventures in the Interior of Southern Africa*. London: Longman. 2 vols.

Steere, J. B. 1876. "Formosa," *Journal of the American Geographical Society of New York*, 6: 302–34.

Stefansson, Vilhjalmur. 1920. "Food Tastes and Food Prejudices of Men and Dogs," *Scientific Monthly*, 11: 540–43.

———. 1937. "Food of the Ancient and Modern Stone Age Man," *Journal of the American Dietetic Association*, 13: 102–19.

———. 1946. *Not by Bread Alone*. New York: Macmillan. 339 pp.

Steiner, Franz. 1956. *Taboo*. London. Cohen & West. 154 pp.

Stevenson, H. N. C. 1944. *The Hill Peoples of Burma*. Burma Pamphlets, No. 6. Calcutta: Longmans, Green. 50 pp.

Stevenson, Margaret Sinclair. 1930. *Without the Pale*. The Religious Life of India Series. London: Oxford Univ. Press. 88 pp.

Strabo, Gnaeus Pompeius. 1854. *The Geography of Strabo*. Trans. by H. C. Hamilton and W. Falconer. London: Henry G. Bohn. 3 vols.

Sumner, William Graham. 1906. *Folkways*. Boston: Ginn. 692 pp.

Sundara Ram, L. L. 1927. *Cow-Protection in India*. George Town, Madras: South Indian Humanitarian League. 202 pp.

Sverdrup, Harald Ulrich. 1938. *Hos Tundrafolket* (With the People of the Tundra). Oslo: Gyldendal Norsk Forlag. 175 pp. Trans. for the Human Relations Area Files.

Sykes, Ella C. 1910. *Persia and Its People*. London: Methuen. 356 pp.

Sykes, P. M. 1906. "The Parsis of Persia," *Journal of the Society of Arts*, 54: 754–67.

Tacitus, Cornelius. 1958. "A Treatise on the Situation, Manners, and Inhabitants of Germany," pp. 286–342 in Volume 2, *The Works of Tacitus*. New York: Harper and Brothers.

Tallgren, A. M. 1936. "Problems concerning the Gorodishche Civilisation," *Eurasia Septentrionalis Antiqua*, 10: 171–85.

Tamai, Kisak. 1896. "Die Erforschung des Tschinwan-Gebietes auf Formosa durch die Japaner," *Globus*, 70: 93–98. Trans. for the Cross-Cultural Survey by M. Switzer.

Tao, L. K. 1928. *Livelihood in Peking*. Peiping: Social Research Department, China Foundation. 158 pp.

Tawney, R. H. 1932. *Land and Labor in China*. New York: Harcourt, Brace. 207 pp.

Tedesche, Sidney, trans. 1950. *The First Book of Maccabees*. New York: Harper and Brothers. 291 pp.

Teichman, Eric. 1921. *Travels of a Consular Officer in Northwest China*. Cambridge: Cambridge Univ. Press. 219 pp.

Temple, O. 1922. *Notes on the Tribes, Provinces, Emirates and States of the Northern Provinces of Nigeria*. Lagos, Nigeria: Church Missionary Society Bookshop. 577 pp.

Tew, Mary. 1950. *Peoples of the Lake Nyasa Region*. Ethnographic Survey of Africa. East Central Africa, Pt. 1. London: International African Institute. 131 pp.

Thomas, Bertram. 1932. *Arabia Felix*. New York: Charles Scribner's Sons. 397 pp.

Thomas, N. W. 1904. "Animal Superstitions among the Zulus, Basutos, Griquas, and Magatese, and the Kafirs of Natal," *Man*, 4: 181–83.

Thomas, P. [19——?] *Hindu Religion, Customs and Manners*. Bombay: D. B. Taraporevala Sons. 161 pp.

Thompson, Laura. 1940. *Southern Lau, Fiji: An Ethnography*. Bernice P. Bishop Museum, Bul. 162. Honolulu. 228 pp.

Thompson, R. Campbell. 1908. *Semitic Magic: Its Origins and Development*. London: Luzac. 286 pp.

Thompson, Virginia. 1937. *French Indo-China*. New York: Macmillan. 517 pp.

———. 1941. *Thailand: The New Siam*. New York: Macmillan. 865 pp.

———. 1943. *Post-Mortem on Malaya*. New York: Macmillan. 323 pp.

Thomson, Joseph. 1885. *Through Masai Land*. Boston: Houghton, Mifflin. 583 pp.

Towne, Charles Wayland, and Edward Norris Wentworth. 1950. *Pigs from Cave to Corn Belt*. Norman: Univ. of Oklahoma Press. 305 pp.

Townsend, Charles W. 1928. "Food Prejudices," *Scientific Monthly*, 27: 65–68.

Trant, Hope. 1954. "Food Taboos in East Africa," *Lancet*, 267: 703–5.

Tregear, Edward. 1904. *The Maori Race*. Wanganni, New Zealand: A. D. Willis. 592 pp.

Tremearne, A. J. N. 1912. *The Tailed Head-Hunters of Nigeria*. London: Seeley, Service. 342 pp.

Trimingham, J. Spencer. 1952. *Islam in Ethiopia*. London: Oxford Univ. Press. 299 pp.

Tseng Chao-lun. 1945. "Liang-Shan I-Ch'ü Kai-Huang" (The Lolo District in Liang-Shan), A Selection from *Ta Liang-shan I-ch'ü k'ao-ch'a chi* (An Account of Investigation Trip to Ta Liang-Shan), pp. 91–139. Chungking. Trans. for the Human Relations Area Files by J. M. Yeu.

Tufnell, Olga. 1953. *Lachish III: The Iron Age*. Vol. 3, Wellcome–Marston Archaeological Research Expedition to the Near East. London: Oxford Univ. Press. 437 pp.

Turner, George. 1884. *Samoa, a Hundred Years Ago and Long Before; Together with Notes on the Cults and Customs of Twenty-Three Other Islands in the Pacific.* London: Macmillan. 395 pp.

Turner, V. W. 1952. *The Lozi Peoples of North-Western Rhodesia.* Ethnographic Survey of Africa. West Central Africa, Pt. 3. London: International African Institute. 62 pp.

Tussing, Lyle. 1939. "A Study of Sex Differences in Food Likes and Dislikes," *Proceedings of the Indiana Academy of Science,* 48: 198–99.

Twitchell, K. S. 1953. *Saudi Arabia.* Princeton: Princeton Univ. Press. 231 pp.

Ungnad, A. 1908. "Zum Genuss von Schweinefleisch im alten Babylonien," Babylonische Miszellen, Teil 7, *Orientalistische Litteratur-Zeitung,* 11: 534–35.

University of California. 1956. *The Economy of India.* Subcontractor's Monograph, HRAF–32, California–1. New Haven: Human Relations Area Files. 2 vols.

Vámbéry, Arminius. 1864. *Travels in Central Asia.* London: John Murray. 443 pp.

VanBuskirk, J. D. 1923. "Some Common Korean Foods," *Transactions of the Korea Branch of the Royal Asiatic Society,* 14: 1–8.

Vanoverbergh, Morice. 1936–38. "The Isneg Life Cycle," Publications of the Catholic Anthropological Conference, 3 (No. 2): 81–186; 3 (No. 3): 187–280. Washington.

Varro. 1912. *On Farming.* Trans. by L. Storr-Best. London: G. Bell and Sons. 375 pp.

Vassal, Gabrielle M. 1910. *On and off Duty in Annam.* London: William Heinemann. 283 pp.

Verrill, Alpheus H. 1946. *Strange Customs, Manners and Beliefs.* Boston: L. C. Page. 302 pp.

Vesey-Fitzgerald, Brian Seymour. 1957. *The Domestic Dog.* London: Routledge and Kegan Paul. 226 pp.

Vickery, Kenton Frank. 1936. *Food in Early Greece.* Illinois Studies in the Social Sciences, Vol. 20. Urbana: University of Illinois. 97 pp.

Virchow, Rudolph. n.d. *The Life of the Trichina.* Trans. by Rufus King Browne. 47 pp.

Viski, Károly. 1932. *Hungarian Peasant Customs.* Budapest: Dr. George Vajna. 187 pp.

Von der Osten, Hans Henning. 1937. *The Alishar Hüyük, Seasons of 1930–32,* Pt. 3. Oriental Institute Publications, Vol. 30. Chicago: Univ. of Chicago Press. 496 pp.

von Schwarz, Franz. 1900. *Turkestan, die Wiege der indogermanischen Völker,* Pt. 3, pp. 140–249. Freiburg im Breisgau. Trans. for the Human Relations Area Files.

Waddell, L. Austine. 1895. *The Buddhism of Tibet.* London: W. H. Allen. 598 pp.

Wagner, Günter. 1949–56. *The Bantu of North Kavirondo.* London: Oxford Univ. Press. 2 vols.

Wallen, Richard. 1943. "Sex Differences in Food Aversions," *Journal of Applied Psychology,* 27: 288–98.

Ward, Artemas. 1923. *The Encyclopedia of Food.* New York: Published by the author. 596 pp.

Watt, George. 1908. *The Commercial Products of India.* London: John Murray. 1189 pp.

Watters, Thomas. 1904–5. *On Yuan Chwang's Travels in India, 629–645 A.D.* Oriental Translation Fund, N.S., Vol. 14. London: Royal Asiatic Society. 2 vols.

Webster, Harrie. 1900. "Korea—The Hermit Nation," *National Geographic Magazine,* 11: 145–55.

Webster, Hutton. 1942. *Taboo: A Sociological Study.* Stanford: Stanford Univ. Press. 393 pp.

Weissenborn, Johannes. 1905. "Tierkult in Afrika," *Internationales Archiv für Ethnographie,* 17: 91–175.

Westermarck, Edward. 1924. *The Origin and Development of the Moral Ideas.* London: Macmillan. 2 vols.

———. 1926. *Ritual and Belief in Morocco.* London: Macmillan. 2 vols.

Wheeler, L. Richmond. 1928. *The Modern Malay.* London: George Allen & Unwin. 300 pp.

White, John. 1823. *History of a Voyage to the China Sea.* Boston: Wells and Lilly. 372 pp.

Whiteley, Wilfred. 1951. *Bemba and Related Peoples of Northern Rhodesia.* Ethnographic Survey of Africa. East Central Africa, Pt. 1 of Pt. 2. pp. 1–76. London: International African Institute.

Whiteway, R. S., trans. and ed. 1902. *The Portuguese Expedition to Abyssinia in 1541–1543.* Hakluyt Society Works, Series 2, No. 10. London: Hakluyt Society. 296 pp.

Wiedfeldt, O. 1914. "Wirtschaftliche, rechtliche und soziale Grundtatsachen und Grundformen der Atayalen auf Formosa," *Mitteilungen der Deutschen Gesellschaft für Natur- und Völkerkunde Ostasiens,* 15 (Pt. C): 7–55. Trans. for the Cross-Cultural Survey.

Wiens, Herold J. 1954. *China's March toward the Tropics.* Hamden, Conn.: Shoe String Press. 441 pp.

Wilkinson, J. Gardner. 1878. *The Manners and Customs of the Ancient Egyptians.* London: John Murray. 3 vols.

Williams, F. E. 1936. *Papuans of the Trans-Fly.* Oxford: Clarendon Press. 452 pp.

Williams-Hunt, P. D. R. 1952. *An Introduction to the Malayan Aborigines.* Kuala Lumpur: Government Press. 102 pp.

Wilson, H. H., trans. 1866–88. *Ṛig-Veda Sanhitá.* London: N. Trübner. 6 vols.

Wilson, Laurence L. 1947. *Apayao Life and Legends.* Publisher unknown. 195 pp.

Winfield, Gerald F. 1948. *China: The Land and the People*. New York: William Sloane Associates. 437 pp.

Winstedt, R. O. 1925. *The Circumstances of Malay Life*. Papers on Malay Subjects. Life and Customs. Kuala Lumpur: Federated Malay States Government Press. 69 pp.

Wiser, Charlotte Viall. 1955. "The Foods of a Hindu Village of North India," *Annals of the Missouri Botanical Garden*, 42: 303–412.

Worthington, E. B. 1946. *Middle East Science*. London: H.M. Stationery Office. 237 pp.

Wrangell, Ferdinand. 1842. *Narrative of an Expedition to the Polar Sea, in the Years 1820, 1821, 1822, and 1823*. New York: Harper and Brothers. 302 pp.

Xenophon. 1958. *Anabasis*. Trans. by W. H. D. Rouse as *The March Up Country*. Ann Arbor: Univ. of Michigan Press. 205 pp.

Yamasaki, N. 1900. "Unsre geographischen Kenntnisse von der Insel Taiwan (Formosa)," *Petermanns Mitteilungen*, 46: 221–34. Trans. for the Cross-Cultural Survey.

Yang, Ch'ing-k'un. 1954. *A Chinese Village and Its Early Change under Communism*. Cambridge: Massachusetts Institute of Technology, Center for International Studies. 375 pp.

Yang, Martin C. 1945. *A Chinese Village: Taitou, Shantung Province*. New York: Columbia Univ. Press. 275 pp.

Yetts, W. Perceval. 1934. "The Horse: A Factor in Early Chinese History," *Eurasia Septentrionalis Antiqua*, 9: 231–55.

Young, Ernest. 1898. *The Kingdom of the Yellow Robe*. Westminster: Archibald Constable. 399 pp.

Zeitlin, Solomon, ed. 1954. *The Second Book of Maccabees*. English trans. by S. Tedesche. New York: Harper and Brothers. 271 pp.

Zwemer, S. M. 1900. *Arabia: The Cradle of Islam*. New York: Fleming H. Revell. 434 pp.

INDEX*

221

among, greater for youth, 109–10; object of food avoidances among, 115; and totemic animals, 118; tamed wild dingo, 179

Austral Islands (Polynesia): spread of pig to, 32; chicken eaten in, 166; M 13b

Avicenna: approved eating of pork, 21; thought horseflesh nutritious, 174

Azande, The (Sudan): use of chickens by, 73; attitude toward dogs and dog eating, 94, 176; M 8b, 8c(14)

Azerbaijan, Persian: 151; M 7b

Babylonia: pig raising in, 17; sacredness of pig in, 18; and origin of Jewish prejudice against pigs and pork, 37; adopted Sumerian beliefs about the bull, 163; position of dog in, 180–81; M 7d

Bactrians, The (Afghanistan): held horses sacred, 174; threw disabled people to dogs, 180

Badjo, The (Congo): 95; M 8c(15)

Baghirmi, The (Chad): eat horseflesh, 83; like dogflesh, 176; M 8b(16)

Bahrein Island: pork available on, 22; dogflesh eaten on, 180; M 7b

Baka, The (Sudan): 170; M 8c(17)

Bakwiri, The (Cameroons). *See* Kpe

Bali (Indonesia): pigs and pork used on, 31; male Brahmans of, avoid beef, 52; M 12

Baluchi, The (Iran): 153

Bangba Chugdso (Tibet): 82; M 10

Bango (Bobango), The (Congo): 94–95, 177

Bango-Bango, The (Congo): 172; M 8e(19)

Banjangi, The (Cameroons): pregnant women avoid pork, 155; have prohibition against eggs, 172; castrate dogs, 176; M 8b(20)

Bantu, The (North Kavirondo, Kenya): 171, 172, 173

Bantu, The (South Africa): uses of chicken among, 170; belief about women eating eggs, 171; do not eat or sacrifice dogs, 177

Banziri, The (Central African Republic): dog eating reported for, 176; M 8b(22)

Barabaig, The (Tanganyika): 154; M 8e(23)

Bari, The (Sudan): attitudes of, toward cattle, 57, 58, 113, 164; eat beef, 165; women do not eat chicken or eggs, 171; M 8c(24)

Baschilambua, The (Congo): 177

Bashkir, The (Soviet Union): 173; M 9

Bassa, The (Nigeria): ate horseflesh, 83; raise pigs, 155; dog eating reported for, 176; M 8b(25)

Basutoland: consumption of cattle in, 165; chickens kept by Sotho of, 170; M 8d

Batak, The (Sumatra): reject chicken eggs, 67; position and use of dog among, 99, 178; pig keeping and pork eating among, 157; eat chicken, 166; M 12(3)

Bates, Marston: 107

Batom, The (Cameroons): 172; M 8b(26)

Baudhāyana Dharma Sūtra: 159

Bauri, The (India): reject dogflesh, 99

Bedde, The (Nigeria): pork eaten by, 155; dog eating reported for, 176; M 8b(27)

Beef: demand for, in Portuguese Goa, 47; upper-caste Hindus despised for eating, 108; definition of use of term, 160, 162; valued as medicine by early Indian doctors, 162

Beef avoidance: diffusion of, 61–63; origin of, 61–63, 114–15; extension of, to water buffalo, 121; as an alien food, 124

Begemder and Semyen (Ethiopia): 154; M 8c

Bel (god), of Nippur: pig sacred to, 18

Belt Cave (Iran): 151; M 7b

Bemba, The (Northern Rhodesia): and craving for meat, 8–9; professional butcher among, 11–12; value chicken highly, 170; have prohibitions against eggs, 172; M 8e(28)

Bena, The (Tanganyika): 172; M 8e(29)

Bengasi (Libya): 102; M 7a

Benguela (Angola): pig raising in, 155; M 8d

Beni, The (Nigeria): 77

Berbers, The (North Africa): persistence in pig keeping and pork eating by, 21–22; eating of dogflesh by, 102–3; M 8a, 8b(30)

Berta, The (Sudan): pig raising among, 153; eat any kind of flesh, 176; M 8c(31)

Besom, The (Cameroons): 172; M 8b(32)

Bhars, The (India): 29

Bhil, The (India): reject pork, 156; worship the horse, 174; M 11a(8)

Bhopal (India): 45; M 11a

Biara, The (New Britain): forbid pork to women, 34; regard dogflesh a delicacy, 178

Bible, N.T.: references to pigs, 17; pig herds described, 37; reference to dogs, 181

Bible, O.T.: passages concerning the pig, 16, 37; references to bull worship, 163; reference to dogs, 181

Bidjuk, The (Cameroons): 172; M 8b(34)

Bihar (India): 29; M 11b

Binbinga, The (Australia): 109–10; M 13a

Birom, The (Nigeria): 177; M 8b(36)

Bisayans, The (Philippines): 173; M 12(4)

Bjakum, The (Cameroons): 172

Bleeding, of cattle: 60, 166

Blinding, of sows: in Melanesia, 33

Blood, of animals, uses of: cattle, 60; camel, 87; dog, 102, 177

Cannibalism: believed to spring from meat eating, 11; and restrictions against eating familiar individuals, 113–14; likened to eating totemic animal, 118

Cape Coast region (Ghana): 154; M 8a

Caria (Asia Minor): pork avoidance in, 18; people claim descent from "dog Apollo," 181; M 7a

Caribs, The (Caribbean area): 117

Caroline Islands (Micronesia): pig care on Ifalik, 33, 35; chickens and chicken eating in, 166, 167; dog eating on Ifalik, 178; M 13a

Castes (India): pig keeping and pork eating by, 29, 36, 156; beef eating and avoidance by, 46, 61–62; and giving up dog eating, 121

Castration: of pigs, among Naga, 29; of bull calves in Lake Victoria region, 60; of dogs in Africa, 94, 176

Cato: on sacrifice of pigs, 20

Cattle: sacrifice of, in Middle East and Mediterranean area, 17, 55; sacrifice of, in India, 47, 48, 50; hides of, in East Africa, 60; horns of, in East Africa, 60, 164–65; definition of use of term, 160; bones of, in ancient China, 162–63; sacrifice of, in China, in Shang times, 163

Cattle and beef: in India, 45–50, 160–62 passim; in Southeast Asia, 50–52, 162; in Tibet, Mongolia, and the Far East, 52–55, 162–63; in the Middle East and Mediterranean, 55–56, 163–64; in Africa south of the Sahara, 56–61, 115, 164–66 passim; origin and diffusion of beef avoidance, 61–63

Cebu (Philippines): 166; M 12

Celebes: dogflesh eating in, 100, 178; pig keeping and pork eating in, 157; chicken sacrifice and eating in, 166, 167; M 12

Central Asia. See Inner Asia

Ceylon: meat eaten in, 10; avoidance of chickens and eggs in, 67, 69; pork eating and avoidance in, 156–57; M 11a

Chaamba, The (Sahara Desert): eat chicken and eggs, 72; raise camels for meat, 88; M 8b(46)

Chad, Baghirmi of: eat horseflesh, 83; sacrifice dogs, 176

Chagga, The (Tanganyika): cattle and beef among, 59, 165, chicken and egg rejection by 73, 170; pig raising among, 155; M 8e(47)

Chaldean Christians, The: 11

Cham, The (Indochina): 31; M 12(7)

Chamar caste, The (India): pork rejection in Kotah State, 29; beef eating abandoned in Kotah State, 46; do not eat horseflesh, 80; reject camel flesh, 89

Chamba, The (Nigeria): 176; M 8b(48)

Chandler, Asa Crawford: 39

Chanhu-Daro (Pakistan): 151; M 11a

Chenchu, The (India): 166; M 11a(10)

Cheremis, The (Soviet Union): pork rejection by, 25; horseflesh eating by, 173; M 9

Chevaline: efforts to popularize in Europe, 85; mentioned, 174

Chewa, The (Nyasaland): 176; M 8e(49)

Chicken: as scavenger, 37, 169, 170; in divination, 65–66, 75, 166; domestication and spread, 65, 67, 70, 72–73; as sacred, 66, 71, 72, 73, 169; care of, 67; as pet, 71, 114; sacrifice of, 71, 166–67, 170, 171; terminology, 166. See also Cock; Cockfighting

Chicken and egg avoidance: origin of, 65, 74–78, 116–17; and primitive magico-religious beliefs, 67–69; and the major religions, 69–70, 71, 74–76 passim, 78, 171

Chicken and eggs: in Southeast Asia, the Pacific Islands, India, Tibet, and Mongolia, 65–70, 166–68 passim; in China and the Far East, 70–71, 168; in the Middle East and Mediterranean area, 71–73, 168, 169; in Africa south of the Sahara, 73–74, 169–73 passim. See also Eggs

Children: food restrictions and discriminations against, 34, 94, 115, 124, 159; role in changing family foodways, 123–24

Chin, The (Burma): 177; M 11b(11)

China: vegetarianism in, 10–11; pigs and pork in, 26–28, 30, 155–56; cattle and water buffalo in, 51, 53, 63, 162–63; chicken and eggs in, 70–71, 76, 167, 168; horse in, 83, 173; dogs and dogflesh in, 95–96; M 10

China, influence of: on pig keeping in adjacent areas, 26, 28, 31–32; on beef consumption in Mongolia and Tibet, 52–53; in spreading use of chickens and eggs, 70–71; in spreading dog eating, 95–96

Chinese: serve as butchers in Thailand, 31; identified with pigs by Mongols, 42, 122; eat dogflesh on Java, 178

Chinghai, eastern (China): 162–63; M 10

Chios (Aegean Sea): 72; M 7a

Chokwe, The (Angola): 155; M 8d(50)

Chopi, The (Mozambique): 172; M 8e(51)

Christianity: failure to adopt pork avoidance, 20; distinguished from Islam in pork eating, 21; preferred because it permits pork, 157

Christians: pigs and pork among various groups of, 21, 22, 23–24, 30, 116, 153, 155, 156, 157; of Ethiopia, food avoidances of, 23, 24, 42, 83, 89, 154; and rejection of camel flesh, 89, 108; among Bantu of Kenya, and eating of chicken flesh, 173

Christians, influence of: on eating of horseflesh, 83–84; on dog eating, 94–95, 100; in diffusion of flesh food avoidance, 122

Kunabembe, The (Cameroons): 172; M 8b (131)
Kundu, The (Cameroons): 171, 172; M 8b (132)
Kurdistan: M 7b, 7d. See also Yezidi
Kurumba, The (India): avoid flesh of cattle, 160; eat buffalo calf ceremonially, 160; M 11a(31)
Kuwait: pork available in, 22: M 7d
Kwangari, The (Angola): 176; M 8d(134)
Kwotto, The (Nigeria): 172; M 8b(135)

Ladakh District (India): and beef avoidance, 52; and fowl and eggs, 70; M 11a
Lake Victoria region (East Africa): 60; M 8e
Lakka, The (Chad): 172; M 8b(136)
Lamaism (of Tibet): and pigs and pork, 26; and beef and beef animals, 52–53; and eating of chicken and eggs, 70. See also Buddhism; Tibet
Lanchow (China): dogs present in, 96; M 10
Land Dyak, The (Borneo): M 12(20) See also Dyak
Lange, The (Congo): 121, 177; M 8d(139)
Lango, The (Uganda): dogflesh used in tests of guilt, 92; forbid eggs to women, 171; M 8c(140)
Laos: and beef rejection, 50; law against killing packs of dogs, 98; eating of chicken and eggs in, 166, 167; M 12
La Pérouse Island (Melanesia): 159; M 13a
Lapps, The: pork rejected by, 25; eat horseflesh, 173; M 9
Larry, Baron: 84–85
Lattimore, Owen: 42
Laufer, Berthold: on cockfighting, 66; on chicken bones in divination, 166; his use of terms "cock," "fowl," and "chicken," 166
Lebanon: eating of pork by Christians, 21; worship of sacred calf among the Druses, 164; chicken and eggs eaten in, 169; M 7c. See also Phoenicia
Legba (god), of Dahomey: 176
Legislation: in Israel against keeping of pigs by Jews, 21; Jewish, ban on various flesh foods, 39; in India, to protect cattle, 46; and slaughter of horned animals in Indochina, 50; by Lamaists, against eating the "cow," 52; among Moslems, against horseflesh, 82; by pope, against eating horseflesh, 84, 122; in Egypt, against slaughtering diseased camels, 88; Levitican code prohibits horseflesh, 89; against dogmeat feasts, in Philippines, 100. See also Sanctions
Lele, The (Congo): craving for animal food, 9; distribution of meat among, 12; privileges to certain foods among, 110; pig raising and pork eating among, 155; for-

bid chicken and eggs to women, 171; M 8d(141)
Lemba, The (Southern Rhodesia and South Africa): 154; M 8e(142)
"Lending": of pigs, on Sakau, New Hebrides, 35; of cattle, in East Africa, 58
Lendu, The (Congo): reserve fresh eggs for old people, 172; never eat dogflesh, 177; M 8c(143)
Lenge, The (Mozambique): pig raising among, 155; women avoid eggs, 171; M 8e (144)
Lhasa (Tibet): pork eating in, 26; M 10
Lhota Naga, The (India): 178; M 11b(32)
Liberia: chickens and eggs in, 171; dog eating reported in, 176; M 8a
Libya: ancient, avoidance of cow's flesh, 55; sale and eating of dogs in, 102; M 7a, 8b
Lissel, The (Congo): 172; M 8b(145)
Lisu, The (China): pigs and pork among, 156; sell dogs for flesh to Burma, 177; M 10, 11b(33)
Loango coast (Congo): 170-71; M 8d
Loeb, Edwin M.: 118
Lokoiya, The (Sudan): 170; M 8c(147)
Lolo, The (China): use chickens in divination, 65; pigs and pork among, 156; M 10
Lotuko, The (Sudan): 171; M 8c(148)
Lovedu, The (South Africa): 172; M 8e (149)
Lozi, The (Northern Rhodesia): 59, 165; M 8d(150)
Luba, The (Congo): pigs and pork among, 155; eat sterile eggs, 172; M 8d(152)
Lubu, The (Sumatra): 158; M 12(21)
Luchazi, The (Angola and Northern Rhodesia): pig raising among, 155; dog fattening and eating reported, 176; M 8d(153)
Lucian: on pigs in Hierapolis, 18
Luena, The (Angola and Northern Rhodesia): pig raising among, 155; and selling of cattle for meat, 165; M 8d(154)
Lugbara, The (Uganda): context of beef eating, 165; forbid eggs and chicken flesh to women, 171; M 8c(155)
Lunda, The (Congo): 155; M 8d(158)
Lushai, The (India): eat flesh of the mithan, 47; pigs and pork among, 156; eat and sacrifice chicken, 166; eat dogflesh, 177–78; M 11b(34)
Luzon: 166, 167; M 12. See also Apayao; Igorot
Lycians, The (Asia Minor): 181
Lydia (Asia Minor): 18, 19; M 7a

Ma (Anatolian goddess): 18
Maadi (Egypt): 151; M 7c
Maanjan, The (Borneo): 158
Maban, The (Sudan): 153; M 8c(159)
Mabum, The (Cameroons): 172; M 8b(160)
Maccabees: 17